WHY ENGLAND LOSE

WHY ENGLAND LOSE

& OTHER CURIOUS FOOTBALL PHENOMENA EXPLAINED

SIMON KUPER & STEFAN SZYMANSKI

HarperCollins*Publishers*

HarperCollins*Publishers*
77–85 Fulham Palace Road,
Hammersmith, London W6 8JB
www.harpercollins.co.uk

First published by HarperCollins*Publishers* 2009

1

A catalogue record of this book
is available from the British Library

ISBN 978-0-00-730111-9

Printed and bound in Great Britain by
Clays Ltd, St Ives plc

Mixed Sources
Product group from well-managed
forests and other controlled sources
www.fsc.org Cert no. SW-COC-1806
© 1996 Forest Stewardship Council

FSC
FSC

FSC is a non-profit international organisation established to promote the
responsible management of the world's forests. Products carrying the FSC
label are independently certified to assure consumers that they come
from forests that are managed to meet the social, economic and
ecological needs of present and future generations.

Find out more about HarperCollins and the environment at
www.harpercollins.co.uk/green

DEDICATION

From Simon: To Pamela, who doesn't know about football, but knows about writing; for her astonishing tolerance. And to Leila, Leo and Joey, for many hundreds of smiles.

From Stefan: to my father. We never saw eye to eye, but he taught me to question everything.

CONTENTS

SECTION II: THE COMPETITIONS: INEQUALITY, A PINT AT THE LOCAL, AND A NEW TRADITION

SECTION III: THE FANS: LOYALTY, SUICIDES, HAPPINESS, AND THE COUNTRY WITH THE BEST SUPPORTERS

SECTION IV: THE COUNTRIES: RICH AND POOR, TOM THUMB, GHIDDINK, SADDAM, AND THE CHAMPIONS OF THE FUTURE

DRIVING WITH A DASHBOARD: IN SEARCH OF NEW TRUTHS ABOUT FOOTBALL

This book began in the Hilton in Istanbul. From the outside it's a squat and brutalist place, but once the security men have checked your car for bombs and waved you through, the hotel is so soothing you never want to go home again. Having escaped the 13-million-person city, the only stress is over what to do next: a Turkish bath, a spot of tennis or yet more overeating while the sun sets over the Bosphorus? For aficionados, there's also a perfect view of the Besiktas football stadium right next door. And the staff are so friendly they are even friendlier than ordinary Turkish people.

The two authors of this book, Stefan Szymanski (a sports economist) and Simon Kuper (a journalist), met here. Fenerbahce football club was marking its centenary by staging the '100th Year Sports and Science Congress', and had flown them both in to give talks.

Simon's talk was first. He said he had good news for Turkish football: as the country's population mushroomed, and its economy grew, the national team was likely to keep getting better. Then it was Stefan's turn. He too had good news for Turkey. As the country's population mushroomed, and its economy grew, the national team was likely to keep getting better. All this may, incidentally, have been lost on the not very Anglophone audience.

The two of us had never met before Istanbul, but over beers in the Hilton bar we confirmed that we did indeed think much the same way about football. Stefan as an economist is trained to torture the data until they confessed, while Simon as a reporter tends to go around interviewing people, but those were just surface differences. We both think that much in football can be explained, even predicted, by studying data – especially data found outside football.

For a very long time football escaped the Enlightenment. Football clubs are still mostly run by people who do what they do because they have always done it that way. These people used to 'know' that black players 'lacked bottle', and they therefore overpaid for mediocre white players. Today they discriminate against black managers, buy the wrong players, and then let those players take penalties the wrong way. (We can, incidentally, explain why Manchester United won the penalty shootout in the Champions League final in Moscow. It's a story involving a secret note, a Basque economist, and Edwin van der Sar's powers of detection.)

Entrepreneurs who dip into football also keep making the same mistakes. They buy clubs promising to run them 'like a business', and disappear a few seasons later amid the same public derision as the previous lot. Fans and journalists aren't blameless either. Many newspaper headlines rest on false premises: 'Newcastle Land World Cup Star', or 'World Cup Will Be Economic Bonanza'. The game is full of unexamined clichés: 'Football is becoming boring because the big clubs always win', 'Football is big business', and, perhaps the greatest myth in the English game, 'The England team should do better'. None of these shibboleths has been tested against the data.

Most male team sports are pervaded by the same overreliance on traditional beliefs. American baseball, too, was until very recently an old game filled with old lore. Since forever players had stolen bases, hit sacrifice bunts, and been judged on their batting averages. Everyone in baseball just *knew* that all this was right.

But that was before Bill James. Like Dorothy in *The Wizard of Oz*, James came out of rural Kansas. He hadn't done much in life beyond keeping the stats in the local Little League, and watching the furnaces in a pork-and-beans factory. However, in his spare time he had begun to study baseball statistics with a fresh eye, and discovered that 'a great portion of the sport's traditional knowledge is ridiculous hokum'. James wrote that he wanted to approach the subject of baseball 'with the same kind of intellectual rigor and discipline that is routinely applied, by scientists great and poor, to trying to unravel the mysteries of the universe, of society, of the human mind, or of the price of burlap in Des Moines'.

In self-published mimeographs masquerading as books, the first of which sold 75 copies, James began demolishing the game's myths. He found, for instance, that the most important statistic in batting was the rarely mentioned 'on-base percentage' – how often a player managed to get on base. James and his followers (statisticians of baseball who came to be known as sabermetricians) showed that good old sacrifice bunts and base-stealing were terrible strategies.

His annual *Baseball Abstracts* turned into real books; eventually they reached the bestseller lists. One year, the cover picture showed an ape, posed as Rodin's *The Thinker*, studying a baseball. As James wrote in one *Abstract*: 'This is *outside* baseball. This is a book about what baseball looks like if you step back from it and study it intensely and minutely, but from a distance.'

Some Jamesians began to penetrate professional baseball. One of them, Billy Beane, the bafflingly successful general manager of the little Oakland A's, is the hero of Michael Lewis's earth-moving book *Moneyball*. (We'll say more later about Beane's brilliant gaming of the transfer market and its lessons for football.)

Eventually even the people inside baseball started to get curious about James. In 2002 the Boston Red Sox actually appointed him 'Senior Baseball Operations Adviser', his first regular job since the pork-and-beans plant. That same year, the Red Sox hired one of James's followers, the 28-year-old Theo Epstein, as the youngest general manager in the history of the major leagues. In 2004 the 'cursed' club won its first World Series in 86 years. In 2007 they won another.

In 2006 *Time* magazine named James in its hundred most influential people in the world. Now football is due its own Jamesian revolution.

A NUMBERS GAME

It's strange that football has been so averse to studying data, because one thing that attracts many fans to the game is precisely a love of numbers.

The man to ask about that is Alex Bellos. He wrote the magnificent book *Futebol: The Brazilian Way of Life,* but he also has a maths degree, and his *The Book of Numbers: Everything You Need to Know about Simple Math* was due to appear at about the same time as *Why England Lose*.

'Numbers are incredibly satisfying,' Bellos tells us. 'The world has no order, and maths is a way of seeing it in an order. League tables have an order. And the calculations you need to do for them are so simple: it's nothing more than your three times table.'

Though most fans would probably deny it, a love of football is often intertwined with a love of numbers. There are the match results, the famous dates, and the special joy of sitting in a pub with the newspaper on a Sunday morning 'reading' the league table. Fantasy Football Leagues are, at bottom, numbers games.

And James Alexander Gordon's incantation of the British football results on Saturday afternoons ('Cow-den-BEATH 1, Sten-house-MUIR [pause] 1') is part timeless ritual, part romance of place names, and part poem of numbers.

In this book we want to introduce new numbers and new ideas to football: numbers on suicides, on wage spending, on countries' populations, on anything that helps to reveal new truths about the game. Though Stefan is a sports economist, this is not a book about money. The point of football clubs is not to turn a profit (which is fortunate, as almost none of them does) and nor are we particularly interested in any profits they happen to make. Rather, we want to use an economist's skills (plus a little geography, psychology and sociology) to understand the game on the pitch, and the fans off it.

Some people may not want their emotional relationship with football sullied by our rational calculations. On the other hand, the next time England lose a penalty shootout in a World Cup quarter-final these same people will probably be throwing their beer glasses at the TV, when instead they could be tempering their disappointment with some reflections on the nature of binomial probability theory.

We think it's a good time to be writing this book. For the first time ever in football, there are a lot of numbers to mine. Traditionally, the only data that existed in the game were goals and league tables. (Newspapers published attendance figures, but these were unreliable.) At the end of the 1980s, when Stefan went into sports economics, only about 20 or 30 academic articles on sport had ever been published. Now there are countless. Many of the new truths they contain have not yet reached most fans.

The other new source of knowledge is the bulging library of football books. When Pete Davies published his *All Played Out: The Full Story of Italia '90,* there were probably only about 20 or 30 good football books in existence. Now – thanks partly to

Davies, who has been described as John the Baptist to Nick Hornby's Jesus – there are thousands. Many of these books (including Bellos's *Futebol*) contain truths about the game that we have tried to present here.

So unstoppable has the stream of data become that even people inside the game itself are finally starting to sift it. Michael Lewis, the author of *Moneyball*, wrote in the *New York Times* in February 2009:

> The virus that infected professional baseball in the 1990s, the use of statistics to find new and better ways to value players and strategies, has found its way into every major sport. Not just basketball and football, but also soccer and cricket and rugby and, for all I know, snooker and darts – each one now supports a subculture of smart people who view it not just as a game to be played but as a problem to be solved.

In football, one of these smart men (it's part of the game's ridiculous hokum that they have to be men) is Arsène Wenger. A trained economist, Wenger is practically addicted to statistics like the number of kilometres run by each player in a game. What makes him one of the heroes of *Why England Lose* is that he understands that in football today, you need data to get ahead. If you are a trainspotter who studies figures, you will see more and win more.

Slowly, Wenger's colleagues are also ceasing to rely on gut alone. Increasingly they use computer programmes like Prozone to analyse games and players. Another harbinger of the impending Jamesian takeover of football is the Milan Lab. Early on, AC Milan's in-house medical outfit found that just by studying a player's jump, it could predict with 70 per cent accuracy whether he will get injured. It then collected millions of data on each of the team's players on computers, and in the process stumbled upon the secret of eternal youth. (It's still a secret: no other club has a

Milan Lab, and the Lab won't divulge its findings, which is why players at other clubs are generally finished by their early thirties.)

Most of Milan's starting 11 that beat Liverpool in the Champions League final of 2007 were 31 or older; Paolo Maldini, the captain, was 38, and Filippo Inzaghi, scorer of both Milan's goals, 33. In large part, that trophy was won by the Milan Lab and its database. It is another version of the Triumph of the Geeks story.

As Stefan and Simon talked more, and began to think harder about football and data, we buzzed around all sorts of questions. Could we find figures to show which country loved football most? Might the game somehow deter people from killing themselves? And perhaps we could have a shot at predicting which clubs and countries – Turkey most likely; perhaps even Iraq – would dominate the football of the future. Stefan lives in London, and Simon in Paris, and so we spent a year firing figures, arguments and anecdotes back and forth across the Channel.

All the while, we distrusted every bit of ancient football lore, and tested it against the numbers. As Jean Pierre Meersseman, the Milan Lab's cigarette-puffing Belgian director, told us: 'You can drive a car without a dashboard, without any information, and that's what's happening in soccer. There are excellent drivers, excellent cars, but if you have your dashboard, it makes it just a little bit easier. I wonder why people don't want more information.' We do.

WHY ENGLAND LOSE

BEATEN BY A DISHWASHER

When the England team fly to South Africa for the World Cup, an ancient ritual will start to unfold. Perfected over England's 14 previous failures to win the World Cup away from home, it follows this pattern:

Phase One, pre-tournament: Certainty that England will win the World Cup.

Alf Ramsey, the only English manager to win the trophy, forecast the victory of 1966. However, his prescience becomes less impressive when you realise that almost every England manager thinks he will win the trophy, including Ramsey in the two campaigns he didn't. When his team were knocked out in 1970 he was stunned, and said: 'We must now look ahead to the next World Cup in Munich, where our chances of winning I would say are very good indeed.' England didn't qualify for that one.

Glenn Hoddle, England's manager in 1998, revealed only after his team had been knocked out 'my innermost thought, which was that England would win the World Cup'. Another manager who went home early, Ron Greenwood, said: 'I honestly thought we could have won the World Cup in 1982.' A month before the World Cup of 2006, Sven Goran Eriksson said: 'I think we will win it.'

The deluded manager is never alone. As England's inside forward Johnny Haynes remarked after elimination in 1958: 'Everyone in England thinks we have a God-given right to win the World Cup.' This belief in the face of all evidence was a hangover from empire: England is football's mother country and should therefore be the best today. The sociologist Stephen Wagg notes: 'In reality, England is a country like many others and the England football team is a football team like many others.' This truth is only slowly sinking in.

Phase Two: During the tournament England meet a former wartime enemy.

In five of their last seven World Cups, they were knocked out by either Germany or Argentina. The matches fit seamlessly into the British tabloid view of history, except for the outcome. As Alan Ball summed up the mood in England's dressing-room after the defeat to West Germany in 1970: 'It was disbelief.'

Even Joe Gaetjens, who scored the winning goal for the US against England in 1950, turns out to have been of German-Haitian origin, not Belgian-Haitian as is always said. And in any case, the US is another former wartime enemy.

Phase Three: The English conclude that the game turned on one freakish piece of bad luck that could happen only to them.

Gaetjens, the accounting student and dishwasher in a Manhattan restaurant who didn't even have an American passport, scored his goal by accident. 'Gaetjens went for the ball, but at the last moment, decided to duck,' England's captain Billy Wright wrote later. 'The ball bounced on the top of his head and slipped past the bewildered Williams.'

In 1970 England's goalkeeper Gordon Banks got a stomach upset before the quarter-final against West Germany. He was OK on the morning of the game, and was picked to play, but a little later was discovered on the toilet with everything 'coming out both ends'. His understudy Peter Bonetti let in three soft German goals.

There was more bad luck in 1973, when England failed to qualify for the next year's World Cup because Poland's 'clown' of a goalkeeper, Jan Tomaszewski, unaccountably had a brilliant night at Wembley. 'The simple truth is that on a normal day we would have beaten Poland 6–0,' England's midfielder Martin Peters says in Niall Edworthy's book on England managers, *The Second Most Important Job in the Country.* Poland went on to reach the semi-finals of the 1974 World Cup.

In 1990 and 1998 England lost in what everyone knows is the lottery of the penalty shootout. In 2002 everyone knew that the obscure, bucktoothed Brazilian kid Ronaldinho must have mishit the free-kick that sailed into England's net, because he couldn't have been good enough to place it deliberately. In 2006 Wayne Rooney would never have been sent off for stamping on Ricardo Carvalho's genitals if Cristiano Ronaldo hadn't tattled on him. These things just don't happen to other countries.

Phase Four: Moreover, everyone else cheated.

The Brazilian crowd in 1950 and the Mexican crowd in 1970 deliberately wasted time while England were losing by keeping the ball in the stands. The CIA (some say) drugged Banks. Diego Maradona's 'hand of God' did for England in 1986. Diego Simeone play-acted in 1998 to get David Beckham sent off, and Cristiano Ronaldo did the same for Rooney in 2006.

Every referee opposes England. Those of his decisions that support this thesis are analysed darkly. Typically the referee's nationality is mentioned to blacken him further. Billy Wright, England's captain in 1950, later recalled 'Mr Dattilo of Italy, who seemed determined to let nothing so negligible as the laws of the game come between America and victory'. The referee who didn't give England a penalty against West Germany in 1970 was, inevitably, an Argentine. The Tunisian referee of 1986 who, like most people watching the game, failed to spot the 'hand of God', has become legendary.

Phase Five: England are knocked out without getting anywhere near lifting the cup.

The only exception was 1990, when they reached the semi-final. Otherwise they have always gone out when still needing to defeat at least three excellent teams. Since 1970, Bulgaria, Sweden and Poland have got as close to winning a World Cup as England have.

Perhaps England should be relieved that they don't come second. As Jerry Seinfeld once said, who wants to be the greatest loser? The science writer Stefan Klein points out that winning bronze at the Olympics is not so bad, because that is a great achievement by any standards, but winning silver is awful, as you will always be tortured by the thought of what might have been.

England have never been at much risk of that. They won only five of their 18 matches at World Cups abroad from 1950 through 1970, and didn't qualify for the next two tournaments in 1974 and 1978, so at least they have been improving since. The general belief in decline from a golden age is mistaken.

Phase Six: The day after elimination, normal life resumes.

The one exception is 1970, when England's elimination may have caused Labour's surprise defeat in the general election four days later. But otherwise the elimination does not bring on a nationwide hangover. To the contrary, England's eliminations are celebrated, turned into national myths, or songs, or Pizza Hut adverts.

Phase Seven: A scapegoat is found.

The scapegoat is never an outfield player who has 'battled' all match. Even if he directly caused the elimination by missing a penalty, he is a 'hero'.

Beckham was scapegoated for the defeat against Argentina in 1998 only because he got himself sent off after 46 minutes. The writer Dave Hill explained that the press was simply pulling out its 'two traditional responses to England's sporting failure: heralding a glorious defeat and mercilessly punishing those responsible for it, in this case Posh Spice's unfortunate fiancé.'

Beckham wrote in one of his autobiographies that the abuse continued for years: 'Every time I think it has disappeared, I know I will meet some idiot who will have a go at me. Sometimes it is at matches, sometimes just driving down the road.' He added that he kept 'a little book in which I've written down the names of those people who upset me the most. I don't want to name them because I want it to be a surprise when I get them back.' One day they will all get tummy bugs.

Often the scapegoat is a management figure: Wright as captain in 1950, Joe Mears as chief selector in 1958, and many managers since. Sometimes it is a keeper, who by virtue of his position just stood around in goal rather than battling like a hero. Bonetti spent the rest of his career enduring chants of 'You lost the World Cup'. After retiring from football, he went into quasi-exile as a postman on the Scottish Isle of Mull.

In 2006 Cristiano Ronaldo was anointed scapegoat. Only after a defeat to Brazil is no scapegoat sought, because defeats to Brazil are considered acceptable.

Phase Eight: England enter the next World Cup thinking they will win it.

The World Cup as ritual has a meaning beyond football. The elimination is usually the most watched British television programme of the year. It therefore educates the English in two contradictory narratives about their country: one, that England has a manifest destiny to triumph, and two, that it never does. The genius of the song 'Three Lions', English football's unofficial anthem, is that it combines both narratives: 'Thirty years of hurt/Never stopped me dreaming.'

There is an alternative universe in which Beckham didn't get sent off, Banks's tummy held up, the referee spotted Maradona's handball and so on. In that universe England have won about seven World Cups. Many English fans think they would have preferred that. But it would have deprived the English of a ritual that marks the passing of time much like Christmas or New Year, and that celebrates a certain idea of England: a land of unlucky heroes who no longer rule the world, although they should.

A PERFECTLY DECENT TEAM

Any mathematician would say it's absurd to expect England to win the World Cup. England win two thirds of their matches. To be precise, from 1970 to 2007 they played 411, won 217, drew 120 and lost 74. If we treat a draw as half a win, this translates into a winning percentage of 67.4 per cent. If we then break this down into seven equal periods of just under four years each, England's winning percentage has never fallen below 62 per cent or risen above 70 per cent. In other words, their performance is very constant.

Yes, these statistics conceal some ghastly mishaps (Poland at Wembley in 1973, the 'Turnip' front page in 1993, Phil Neville against Rumania in 2000) as well as some highs (John Barnes slaloming through the Brazilian defence in 1984, revenge on Holland at Euro 96, the 5–1 in Munich), but the statistics tell us that the difference between anguish and euphoria is a few percentage points.

On the face of it, winning two thirds of the time – meaning bookies' odds of 2–1 on – is not too shabby in a two-horse race. Of course, some countries do even better. Brazil win about 80 per cent of their games. But against most teams, England are the deserved favourites. In the fairly typical period of 1980 to 2001, England's win percentage was 10th best in the world.

The problem comes when we try to translate this achievement into winning tournaments. England's failure to win anything since the holy year of 1966 is a cause of much embarrassment in bars on the Costa del Sol. But next time you are mocked by German or Italian fans, try explaining to them the rules of multiplicative probability.

It is tricky to calculate the exact probability of England qualifying for a tournament, because it requires an analysis of many permutations of events. However, we can reduce it to a simple problem of multiplicative probability if we adopt the 'must win' concept. For example, England failed to qualify for Euro 2008 by coming third in their group behind Croatia and Russia. In doing so they won seven matches, lost three and drew two (for an average winning percentage of exactly 66.66 per cent). They were pipped by Russia, who won seven, lost two and drew three (a winning percentage of 70.83 per cent).

Suppose that to guarantee qualification you have to win eight games outright. Then the problem becomes one where you have to win eight from 12, where your winning probability in each game is 66 per cent. Calculating this probability is a bit more complicated, since it involves combinatorics.

The answer is a probability of qualification of 63 per cent. That means that England should qualify for fewer than two thirds of the tournaments they enter. In fact, from 1970 through 2008 England qualified two thirds of the time: for six out of nine World Cups and six out of nine European Championships. Given that the number of qualifying matches has risen over time, England's performance is in line with what you might have expected.

Every time that England have qualified for a World Cup since 1982, they have reached at least the last 16. But even at that stage of the tournament, when hysteria grips the nation, England's chances of winning remain modest. If the probability of reaching the quarter-final from the second round is theoretically 66 per cent, your chance of getting to the semi-final is 66 per cent x 66 per cent = 44 per cent; your chance of making it to the final is 66 per cent x 44 per cent = 30 per cent, and your chance of winning is 66 per cent x 30 per cent = 20 per cent. In fact, at this stage of a tournament England's chances of winning any game are rather lower than 66 per cent, as this is the phase when they meet sides like Germany and Argentina.

The sad fact is that England are a good team that does better than most. This means they are not likely to win many tournaments, and they don't.

The English tend to feel that England should do better. The team's usual status around the bottom of the world's top 10 is not good enough. The national media, in particular, feel almost perpetually let down by the team. England are 'known as perennial underachievers on the world stage', according to the *Sun;* their history 'has been a landscape sculpted from valleys of underachievement', says the *Independent*; while Terry Butcher grumbled in the *Sunday Mirror* in 2006 that 'historical underachievement has somehow conspired to make England feel even more important.'

'Why do England lose?' is perhaps the greatest question in English sport. In trying to answer it, we hear strange echoes from the field of development economics. The central question in that field is, 'Why are some countries less productive than others?' The two main reasons why England lose would sound familiar to any development economist. So would the most common reason *falsely* cited for why England lose. Here are those three reasons for England's eliminations – first the false one, then the correct ones.

BRITISH JOBS FOR BRITISH WORKERS?
WHY THERE ARE TOO MANY ENGLISHMEN
IN THE PREMIER LEAGUE

When pundits gather to explain why England lose, their favourite scapegoat of the moment is imports: the hundreds of foreigners who play in the Premier League. Here is Steven Gerrard speaking before England lost to Croatia and failed to qualify for Euro 2008: 'I think there is a risk of too many foreign players coming over, which would affect our national team eventually if it's not already. It is important we keep producing players.'

After all, if our boys can barely even get a game in their own league, how can they hope to mature into internationals? After England lost to Croatia, Sepp Blatter, Alex Ferguson, and UEFA's president Michel Platini all made versions of Gerrard's argument.

These men were effectively blaming imports for the English lack of skills. The reasoning is that our own workers don't get a chance because they are being displaced by foreign workers. Exactly the same argument is often made in development economics. Why are some countries not very productive? Partly because their inhabitants don't have enough skills. The best place to learn skills – such as making toothpaste, or teaching maths, or playing football – is on the job. To learn how to make toothpaste you have to actually make it, not just go on courses to learn how to make it. But if you are always importing toothpaste, you will never learn.

That is why, for over half a century, many development economists have called for 'import substitution'. Ban or tax certain imports so that the country can learn to make the stuff itself. Import substitution has worked for a few countries. Japan after the war, for instance, managed to teach itself from scratch how to make all sorts of high-quality cars and electrical gadgets.

The idea of 'import substitution' in the Premier League has an emotional appeal to many English fans. Britons often complain about feeling overrun by immigrants, and few spots in the country are more foreign than a Premier League pitch on match day. Arsenal, in particular, have wisely almost dispensed with Englishmen entirely. Altogether Englishmen accounted for only 37 per cent of the minutes played by footballers in the Premier League in the 2007–08 season before Croatia's night at Wembley. To some degree, *English* football no longer exists.

'It is my philosophy to protect the identity of the clubs and country,' said Platini. 'Manchester United against Liverpool should be with players from Manchester and Liverpool, from that region. Robbie Fowler was from Liverpool. He grew up in that city, it was nice, but now you don't have the English players.'

Imagine for a moment that Platini somehow managed to suspend EU law, and force English football clubs to discriminate against players from other EU countries. If that happened, Platini and Gerrard would probably end up disappointed. If inferior English players were handed places in Premier League teams, they would have little incentive to improve. This is a classic problem with import substitution: it protects bad producers. What then tends to happen is that short-term protection becomes long-term protection.

In fact, however, Platini's entire premise is wrong. If people in football understood numbers better, they would grasp that the problem of the England team is not that there are too few Englishmen playing in the Premier League. To the contrary: there are too *many*. England would do better if the country's best clubs fielded even fewer English players.

You could argue that English players accounted for 'only' 37 per cent of playing time in the Premier League. Or you could argue that they account for a massive 37 per cent of playing time, more than any other nationality in what is now the world's toughest league.

This means that English players get lots of regular experience of top-level club football. Even if we lump together the continent's three toughest leagues – the Premier League, the Primera Liga and Serie A – then only Italians, Spaniards and perhaps Brazilians and Frenchmen play more tough club football.

In fact the English probably get too much of this kind of experience. The Premier League is becoming football's NBA, the first global league in this sport's history. So the players earn millions of pounds. So the league is all-consuming, particularly if you play for one of the Big Four clubs, as almost all regular England internationals do. The players have to give almost all their energy and concentration every match. Life is a little more relaxed even in the Serie A or La Liga, where smaller teams like Siena, Catania or Santander cannot afford to buy brilliant foreigners.

Clearly an athlete can't peak in every match. If you are running in the Olympics, you plan your season so that you will peak only at the Olympics, and not before. If you play football for (say) Croatia, and for a club in a smaller league (even the Bundesliga), you can husband your energy so as to peak in big international matches – for instance, when you are playing England at Wembley.

By contrast, English players have to peak every week for their clubs. In no other country do footballers play as many demanding games a season. Clubs in no other country play as many European games as the English do. Daniele Tognaccini, chief athletics coach at AC Milan's 'Milan Lab', probably the most sophisticated medical outfit in football, explains what happens when a player has to play 50 tough games a year: 'The performance is not optimal. The risk of injury is very high. We can say the risk of injury during one game, after one week's training, is 10 per cent. If you play after two days, the risk rises by 30 or 40 per cent. If you are playing four or five games consecutively without the right recovery, the risk of injury is incredible. The probability of having one lesser performance is very high.'

So when English footballers play internationals, they start tired, hurting, and without enough focus. Often they cannot raise their game. Harry Redknapp said when he was Portsmouth manager:

'I think England games get in the way of club football for the players now. Club football is so important, the Champions League and everything with it, that England games become a distraction to them.' Moreover, players in the intense Premier League are always getting injured, and their clubs don't give them time to recover. That may be why half of England's regulars couldn't play against Croatia.

In short, if England wanted to do better in internationals, it should export English players to more relaxed leagues, like for example Croatia's.

Eriksson understood the problem. When one of the authors of this book asked him why England lost in the quarter-finals in the World Cup 2002 and Euro 2004, he said his players were tired after tough seasons. Was that really the only reason? 'I would say so,' Eriksson replied. 'If you're not fit enough … in Japan, we never scored one goal in the second half.'

In any case, English fans *want* to see teams full of foreign play-ers. Platini wonders whether Liverpudlians can identify with a Liverpool team full of foreigners. Well, they seem to manage. Judging by the Premiership's record crowds despite its record ticket prices, fans still identify enough. Arsenal's all-foreign team now draws 60,000 fans weekly, the highest average crowd of any London team in history. England can have an excellent league, or it can have an English league, but it can't have both. Given the choice, fans seem to prefer excellence. In that sense, they are typical consumers. If you try to substitute imports, then, at least at first, consumers have to put up with worse products. They generally don't like that.

THE PROBLEM OF EXCLUSION: HOW ENGLISH FOOTBALL DRIVES OUT THE MIDDLE CLASSES

The Romans built their empire with an army drawn from every part of society. Only when the militia became an elite profession open just to particular families did the empire start to decline. When you limit your talent pool, you limit the development of skills. The bigger the group of people you draw from, the more new ideas are likely to bubble up. That's why large networks like the City of London or Silicon Valley, which draw talent from around the world, are so creative. So is the Premier League.

The problem of English football is what happens *before* our best players reach the Premier League. The Englishmen who make it to the top are drawn very largely from one single and shrinking social group: the traditional working-class. The country's middle classes are mostly barred from professional football. That holds back the national team.

There are many ways to classify which social class someone was born into, but one good indicator is the profession of that person's father. Joe Boyle, with some help from Dan Kuper, researched for us the jobs of the fathers of England players who played at the World Cups of 1998, 2002 and 2006. Boyle ignored jobs the fathers might have been handed after their sons' rise to stardom. As much as possible, he tried to establish what the father did while the son was growing up. Using players' auto-biographies and newspaper profiles, he came up with the list below. It doesn't include every player (asked what Wayne Bridge's dad did for a living, we throw up our hands in despair), but most are here. Another caveat: some of the dads on the list were absent while their boys were growing up. That said, here are their professions:

Player	Father's job
Tony Adams	Roofer
Darren Anderton	Ran removals company; later taxi driver
David Batty	Dustbin man
David Beckham	Heating engineer
Sol Campbell	Railway worker
Jamie Carragher	Pub landlord
Ashley Cole	None given, but in his autobiography he describes 'a grounded working-class upbringing in East London'

Joe Cole	Fruit and vegetable trader
Peter Crouch	Creative director at international advertising agency
Stewart Downing	Painter and decorator on oil rigs
Kieron Dyer	Manager of Caribbean social club
Rio Ferdinand	Tailor
Robbie Fowler	Labourer; later worked night-shift at railway maintenance depot
Steven Gerrard	Labourer (bricklaying, tarmacking etc.)
Emile Heskey	Security worker at nightclub
Paul Ince	Railwayman
David James	Artist who runs gallery in Jamaica
Jermaine Jenas	Soccer coach in US
Frank Lampard	Footballer
Rob Lee	'Involved in a shipping company'
Graeme Le Saux	Ran fruit and vegetable stall
Steve McManaman	Printer
Paul Merson	Coalman
Danny Mills	Coach in Norwich City's youth academy
Michael Owen	Footballer
Wayne Rooney	Labourer, mainly on building sites; often unemployed
Paul Scholes	Gas-pipe fitter
David Seaman	Garage mechanic, later ran sandwich shop, then worked at steelworks
Alan Shearer	Sheet-metal worker
Teddy Sheringham	Policeman
Gareth Southgate	Worked for IBM
John Terry	Forklift-truck operator
Darius Vassell	Factory worker
Theo Walcott	RAF administrator; later joined services company working for British Gas

Many of these job descriptions are imprecise. What exactly did Rob Lee's dad do at the shipping company, for instance? Still, it's possible to break down the list of 34 players into a few categories:

Eighteen players, or more than half the total, were sons of skilled or unskilled manual labourers: Vassell, Terry, Shearer, Seaman, Scholes, Rooney, Merson, McManaman, Ince, Heskey, Gerrard, Fowler, Adams, Batty, Beckham, Campbell, Ferdinand and Downing. Ashley Cole with his 'working-class upbringing' is probably best assigned to this category, too.

Four players (Jenas, Lampard, Mills and Owen) had fathers who worked in football. Le Saux and Joe Cole were both sons of fruit and vegetable traders. Anderton's dad ran a removals business, which seems to have failed, before becoming a cab driver. Sheringham's father was a policeman. Carragher's and Dyer's dads ran a pub and a social club respectively.

That leaves only five players out of 34 – Crouch, James, Lee, Southgate and Walcott – whose fathers seem to have worked in professions that required more than a basic formal education. If we define class by education, then only 15 per cent of England players of recent years had 'middle-class' origins.

The male population as a whole was much better educated. Of British men aged between 35 and 54 in 1996 – the generation of most of these footballers' fathers – a little over half had qualifications beyond O-level, according to the British Household Panel Study.

English football's reliance on an overwhelmingly working-class talent pool was only moderately damaging in the past, when most English people were working class. In the late 1980s, 70 per cent of Britons still left school aged 16, often for manual jobs. But by then, the growth of the middle classes had already begun. In fact, middle-class values began to permeate the country, a process that sociologists call 'embourgeoisement'. It happened on what used to be the football terraces, which because of high ticket prices are now slightly more middle-class than even the country at large.

Nowadays over 70 per cent of Britons stay in school after 16, and over 40 per cent enter higher education. More and more, this is a middle-class nation. Yet because football still recruits over-whelmingly from the traditional working classes, it excludes an ever-growing swathe of the population. That must be a brake on the England team.

The shrinking of the talent pool is only part of the problem. Until at least the late 1990s British football was suffused, without quite knowing it, by British working-class habits. Some of these were damaging, such as the sausages-and-chips diet, or the idea that binge-drinking is a hobby. 'Maybe in earlier generations the drinking culture carried over from the working-class origins of the players,' wrote Alex Ferguson in his autobiography. 'Most of them came from families where many of the men took the view that if they put in a hard shift in a factory or a coalmine they were enti-tled to relax with a few pints. Some footballers seem determined to cling to that shift-worker's mentality ... Also prevalent is the notion that Saturday night is the end of the working week and therefore a good time to get wrecked.'

Of course 'problem drinking' exists in the middle classes too, and of course most working-class people have no issues with drink. However, Ferguson is explicitly describing a traditional working-class attitude.

Furthermore, the working classes tended to regard football as something you learnt on the job, rather than from educationalists with diplomas. It was the attitude you would expect of an industry in which few people had much formal education. One British national football administrator, who worked for decades to intro-duce coaching courses, told us that clubs mocked his attempts as 'some new-fangled thing got up by college boys – as if there was shame in being educated'. He recalls that 'coaching' and 'tactics' became 'shame words'. 'People would say, "The trouble with foot-ball today is that there is too much coaching." That's like saying, "The trouble with school is that there's too much education."'

It would be crazy to generalise too much about the working classes. There is a strong working-class tradition of self-education. Large numbers of post-war Britons became the first people in their families to go to university. Nonetheless, the anti-intellectual attitudes that the football administrator encountered do seem to be widespread in the English game.

These attitudes may help explain why English managers and English players are not known for thinking about football. When the Dutchman Johan Cruijff said, 'Football is a game you play with your head,' he wasn't talking about headers.

Over the last decade these traditional working-class attitudes have begun to fade in British football. Foreign managers and play-ers have arrived, importing the revolutionary notions that profes-sional athletes should think about their game and look after their bodies. But one working-class custom still bars middle-class Britons from professional football: what you might call the 'anti-education requirement'.

Most British footballers still leave school at 16. The belief persists that only thus can they concentrate fully on the game. The argument that many great foreign footballers – Ruud Gullit, Dennis Bergkamp, Tostao, Socrates, Osvaldo Ardiles, Jorge Valdano, Fernando Redondo, Kaká, etc – stayed in school after 16, or even attended university, is ignored. This is probably because British coaches and players tend to be suspicious of educated people.

It is true that the clubs' new academies are meant to help play-ers keep studying, but in practice this barely happens. A few years ago one of us visited the academy of an English club. It's an academy of some note: two of its recent graduates won their first international caps while still teenagers. But all the boys we met there, bright or otherwise, were sent to do the same single GNVQ in Leisure and Tourism to fulfil the academy's minimum education requirement. Together the boys caused such havoc in class that all the other students had dropped out of the course. It's not that footballers are too busy to study, as they rarely train more than a couple of hours a day; rather, being studious is frowned upon.

Football consequently remains unwelcoming to middle-class teenagers. To cite just one example, Stuart Ford, who at 17 played for England Schools, gave up on becoming a professional because he got tired of listening to rants from uneducated coaches. Being middle-class, he always felt an outsider. He recalls: 'I was often goaded about my posh school or my gross misunderstanding of street fashion. That was just from the management.' Instead he became a Hollywood lawyer. Later, as a senior executive at one of the Hollywood studios, he was one of the people behind an unsuccessful bid to buy Liverpool FC.

If the working classes get little education, that is mainly the fault of the middle-class people who oversee the British schools system. Nonetheless, the educational divide means that any middle-class person entering British football feels instantly out of place.

Many middle-class athletes drift to cricket or rugby instead. Often, this represents a direct loss to football. In most people, sporting talent is fairly transferable until they reach their late teens. Many English footballers, like Phil Neville and Gary Lineker, were gifted cricketers too. Some well-known rugby players took up rugby only as teenagers, when they realised they weren't going to make it as footballers. And in the past, several paragons represented England in more than one sport. Only a few sports demand very specific qualities that can't be transferred: it's hard to go from being a jockey to being a basketball player, for instance. But football competes with other ball games for talent, and it scared away the educated middle classes.

This is particularly sad because there is growing evidence that sporting talent and academic talent are linked. The best athletes have fast mental reactions, and those reactions, if properly trained, would make for high-calibre intellects.

All this helps explain why even though the academies of English clubs are the richest in the world, England doesn't produce better players than poor nations. Instead of trying to exclude foreigners from English football, it would be smarter to include more middle-class English people. Only when there are England players with educated accents – as happens in Holland, Argentina, and even Brazil (Dunga and Kaká, for instance) – might the national team maximise its potential.

CLOSED TO INNOVATIONS: ENGLISH FOOTBALL'S SMALL NETWORK

When the internet arrived, many pundits predicted the decline of the city. After all, why live in a flat in Hackney when you could set up your laptop in an old farmhouse overlooking a sheep meadow?

The prediction turned out to be wrong. Cities have continued their growth of the last 200 years, which is why Hackney flats became so expensive. Meanwhile the countryside has turned into something of a desert, inhabited by a few farmers and old people, and used by the rest of us mostly for long walks. It turns out that people still want to live in dirty, overcrowded, overpriced cities. And the reason they do is the social networks. To be rural is to be isolated. Networks give you contacts.

Someone you meet at a party or at your kids' playground can give you a job or an idea. Just as the brain works by building new connections between huge bundles of neurons, with each connection producing a new thought, so we as individuals need to find ourselves in the centre of the bundle in order to make more connections.

Networks are key to the latest thinking about economic development. Better networks are one reason why some countries are richer than others. As it happens, networks also help explain why some countries have done better at football than England. English football's biggest problem until very recently was probably geography. The country was too far from the networks of continental western Europe, where the best football was played.

Once upon a time, England was at the centre of football's knowledge network. From the first official football international in 1872, until at least the First World War, and perhaps even until England's first home defeat against Hungary in 1953, you could argue that England was the dominant football nation. It was the country that exported football know-how to the world in the form of managers. The English expat manager became such a legendary figure that to this day in Spain and Italy a head coach is known as a *'mister'*.

Many English people clung to the belief in England's footballing centrality long after it had ceased to be true. The astonishment each time England didn't win the World Cup ended only with the team's abject failures in the 1970s.

This gradual shift away from British dominance in football echoes the decline in Britain's economic status. The country went from supreme economic power under Victoria to having its hand held by the International Monetary Fund in the late 1970s. Admittedly, in football as in economics, most observers exaggerated Britain's decline. The country's position in the top 10 of economies was never much in doubt, but in football it became clear by 1970 at the latest that dominance had shifted across the Channel to core western Europe. For the next 30 years, this part of the continent was the most fertile network in football. And Britain was just outside it.

The German World Cup of 2006 demonstrated western Europe's grip on global football. The region has only about 400 million inhabitants, or 6 per cent of the world's population, yet only once all tournament did a western European team lose to a team from another region: Switzerland's insanely dull defeat on penalties by Ukraine.

That summer even Brazil couldn't match western Europe. Argentina continued its run of failing to beat a western European team in open play at a World Cup since the final against West Germany in 1986 (though it has won two of the eight subsequent encounters against Europeans on penalties). Big countries outside the region like Mexico, Japan, the US and Poland could not match little western European countries like Portugal, Holland or Sweden. If you understood the geographical rule of the last World Cup, you could sit in the stands for almost every match before the quarter-finals confident of knowing the outcome.

Western Europe excels at football for the same fundamental reason why it had the Scientific Revolution and was for centuries the world's richest region. The region's secret is what the historian Norman Davies calls its 'user-friendly climate'. Western Europe is mild and rainy. Because of that, the land is fertile, allowing hundreds of millions of people to inhabit a small area of land. That creates networks.

From the World Cup in Germany, you could have flown in two-and-a-half hours to about 20 countries containing about 300 million people. That is the densest network on earth. There was nothing like that in Japan at the previous World Cup: the only foreign capital you can reach from Tokyo within that time is Seoul. South Africa, host of the next World Cup, is even more isolated.

For centuries now, the interconnected peoples of western European have exchanged ideas fast. The 'Scientific Revolution' of the sixteenth and seventeenth centuries could happen in western Europe because its scientists were near each other, networking, holding a dialogue in their shared language: Latin. Copernicus, Polish son of a German merchant, wrote that the earth circled the Sun. Galileo in Florence read Copernicus and confirmed his findings through a telescope. The Englishman Francis Bacon described their 'scientific method': deductions based on data. England at the time was very much part of the European network.

A typical product of that network was the lens grinder, a crucial new machine in the development of the microscope in the early 1660s. Robert Hooke in London invented a new grinder, which made lenses so accurate that Hooke could publish a detailed engraving of a louse attached to a human hair. But meanwhile Sir

Robert Moray, a Scot in London who knew what Hooke was up to, was sending letters in French about the new grinder to the Dutch scientist Christiaan Huygens. Thanks to Moray, Huygens had previously got hold of details of Hooke's balance-spring watch.

Moray and Huygens 'sometimes wrote to each other several times a week', writes the historian Lisa Jardine. Their letters crossed the Channel in days, or about as quickly as mail does now. Meanwhile, in Paris the French astronomer Adrien Auzout was getting copies of some of their letters. So Hooke's breakthroughs were being spread to his European competitors almost instantly.

All this irritated Hooke. But the proximity of many thinkers in western Europe created an intellectual ferment. That is why so many of the great scientific discoveries were made there. These discoveries then helped make the region rich.

Centuries later, football spread the same way. In the nineteenth century the game infected western Europe first, because there it had the shortest distances to travel. Later, the proximity of so many peoples brought the region two world wars. After 1945, western Europeans decided they could live crammed together only under a sort of single government: the European Union. Borders opened, and the region became the most integrated in the history of the world.

Again the best ideas spread fastest here, just as they had in the Scientific Revolution. The region's soccer benefited. One of the men who carried tactical ideas around Europe was Arrigo Sacchi. His father was a shoe manufacturer in Ravenna, Italy, and the young Sacchi used to accompany him on business trips. He saw lots of games in Germany, Switzerland, France and the Netherlands. 'It opened my mind,' he later said. As manager of AC Milan in the 1980s, he imported a version of Dutch football that revolutionised the Italian game.

Ideas spread even more quickly in European football than in other economic sectors, because football is the most integrated part of the continent's economy. Only about 2 per cent of all western Europeans live in a different European Union country from the one in which they were born, because few companies bother hiring bus drivers or office administrators from neighbouring countries. In some professions, language barriers stop workers moving abroad.

But many footballers do find work abroad, largely because TV advertises their wares to employers across Europe. And so most of the EU's best players have gathered in the English, Spanish and Italian leagues, and meet each other on weekday nights in the Champions League. This competition is the European single market come to life, a dense network of talent.

The teams in the Champions League can draw talent from anywhere in the world. Nonetheless, an overwhelming majority of their players are western Europeans. With the world's best footballers and coaches packed together, the world's best football is constantly being refined here.

The best football today is Champions League football, western European football. It's a rapid passing game played by athletes. Rarely does anyone dribble, or keep the ball for a second; you pass instantly. It's not the beautiful game – dribbles are prettier – but it works best. All good teams everywhere in the world now play this way. Even the Brazilians adopted the Champions League style in the 1990s. They still have more skill than us, but they now try to play at our pace.

In other words, western Europe has discovered the secret of football. More precisely, a core group of western European countries has: namely five of the six nations that in 1957 founded the European Economic Community, ancestor of the European Union. (We'll leave out the sixth founding nation, the pathetic minnows Luxembourg.) West Germany, France, Italy, Holland and even Belgium don't all play in exactly the same style. Holland and Italy, say, are rather different. But they all adhere to the basic tenets of rapid collectivised western European football. Here are some results from the last 30 years:

- ⚽ The five core countries have won eight European Championships and World Cups between them.
- ⚽ The countries at the corners of Europe – the Brits, former Soviet bloc, Balkans, and Scandinavian nations north of the Baltic Sea – between them have won one: Greece's European Championship of 2004, delivered by a German coach.
- ⚽ Belgium has played as many finals in this period (one) as England, Russia, Ukraine, Poland and Turkey put together.
- ⚽ Europe's only other trophy in these 30 years has gone to Denmark, which enjoys an utterly permeable border with the five core countries.

Countries separated from the core EU – either by great distance, or by poverty, or by closed borders under dictatorships – often underperform in football.

In the vast landmass running from Portugal in the west to Poland in the east, every country of more than one million inhabitants except Belgium qualified. The nations that didn't make it are on Europe's margins: the Brits, most of Scandinavia, and most of Europe's eastern edge. The countries at great distance – and it can be a distance of the mind, rather than geographical distance – are often out of touch with core European football. Many countries on the margins have traditionally had dysfunctional indigenous styles of football. The Greeks, for instance, dribbled too much. The Brits played mindless kick-and-rush.

Again, this is explained by theories of networks. If you are on the periphery, as the British were until recently in football, it's harder to make new connections, because you have to travel further. Worse, those not on the periphery see you only as a second-best connection. You are the end of the line, not the gateway to a new set of connections. That's why foreign countries stopped hiring English coaches or even English players. As a result, the people on the periphery become more and more isolated and insular. The Ukrainian manager Valeri Lobanovski was a football genius, but during the

days of the Soviet Union he was so isolated that when a Dutch journalist came to interview him in the mid-1980s, Lobanovski pumped
him for information about Dutch footballers. Spain, to some
degree, had the same problem under Franco. 'Europe ends at the
Pyrenees,' was the saying in those days.

Gradually isolation becomes your mindset: after a while you
don't even *want* to adopt foreign ideas anymore. Anyone who has
spent time in England – particularly before 1992 – has witnessed
this attitude. Isolation can lead you into your own blind alleys that
nobody else appreciates. For instance, the long refusal of English
players to dive may have been an admirable cultural norm, but
they might have won more games if they had learnt from continental Europeans how to buy the odd penalty.

Happily, the era of British isolationism has now finished. The
era began on Sunday, 3 September 1939, when the country's
borders closed at the outbreak of the Second World War. In football, that isolation deepened when English clubs were banned
from European competitions after the Heysel disaster of 1985.
They lost what modest network they had.

Between 1990 and 1994, however, British isolation began to
break down: English clubs were readmitted to European competitions, new laws enforced free movement of labour and capital
within the EU, and Eurostar trains and budget airlines connected
Britain to the continent. London turned into a global city. Nowadays southern England, at least, belongs to core Europe, just as
it did during the Scientific Revolution.

The end of isolationism meant the end of English football
managers managing England or the best English clubs. You
wouldn't appoint a Frenchman to manage your baseball team,
because the French don't have a history of thinking hard about
baseball. And you wouldn't appoint an Englishman to manage
your football team, because the English don't have a history of
thinking hard about football. After Graham Taylor in his time as
England manager unintentionally discredited kick-and-rush, the

English embraced EEC football. The FA hired a manager drawn from Italian football, Sven Goran Eriksson.

At this, the *Daily Mail* lamented, 'The mother country of football, birthplace of the greatest game, has finally gone from the cradle to the shame.' It was a wonderful statement of 'English exceptionalism': the belief that England is an exceptional football country that should rule the world playing the English way. However, the obvious statistical truth is that England is not exceptional. It is typical of the second-tier football countries outside core western Europe.

Other peripheral countries from Greece to Japan soon followed the English example. Importing know-how from the core EEC turned out to be an excellent remedy for the problem of isolation, which makes it even odder that in 2006 England did an about-face and appointed Steve McClaren. The FA didn't realise that England, as a recovering isolationist, still needed foreign help.

Many of the countries that imported knowledge did very well indeed. Under Eriksson, England always reached the quarter-finals of major tournaments. Russia under Guus Hiddink got to the semi-finals of Euro 2008, their best performance since the USSR collapsed. At the same tournament Turkey also reached the semi-finals, in their case chiefly by importing fitness. Over Sunday lunch in a Lebanese restaurant in Geneva during the tournament, a Turkish official explained how the team kept coming back to win matches in the last few minutes. They had hired a fitness coach, Scott Peri, from the US company Athletes' Performance. Despite Peri's American passport, he was really a borrowing from core Europe: in 2006 the German manager Jürgen Klinsmann had used Athletes' Performance to turn Germany into the fittest side at the World Cup. When Peri arrived in the Turkish camp, the official explained, the players had complained that he worked them too hard. They said he was causing them injuries. But soon they got used to the workload. They then became extremely fit, and achieved a string of last-ditch comebacks.

Spain in 2008 no longer needed much foreign help. Spanish football had been opening to Europe since the early 1970s, as the Franco regime slowly began to give up on isolation and FC Barcelona imported the Dutch football thinkers Rinus Michels and Johan Cruijff. It also helped that Spain was then starting to grow richer. By now the country is fully networked in Europe. Its best players experience the Champions League every season. At Euro 2008, Spain won their first prize in 44 years.

England now seem to have accepted the need for EEC know-how. McClaren's successor, Fabio Capello, is like one of the overpaid consultants so common in development economics, flying in on business class to tell the natives what to do. His job is to teach the English some of the virtues of western European football. To cite just one of those virtues:

A GAME LASTS 90 MINUTES

Habitually English footballers charge out of the gate, run around like lunatics, and exhaust themselves well before the match is over, even if they aren't hung over.

You see this in England's peculiar scoring record in big tournaments. In every World Cup ever played, most goals were scored in the second halves of matches. That is natural: in the second half players tire, teams start chasing goals, and gaps open up on the field. But England, in their last five big tournaments, scored 22 of their 35 goals in the first halves of matches. Their record in crucial games is even starker: in the matches in which they got eliminated from these tournaments, they scored seven of their eight goals before half-time. In other words, England perform like a cheap battery. This is partly because they play in such an exhausting league, but also because they don't seem to have thought about pacing themselves.

Italians know exactly how to measure out the 90 minutes. They take quiet periods, when they sit back and make sure nothing happens, because they know that the best chance of scoring is in the closing minutes, when exhausted opponents will leave holes. That's when you need to be sharpest. In the World Cup of 2006, typically, Italy knocked out Australia and Germany with goals in the final three minutes.

England has already bought Italian know-how. Now all it needs to do is include its own middle classes, and stop worrying about foreigners in the Premier League, and it will finally stop under-achieving and perform as well as it should do. Hang on a moment: who says England underachieve?

SHOULD DO BETTER: ARE ENGLAND WORSE THAN THEY OUGHT TO BE?

That England underachieve is usually taken for granted in the British media. After all, the team haven't won anything since 1966, and sometimes don't even qualify for tournaments. Clearly that is not good enough for 'the mother country of football, birth-place of the greatest game'.

But are England really underachievers? Or is it just that the English expect too much of them? To answer this, we first need to work out how well England should do *given their resources.*

Before we are accused of looking for excuses, let's consider what is and isn't possible. A five-year-old can't win the 100-metre finals at the Olympics, and neither can a 70-year-old. You aren't going to have a career in the NBA if you are only five foot tall, and you'll never cox Oxford in the Boat Race if you are six foot eight. It is very unlikely that you will have a career in show-jumping if your parents earn less £20,000 per year, you probably won't win a boxing match if you've never had any train-ing as a boxer, and you won't have a shot at being world chess champion unless you can persuade a team of grandmasters to act as your seconds. Genetics are beyond our control; training depends partly on our own effort, but partly on the resources that other people give us.

What is true for the individual is also true for the nation. During his tenure an England football manager cannot easily (a) increase the size of the population from which he will have to draw the talent, (b) increase the national income so as to ensure a significant increase in the financial resources devoted to developing football, or (c) increase the accumulated experience of the national team by very much. (England have played over 800 games since their first game in 1872, and currently play around a dozen games per year, so each extra game doesn't add much to the history.)

Yet in any international match, these three factors – the size of the nation's population, the size of the national income and the country's experience in international football – hugely affect the outcome. It's unfair to expect Belarus, say, to perform as well as much larger, more experienced and richer Germany. It is fairer to assess how well each country *should* perform given its experience, income and population, and then to measure that expected performance against reality. Countries like Belarus or Luxembourg will never win a World Cup. The only measure of performance that makes any sense for them is one based on how effectively they use their limited resources. The same exercise makes sense for England too, if only as a check on tabloid hysteria: do England really underperform given what they have to work with?

In absolute terms England are about 10th in the world. But we want to know how well they do in relative terms – not relative to the expectations of the media, but relative to English resources. Might it be that England in fact *overachieve* given the country's experience, population and income?

To work this out, we need to know the football results for all the national teams in the world. Luckily, we have them. There are a number of databases around of international matches, but one of the best is maintained by Russell Gerrard, a mathematics professor at Cass Business School in the City of London. By day Russell worries about mathematical ways to represent the management problems of pension funds. For example, his most recent paper is snappily entitled 'Mean-Variance Optimization Problems for the Accumulation Phase in a Defined Benefit Plan'. It concerns, among other things, Lévy diffusion financial markets, the Hamilton–Jacobi–Bellman equation and the Feynman–Kac representation. As you might expect, Russell has been meticulous in accumulating the football data, which took him seven years of his life. His database runs from 1872 to 2001, and includes 22,130 games.

RUSSELL GERRARD: BRILLIANT FOOTBALL DATABASE

Later in the book, we will crunch Russell's data to discover which is the best football country on earth, and which punches most above its weight. But here, let's limit ourselves to a sneak preview of where England stand.

The distant past is of limited relevance. Let's therefore concentrate on the most recent period of Russell's database, 1980 to 2001.

This was by no means a golden age for England. The country didn't even qualify for the European Championship of 1984, or for the World Cup 10 years later, and their best moments in these 22 years were two lost semi-finals. Altogether in the period England played 228 matches. They won 49 per cent of them, and drew 32 per cent, for a 'win percentage' of 65 per cent (remember that for these purposes we treat a draw as half a win). That is near the middle of their historical range.

We want to see how much of a team's success, match by match, can be explained by population, wealth and experience. However, 'win percentage' is not the best measure of success, because any two wins are not the same. We all know that a 5–1 away win against a certain someone is not the same as a tame 1–0. To put it another way, if England play Luxembourg and win only 1–0, it's more likely that the Luxembourgeois press will be in ecstasy than the *Sun*.

Instead we chose goal difference as our measure, since for any match we expect that the greater the difference between the two teams' population, wealth and experience, the greater will be the disparity in scores. (Of course, a positive goal difference tends to be closely correlated with winning.)

We then analysed Russell's database of matches using the technique of multiple regression. Quite simply, multiple regression is a mathematical formula (first identified by the mathematician Carl Friedrich Gauss in 1801) for finding the closest statistical fit between one thing (in this case success of the national team) and any other collection of things (here experience, population and income per head). The idea is beautifully simple. The problem used to be the endless amount of computation required to find the closest fit. Luckily, modern computers have reduced this process to the press of a button (just look up 'regression' on your spreadsheet package). For each international match you simply input the population, income per head and team experience of the two nations at that date, and in seconds you get a read-out telling you how sensitive (on average) the team's performance is to each factor. We will also take account of home advantage for each match.

Collecting the data is usually the toughest part. We have assembled figures for the population, football experience and income per capita of 189 countries. We will unveil our findings about the other 188 countries later in the book. Here, we will just focus on England and their supposed underperformance.

We ran our regression, and immediately made several discoveries about international football. First, home advantage alone is worth a lead of about two thirds of a goal. Obviously that is a nonsense if applied to single game, but think of it this way: playing at home is like having a goal's head start in two out of every three games.

Second, having twice as much international experience as your rival is worth just over half a goal. In fact, experience turns out to matter much more than the size of your population, which is why the Swedes and Czechs do better at World Cups than very large but inexperienced Nigeria. The finding suggests that experienced Scotland should win rather more than they have been recently.

Having twice your opponent's population is worth only about one 10th of a goal. Having twice the GDP per head is worth about as little. In other words, although being large and rich helps a country win football matches, being experienced helps a lot more.

It should be added that our estimates are statistically very reliable. Not only is there not much doubt that these factors matter, but there is little doubt about the size of the effects. It is these effects that make the first rounds of World Cups fairly predictable.

However, much still remains unexplained. Experience, population and income per head combined explain only just over a quarter of the variation in goal difference. That is good news: if we could predict outcomes perfectly by just these three factors there would not be much point in watching World Cups at all. Nonetheless, the fact that these three factors explain so much tells us that, up to a point, football is rational and predictable.

For now, we are only interested in England. Are its resources so outstanding that it should do better than merely ranking around 10th in the world?

First let's look at experience. England is one of the most experienced countries in football. It played 790 internationals between 1872 and 2001. According to Russell's data, only Sweden played more (namely 802). However, England's much vaunted history is not worth much against the other leading football nations, because most of them have now accumulated similar amounts of experience. Brazil, Argentina and Germany had all played more than 700 internationals by 2001.

When it comes to our second variable, national income, England scores highly too. It is usually one of the richest of the serious football countries. Where England falls short is in size.

What often seems to go unnoticed is that without the other home nations, England's population of 51 million puts it at a major disadvantage to the countries it likes to measure itself against in football. Not only is Germany much bigger, with 80 million inhabitants, but France and Italy have around 60 million each. Among the leading European nations, England are ahead only of those other 'notorious underachievers', Spain (40 million). So in football terms, England is an experienced, rich, but medium-sized competitor.

Then we ran the numbers. We calculated that England, given their population, income and experience, 'should' score on average 0.63 goals per game more than their opponents.

To get a feel for how this works, consider England's performance at the World Cup of 1998. England played Tunisia, Romania, Colombia and Argentina, all on neutral ground, so there was no 'home field' effect. Facing Tunisia in their opening game, England had a population five times larger, a GDP per head four times larger and two times more international experience than their opponents. That combination gave an expected goal difference of one goal in England's favour. In the event, England won 2–0 and so did better than expected.

Against Romania, England had the advantage of twice the population, five times the income per head and a bit more experience (other countries have been playing football for longer than we sometimes like to think). All this gave England an expected advantage of about half a goal. England's 1–0 defeat meant that they underperformed by 1½ goals.

Next, England played Colombia, with a slight advantage in population, four times the income per head and double the experience. The package was worth an advantage of almost an entire goal (you start to see how the Tom Thumb World Cup might be organised) but again England overperformed, winning 2–0.

Then came Argentina: that goal, that sending-off, that disallowed header and that penalty shootout. (If you are under 16, well done for reading for this book, and now go ask your parents what we're talking about.) Should England have done better? Well, they had a slight advantage in population over Argentina, double the income per head, but slightly less experience (Argentina play a lot of games). Putting all that together, a fair score would have been a draw, which is exactly what happened after 120 minutes. Pity about the penalties, but more about those later in the book.

Our model allows us to re-examine every game ever played. The glorious uncertainty of football means that there are many deviations from expectations. However, if we average the difference between expectations and results for each country, we get a picture of whether any national team systematically overperforms or underperforms relative to its resources.

Our finding: England in the 1980–2001 period outscored their opponents by 0.84 goals per game, or 0.21 more than expected. In short, they were not underperforming at all. Contrary to popular opinion, they were overperforming.

As an example, take England's games against Poland. England played them 11 times in the period, won seven and drew four, with a goal difference of plus 16. Over the period England's population was about 25 per cent larger than Poland's, its income per head about three times greater and its international experience about 20 per cent more. These should have contributed to a positive goal difference of about one, three and one goals respectively, or a total of plus five. So England's goal difference of plus 16 was 11 goals better than you might have expected. That is not too shabby.

Later in the book we will reveal our global table for relative performance from 1980 to 2001: a ranking of the teams that did best relative to their countries' experience, income and population. For now, we'll just say that England came in 67th out of 189 countries. That put them in a group of moderate overachievers just below Russia, Azerbaijan and Morocco, and just above Ivory Coast and Mozambique. Like England, all these teams scored about a fifth of a goal per game more than they 'should' have given their population, income and experience.

However, England doesn't benchmark itself against Azerbaijan. It's more interesting to see whether England overperforms 'more' than the teams it sees as its rivals: the best countries in the world. Here's a ranking of the game's giants, plus England, based on how many goals per game each scores above expectations:

'ADDITIONAL' GOALS PER GAME ABOVE EXPECTATIONS

	Country				Country	
1	Brazil	0.67		5	Italy	0.20
2	France	0.35		6	United Germany	0.18
3	West Germany	0.28		7	Argentina	0.08
4	England	0.21				

It turns out that England compare pretty well to the giants. Their 'overperformance' is near the average for the world's leading nations, once we strip out the phenomenon that is Brazil.

Now let's look only at matches between European countries – the arena where England plays most of its football. The match results in Russell's database show that home advantage and experience count for a little less in Europe than in the world in general. On the other hand, population and GDP count for a bit more in Europe than in the world.

Taking all that into account, against European teams England overperform very slightly. From 1980 to 2001 they averaged 0.05 goals per game more than you would predict given their experience, income and population. That put them in 23rd place of the 49 European countries we ranked. They were just behind West Germany in 20th place, but ahead of France (25th) and Italy (31st), even though those countries won tournaments in this period and England didn't.

Our conclusion: England do just fine. They perform even better than expected, given what they have to start with. All they need to bring home some trophies is better timing – they must win fewer friendlies and more World Cup semis – and a few million more inhabitants. Consider the England–Germany semi-final at Euro 96. Both countries had similar levels of experience, and by 1996 German's lead over Britain in income per capita had slipped to only about 7 per cent. However, according to our analysis, England's home advantage (worth just under half a goal in a game between Europeans) was largely wiped out by Germany's much larger population. That made the expected goal difference only 0.26 in favour of the English home team, not far short of the draw that materialised in open play. In the end Gareth Southgate missed his penalty and England lost.

Overall in the 1980–2001 period, England played Germany 10 times. Taking the results at the end of normal time, England won two, drew three and lost five. Their goal difference over the 10 games was minus 2. Given Germany's slight lead in GDP per head in these years, but particularly given England's shortage of people, that is almost exactly the goal difference we would have predicted. The '30 years of hurt' shouldn't be a mystery.

If Britain keeps letting in immigrants, and if the German population drops by millions as predicted, and if English football finally enfranchises the middle classes, then that same match at Euro 2032 might have a different outcome; though given everything we know about life, possibly not.

PHASE EIGHT: ENGLAND ENTER THE NEXT WORLD CUP THINKING THEY WILL WIN IT

Famously, there is a manic depressive quality to supporting England. The nation tends to feel either very high or very low about the team. The night of that home defeat by Croatia in November 2007 was a low. As we write, in spring 2009, most English fans feel high again. Capello's team are eating up their qualifying group. People are starting to daydream about 11 July

2010, when a certain side might just be walking out for the World Cup final in Soccer City outside Johannesburg.

It sounds reasonable to presume that a good qualifying performance presages a good tournament. But is this belief backed up by the facts? When England qualify in style, are they really more likely to excel at the final tournament? We checked the data.

England have tried to qualify for 14 World Cups and Euros since 1980 (they didn't have to qualify for Euro 96). Of those 14 tournaments, they failed to qualify for three, and got knocked out in the first round four times. That means that half the England teams in this period can be considered failures. Collectively, we'll label these teams 'Bad England'.

Of the remaining seven tournaments, England reached the round of 16 twice, the quarter-finals four times, and the semi-final once, in 1990. We'll label these seven teams 'Good England'.

You would assume that Good England did much better in qualifying matches than Bad England. After all, Bad England regularly failed even to qualify. Yet the data show otherwise: in qualifiers, Good England and Bad England were much of a muchness.

The England team at Euro 88, for instance, were unmistakably Bad England. They lost all their three games in West Germany before going home with the hooligans. Yet they had qualified gloriously: five wins, one draw, no losses, and a goal difference of 19 for and just one against. By contrast, the Good England team of 1990 had muddled through qualifying, winning three and drawing three.

Even more curiously, England often performed just as well in qualifiers when it failed to make the tournament as when it succeeded. For example, in missing Euro 2008, England got exactly the same percentage of the available qualifying points (namely 66 per cent) as when it managed to qualify for Euro 2000 or for the World Cup of 1982.

Opposite is a comparison of the qualifying records of Good England (teams that made at least the round of 16) versus Bad England (teams that either missed the final tournament or went home after the first round):

ENGLANDS'S QUALIFYING RECORD SINCE 1980

Team	Played	Won	Drawn	Lost	For	Against
Bad England	60	36	16	8	140	33
Good England	56	36	13	7	106	28

The chart shows that Good England and Bad England had almost indistinguishable win–loss records in qualifying. Indeed, Bad England scored many more goals than Good England while conceding only slightly more. The lesson of history: England's performance at specific World Cups and European championships is almost entirely unpredictable.

What we see here is partly the enormous role of luck in history. We tend to think with hindsight that a team that did well in a particular tournament was somehow always going to do well, and a team that lost was doomed to do so. The winner's victory comes to seem inevitable. This is a common flaw in the writing of any kind of history.

But in fact, inevitable victories hardly ever happen in football tournaments. Perhaps the only recent case was Brazil at the World Cup of 2002. Just how dominant they were dawned on a leading European club manager a few months after the final. This manager was trying to sign Brazil's goalkeeper, Marcos. After all, Marcos was a world champion. Marcos visited the club and did some physical tests, in which he didn't perform particularly well. Never mind, thought the manager, the guy won the World Cup. So he offered Marcos a contract.

At two o'clock that morning, the manager was awoken at home by a phone call. It was Marcos's agent.

The agent said, 'I'm sorry but Marcos won't sign for you.'

The sleepy manager said, 'All right, but why not?'

Then the agent confessed. A couple of years before the World Cup, Marcos had broken his wrist. It had never healed properly. But his old club manager, Luiz Felipe Scolari, became manager of Brazil and put Marcos in the team. Suddenly Marcos was going to a World Cup.

Every day at the tournament, the agent explained, Marcos was in pain. He could barely even train. In matches he could barely catch a ball. Every day Marcos told himself, 'I really must tell Scolari about my wrist.' But he could never quite bring himself to. So he went on, day by day, until he found that he had won the World Cup. Brazil were so superior that they won the World Cup with a crocked goalkeeper.

However, such dominance is very rare. Normally the differences between teams in the final stages of a World Cup are tiny. The difference between an England team being considered legendary or a failure is two to three games, each generally decided by a single goal, in two years.

After all, the difference between making a World Cup and spending the summer on the beach can be just one point. Sometimes it's a point that you lost by hitting the post. Sometimes it's a point garnered by a rival in a match you didn't even play in.

Once you're at the World Cup, the difference between going home ignominiously in the first round and making the semi-finals is often a matter of a few inches here or there on a couple of shots. In 1990, for instance, England got out of the first round by drawing with Holland and Ireland, and then beating Egypt 1–0. Had a single Dutch or Irish shot happened to go in, or had Mark Wright's header against Egypt missed, Gazza would never have been able to parade around Luton in false breasts after the semi-final and unleash the 'New Football'.

That World Cup was considered a success; the quarter-final of 2006 a failure. Yet it could almost as easily have been the other way around, if Paul Robinson had guessed right on a couple of

Portuguese penalties in 2006. The greatest prize in sport hinges on a very few moments. It's the same in baseball, notes Michael Lewis in *Moneyball*: 'The season ends in a giant crapshoot. The play-offs frustrate rational management because, unlike the long regular season, they suffer from the sample size problem.'

Lewis means that because there are so few games in the play-offs – because the 'sample size' is so small – random factors play an outsize role in determining the winner. It's the same in football World Cups, and even more so in European Championships. 'Euros' only last three weeks, and as Arsène Wenger notes, any team in a league can be top of the table after three weeks.

Most fans understand that luck matters, even if they construct a post-fact story about the tournament that makes either the false breasts or the turnips seem fated from the start. But our data point to an even scarier truth than the existence of fluke: namely, that there is barely any difference between 'brilliant' and 'terrible' England teams. It looks suspiciously as if England are always more or less equally good.

This may sound hard to credit. Fans feel strongly about the qualities of managers and players. There are periods of national optimism, and national pessimism, associated with the view that the England team is either strong or disgraceful.

But in fact, watching England play resembles watching a coin-tossing competition. If we focus on outright victories, then England on average win just over 50 per cent of their games; the rest they either draw or lose. So just as a coin has half a chance of landing heads, and half tails, England in the average game have about half a chance of winning and half of not winning. We assigned a '1' for each win and '0' for a loss or a draw, and examined the sequence of the England's 400 games since 1980.

Before we discuss this sequence, let's look at coin-tossing. If you tossed a coin 400 times, you would expect on average to get 200 heads and 200 tails. However, there is no reason to think that the outcomes would alternate (heads, tails, heads, tails ...).

Sometimes you will get sequences of a few heads, sometimes a few tails. Crucially, though, there would be no relationship at all between the current coin toss and the last one. If you toss a fair coin there is always a 50/50 chance of heads, whatever sequence has occurred up to this point. There is no statistical correlation between current coin tosses and past coin tosses, even if the average of any sequence is always around 50 per cent.

Here is our finding: England's win sequence over the 400 games is indistinguishable from a random series of coin tosses. There is no predictive value in the outcome of England's last game, or indeed in any combination of England's recent games. Whatever happened in the last match appears to have no bearing on what will happen tonight. The only thing you can predict is that over the medium to long term, England will win about half their games outright. We have seen that the outcome of matches can be largely predicted by a country's population, income and experience. However, this only explains the *average* outcome. In other words, if England were smaller, poorer or less experienced, it would have a lower percentage of wins, but the sequence of these wins would still be unpredictable.

To make sure that our finding was right, we constructed a few random sequences of ones and zeros to see if they looked like England results. Often we found more apparent correlation in our random sequences than in England's results.

Contrary to all popular opinion, it may be that the strength of the England team barely ever changes (which would make the entire apparatus of punditry attached to the team instantly redundant). A star player might fade or retire, but in a country of 50 million people, there is always someone coming up who is near enough his level as to make almost no difference. Over the long term, the three key factors that determine a country's performance are very stable. The British economy may have boomed in the 1990s, and is now dropping down the global wealth rankings, but measured over the last century Britain has always been one of the wealthiest nations in the world. Equally, its share of the football population changes only glacially. And while the England team gains experience, so do its main rivals. The only key factor that changes is home advantage. Given that playing at home is worth a lead of two thirds of a goal per game in global football, it's little wonder that England won the World Cup in 1966.

Otherwise, England's performances in good or bad times are much the same; it's just that fans and media seek to see patterns even though none exists. Nick Taleb, the financial investor who wrote *The Black Swan: The Impact of the Highly Improbable*, famously explained that we are constantly fooled by randomness. In neuroscientific terms, our rational brains are egged on by our emotional brains to find patterns where there aren't any. In the end, the best explanation for the short-term ups and downs of the England team is randomness.

SECTION I

THE CLUBS:
Racism, Stupidity, Bad Transfers, Capital Cities, and What
Actually Happened in that Penalty Shootout in Moscow

GENTLEMEN PREFER BLONDS: HOW TO AVOID SILLY MISTAKES IN THE TRANSFER MARKET

In 1983 AC Milan spotted a talented young black forward playing for Watford. The word is that the player they liked was John Barnes, and that they then confused him with his fellow black teammate Luther Blissett. Whatever the truth, Milan ended up signing Blissett for £1 million. As a player Blissett became such a joke in Italy that the name 'Luther Blissett' is now used as a pseudonym by groups of anarchist writers. He spent one unhappy year in Milan, before the club sold him back to Watford for just over half the sum they had paid for him. However, that year did give football one of its best quotes. 'No matter how much money you have here,' Blissett lamented, 'you can't seem to get Rice Krispies.' More on Rice Krispies later.

Clubs are always spending fortunes on the wrong transfers. Newcastle United are perhaps the most humorous example, but in fact, the amount that almost any club spends on transfer fees bears little relation to where it finishes in the league. We studied the spending of 40 English clubs between 1978 and 1997, and found that their outlay on transfers explained only 16 per cent of their total variation in league position. By contrast, their spending on salaries explained 92 per cent of that variation. In the 1998–2007 period, spending on salaries by clubs in the Premier League and Championship still explained 89 per cent of the variation in league position. It seems that high wages help a club much more than do spectacular transfers.

THE MORE YOU PAY YOUR PLAYERS, THE HIGHER YOU FINISH (UNLESS YOU ARE MANCHESTER CITY): AVERAGE LEAGUE POSITION AND WAGE SPENDING RELATIVE TO THE AVERAGE FOR PREMIER LEAGUE AND CHAMPIONSHIP CLUBS 1998–2007

Club	Average league Position	Wage spending relative to the average spending of all clubs
1 Manchester United	2	3.16
2 Arsenal	2	2.63
3 Chelsea	3	3.50
4 Liverpool	4	2.68
5 Newcastle United	9	1.93
6 Aston Villa	9	1.34
7 Tottenham Hotspur	10	1.60
8 Everton	12	1.41
9 Middlesbrough	12	1.32
10 Leeds United	13	1.70
11 West Ham United	14	1.31
12 Blackburn Rovers	14	1.48
13 Charlton Athletic	15	0.98
14 Bolton Wanderers	16	0.92
15 Fulham	16	1.24
16 Southampton	16	0.92
17 Sunderland	18	1.00
18 Manchester City	18	1.24
19 Wigan Athletic	19	0.59

20	Wimbledon	19	0.94
21	Birmingham City	20	0.74
22	Leicester City	21	0.88
23	Derby County	23	0.82
24	Ipswich Town	24	0.65
25	Bradford City	24	0.55
26	West Bromwich Albion	25	0.52
27	Reading	26	0.50
28	Portsmouth	26	0.73
29	Wolverhampton Wanderers	26	0.61
30	Coventry City	27	0.70
31	Sheffield United	27	0.50
32	Barnsley	28	0.45
33	Preston North End	28	0.26
34	Watford	29	0.48
35	Norwich City	29	0.50
36	Sheffield Wednesday	29	0.68
37	Crystal Palace	30	0.47
38	Nottingham Forest	31	0.62
39	Millwall	31	0.30
40	Cardiff City	33	0.37
41	Burnley	33	0.28
42	Huddersfield Town	34	0.35
43	Plymouth Argyle	34	0.16
44	Stoke City	35	0.26
45	Gillingham	36	0.19
46	Tranmere Rovers	37	0.25
47	Stockport County	37	0.20
48	Oxford United	38	0.23
49	Crewe Alexandra	38	0.13
50	Grimsby Town	38	0.20
51	Queens Park Rangers	39	0.55
52	Hull City	40	0.23
53	Bury	40	0.21

54	Swindon Town	40	0.28
55	Walsall	40	0.19
56	Port Vale	41	0.24
57	Rotherham United	41	0.15
58	Brighton & Hove Albion	42	0.15

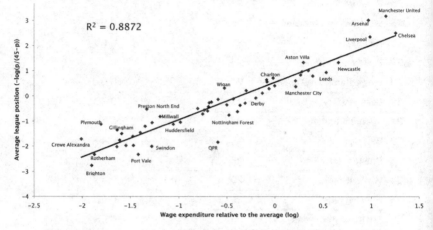

Premier League and Championship Teams 1998–2007

In short, the more you pay your players in wages, the higher you will finish; but what you pay *for* them in transfer fees doesn't seem to make much difference. (This suggests that, in general, it may be better to raise your players' pay than risk losing a couple of them and have to go out and buy replacements.)

While the market for players' wages is pretty efficient – the better a player is, the more he earns – the transfer market is inefficient. Much of the time, clubs buy the wrong players. Even now that they have brigades of international scouts, they still waste fortunes on flops like Blissett. (The transfer market is also of dubious legality – do clubs really have a right to 'buy' and 'sell' employees? – but that's another matter.)

Any inefficient market is an opportunity for somebody. If most clubs are wasting most of their transfer money, then a club that spends wisely is going to overperform. In fact, a few wise buyers have consistently outperformed the transfer market: Brian Clough and his assistant-cum-soulmate Peter Taylor in their years at Nottingham Forest, Arsène Wenger during his first decade at Arsenal, and, most mysteriously of all, Olympique Lyon, who have progressed from obscure provincial club, a sort of French Southampton, to a dictatorial rule over French football. From 2002 through 2008, Lyon won the French league seven times running. The usual way to win things in football is to pay high salaries. These clubs have found a different route: they have worked out the secrets of the transfer market.

There is a fourth master of the transfer market who is worth a look, even if he works in a different sport across an ocean: Billy Beane, general manager of the Oakland A's baseball team. Michael Lewis's book *Moneyball* explains how Beane turned one of the poorest teams in baseball into one of the best by the simple method of rejecting what everyone in the sport had always 'known' to be true about the transfer market. Lewis writes, 'Understanding that he would never have a Yankee-sized checkbook, Beane had set about looking for inefficiencies in the game.' It's odd how many of the same inefficiencies exist in soccer too.

If we study these masters of transfers, it will help us uncover the secrets of the market that all the other clubs are missing.

First of all, though, here are a few of the most obvious inefficiencies in the market. Although it doesn't take a Wenger or a Beane to identify these, they continue to exist:

✪ A new manager wastes money.

Typically, the new manager wants to put his mark on his new side. So he buys his own players. He then has to 'clear out' some of his predecessor's purchases, usually at a discount.

Strangely, it's Alan Sugar's tight-fisted Tottenham that provides the worst example. In May 2000 the club's manager George Graham paid Dynamo Kiev £11 million – nearly twice Spurs's previous record fee – for the Ukrainian striker Sergei Rebrov. Clearly, Rebrov was meant to be a long-term investment.

But nine months later, Sugar sold his stake in Tottenham, whereupon the new owners sacked Graham and replaced him with Glenn Hoddle. Hoddle didn't rate Rebrov. The record signing ended up on the bench, was sent on loan to Turkey, and in 2004 moved to West Ham on a free transfer.

A few years later Spurs discovered a new method for short-term money-burning: sell and then buy back exactly the same players. In January 2008, they transferred Jermain Defoe to Portsmouth for £7.5 million, and six months later sent Robbie Keane to Liverpool for £19 million. Then, in January 2009, under their new manager Harry Redknapp, they bought both players back again. They paid out about the same total sum that they had received for the duo the year before, though their outlay could rise by about another £7 million depending on how often Keane plays. If you add in agents' fees, taxes, the loss of a year of Defoe's services, and six months of Keane's, plus the twofold disruption to the team, this sort of waste helps explain why Spurs got left behind by Wenger's Arsenal. Perhaps Redknapp was right to buy the duo back. The point is that Spurs were wrong to have let them be dealt away so blithely in the first place.

Yet Spurs and Newcastle are only slightly sillier than most clubs. This form of waste is common across football: a new manager is allowed to buy and sell on the pretence that he is reshaping the club for many years to come, even though in practice he almost always leaves pretty rapidly. He doesn't care how much his wheeler-dealing costs: he doesn't get a bonus if the club makes a profit.

Other inefficiencies of the market:

⚽ **Stars of recent World Cups or European championships are overvalued.**

The worst time to buy a player is in the summer when he's just done well at a big tournament. Everyone in the transfer market has seen how good the player is, but he is exhausted and quite likely sated with success. Overpaying for these shooting stars fits what *Moneyball* calls 'a tendency to be overly influenced by a guy's most recent performance: what he did last was not necessarily what he would do next.'

Newcastle are of course the supreme suckers for shooting stars. This is largely because their fans demand it. Newcastle (or Spurs, or Marseille in France) probably aren't even trying to be 'rational' in the transfer market. Their aim is not to buy the best results for as little money as possible; rather, their big signings (like buying fragile Michael Owen for £17 million) are best understood as marketing gifts to their fans. Buying a big name is a way of saying, 'Yes, we are a big club.' It gives the supporters the thrill of expectation, a sense that their club is going somewhere, which may be as much fun as actually winning things. Buying big names is how these clubs keep their customers satisfied during the three-month summer shutdown.

So addicted are Newcastle to buying big names that even their high spending on salaries doesn't bring them the high league position you would expect. When Francisco Pérez Cutiño analysed data for the Premier League for the 2006–07 season, for an unpublished MBA paper at Judge Business School in Cambridge, he found that 'only Newcastle United seemed to significantly underperform taking into account its wage expenditure'.

⚽ **Certain nationalities are overvalued.**

Clubs will pay more for a player from a 'fashionable' football country. The American goalkeeper Kasey Keller says that in the transfer market, it's good to be Dutch. 'Giovanni van Bronckhorst is the best example,' Keller told the German journalist Christoph Biermann. 'He went from Rangers to Arsenal, failed there, and then where did he go? To Barcelona! You have to be a Dutchman to do that. An American would have been sent straight back to DC United.'

The most fashionable nationality of all in the transfer market is Brazilian. As Alex Bellos writes in *Futebol: The Brazilian Way of Life*: 'The phrase "Brazilian footballer" is like the phrases "French chef" or "Tibetan monk". The nationality expresses an authority, an innate vocation for the job – whatever the natural ability.' A Brazilian agent who had exported very humble Brazilian players to the Faroe Islands and Iceland told Bellos: 'It's sad to say, but it is much easier selling, for example, a crap Brazilian than a brilliant Mexican. The Brazilian gets across the image of happiness, party, carnival. Irrespective of talent, it is very seductive to have a Brazilian in your team.'

A wise club will buy unfashionable nationalities – Bolivians, say, or Belorussians – at discounts.

And, lastly, a less obvious inefficiency:

⚽ Gentlemen prefer blonds.

At least one big English club noticed that its scouts kept recommending blond players. The likely reason: when you are scanning a field of 22 similar-looking players, the blonds tend to stand out (except, presumably, in Scandinavia). The colour catches the eye. So the scout notices the blond player without understanding why. The club in question began to take this distortion into account when judging scouting reports.

Similarly, Beane at the Oakland A's noticed that baseball scouts had all sorts of 'sight-based prejudices'. They were suspicious of fat guys or skinny little guys or 'short right-handed pitchers', and they overvalued handsome strapping athletes of the type that Beane himself had been aged 17. Scouts look for players who *look* the part. Perhaps in soccer, blonds are thought to look more like superstars.

This taste for blonds is an example of the 'availability heuristic': the more available a piece of information is to the memory, the more likely it is to influence your decision, even when the information is irrelevant. Blonds stick in the memory.

The inefficiencies we have cited so far are so-called 'systemic failures': more than just individual mistakes, they are deviations from rationality. All this is what you might call 'transfer market 101'. To learn more about how to play the market, we need to study the masters.

DRUNKS, GAMBLERS AND BARGAINS: CLOUGH AND TAYLOR AT FOREST

'Cloughie likes a bung,' Alan Sugar told the High Court in 1993. Sugar's former manager at Spurs, Terry Venables, had told him so. The court heard that when Clough bought or sold a player for Nottingham Forest, he liked to receive a personal bonus, which in a perfect world would be handed over in a motorway service café. Clough denied everything – 'A bung? Isn't that something you get from a plumber to stop up the bath?' – and was never prosecuted. Yet what seems likely is this: 'Old Big Head' was so good at transfers, making profits even while turning a little provincial club into European champions, that he felt he deserved the odd bonus. More than anyone else in his day, Clough and his right-hand man Peter Taylor had succeeded in gaming the transfer market.

Clough and Taylor met while playing in a 'Probables versus Possibles' reserve game at Middlesbrough in 1955. They seem to have fallen in love at first sight. Pretty soon they were using their free time to travel around the north watching football and coaching children together. Taylor never became more than a journeyman keeper, but Clough scored the fastest 200 goals ever notched in English football until, at the age of 27, he wrecked his right knee skidding on a frozen pitch on Boxing Day 1962. Three years later he phoned Taylor and said: 'I've been offered the managership of Hartlepool and I don't fancy it, but if you'll come, I'll consider it.' He then immediately hung up. Taylor took the bait, though to get in he had to double as Hartlepool's medical department, running on with the sponge on match days. It was the prelude to their legendary years together at Derby and Nottingham Forest.

David Peace's novel *The Damned United* – and Tom Hooper's film of it – is in large part the love story of Clough and Taylor. The men's wives only have walk-on parts. As in all good couples, each partner has his assigned role. As Peace's fictional Clough tells himself: 'Peter has the eyes and the ears, but you have the stomach and the balls.' Taylor found the players, and Clough led them to glory.

The relationship ended in 'divorce' in 1982, with Taylor's resignation from Forest. It seems that the rift had opened two years before, when Taylor published his excellent but now forgotten memoir *With Clough by Taylor*. More of this in a moment, because it is the closest thing we have to a handbook to the transfer market.

But clearly the couple had other problems besides literature. Perhaps Clough resented his partner because he needed him so badly – not the sort of relationship Clough liked. Indeed, the film *The Damned United* depicts him failing at Leeds partly because Taylor is not there to scout players, and finally driving down to Brighton with his young sons to beg his partner's forgiveness. He finds Taylor doing the gardening. At Taylor's insistence, he gets down on his knees in the driveway, and recites: 'I'm nothing without you. Please, please, baby, take me back.' And Taylor takes him back, and buys him the cut-price Forest team that wins two European Cups. Because, whatever their precise relationship, the duo certainly knew how to sign footballers. Here are a few of their coups:

⚽ Buying Gary Birtles from the non-league club Long Eaton for £2,000 in 1976, and selling him to Manchester United four years later for £1.25 million. A measure of what a good deal this was for Forest: United forked out £250,000 more for Birtles than they would pay to sign Eric Cantona from

Leeds 12 years later, in 1992. Birtles ended up costing United about £86,000 a goal, and after two years was sold back to Forest for a quarter of the initial fee.

⚽ Buying Roy Keane from an Irish club called Cobh Ramblers for £47,000 in 1990, and selling him to Manchester United three years later for £3.75 million, then a British record fee.

⚽ Buying Kenny Burns from Birmingham City for £145,000 in 1977. Taylor writes in *With Clough by Taylor* that Burns was then regarded as 'a fighting, hard-drinking gambler ... a stone overweight'. In 1978, English football writers voted Burns Footballer of the Year.

⚽ Twice buying Archie Gemmill cheaply. In 1970, when Gemmill was playing for Preston, Clough drove to his house and asked him to come to Derby. Gemmill refused. Clough said that in that case he would sleep outside in his car. Gemmill's wife invited him to sleep in the house instead. The next morning at breakfast Clough persuaded Gemmill to sign. The fee was £60,000, and Gemmill quickly won two league titles at Derby. In 1977 Clough paid Derby £20,000 and the forgotten goalkeeper John Middleton to bring Gemmill to his new club, Forest, where the player won another league title.

If there is one club where almost every pound spent on transfers bought results, it was Forest under Clough. In the 1970s the correlation must have been off the charts: they won two European Cups with a team assembled largely for peanuts. Sadly there are no good financial data for that period, but we do know that even from 1982 to 1992, in Clough's declining years, after Taylor had left him, Forest performed as well on the field as clubs that were spending twice as much on wages. Clough had broken the usually iron link between salaries and league position.

It's hard to identify all of the duo's transfer secrets, and if their rivals at the time had understood what they were up to, everyone would simply have imitated them. Taylor's book makes it clear that he spent a lot of time trying to identify players (like Burns) whom others had wrongly undervalued owing to surface characteristics; but then everyone tries to do that. Sometimes Forest did splash out on a player who was rated by everybody, like Trevor Francis, the first 'million-pound man', or Peter Shilton, whom they made the most expensive goalkeeper in British history.

Yet thanks to *With Clough by Taylor*, we can identify three of the duo's rules:

⚽ **Be as eager to sell good players as to buy them.**
'It's as important in football as in the stock market to sell at the right time,' wrote Taylor. 'A manager should always be looking for signs of disintegration in a winning side and then sell the players responsible before their deterioration is noticed by possible buyers.' (Or in Billy Beane's words: 'You have to always be upgrading. Otherwise you're fucked.')

The moment when a player reaches the top of his particular hill is like the moment when a stock market peaks. Clough and Taylor were always trying to gauge that moment, and sell. Each time they signed a player, they would give him a set speech, which Taylor recorded in his book: 'Son, the first time we can replace you with a better player, we'll do it without blinking an eyelid. That's what we're paid to do – to produce the best side and to win as many things as we can. If we see a better player than you but don't sign him then we're frauds. But we're not frauds.' In 1981, just after Kenny Burns had won everything with Forest, the club flogged him to Leeds for £400,000.

⚽ **Older players are overrated.**
'I've noticed over the years how often Liverpool sell players as they near or pass their thirtieth birthday,' notes Taylor in his book. 'Bob Paisley [Liverpool's then manager] believes the average First Division footballer is beginning to burn out at thirty.' Taylor added,

rather snottily, that that was true of a 'running side like Liverpool', but less so of a passing one like Forest. Nonetheless, he agreed with the principle of selling older players.

The master of that trade today is Wenger. Arsenal's manager is one of the few people in football who can view the game from the outside. In part, this is because he has a degree in economic sciences from the University of Strasbourg. As a trained economist, he is inclined to trust data rather than the game's received wisdom. Wenger sees that in the transfer market, clubs tend to overvalue a player's past performance. That prompts them to pay fortunes for players who have just passed their peak. Probably because Wenger was one of the first managers to use statistics to assess players, he spotted that older players declined sooner than was conventionally realised. When Dennis Bergkamp was in his early thirties, Wenger began to substitute him late in games. If Bergkamp complained about it afterwards, Wenger would simply produce the match statistics: 'Look, Dennis, after 70 minutes you started to run less. And your speed decreased.'

Wenger often lets defenders carry on until their mid-thirties, but he usually gets rid of his midfielders and forwards much younger. He flogged Thierry Henry for £16 million aged 29, Patrick Vieira for £14 million aged 29, Emmanuel Petit for £7 million aged 29 and Marc Overmars for £25 million aged 27, and none of them ever did as well again after leaving Arsenal.

Curiously, precisely the same overvaluation of older players exists in baseball too. The conventional wisdom in the game had always been that players peaked in their early thirties. Then along came Bill James from his tiny town in Kansas. In his mimeographs, the father of sabermetrics showed that the average player peaked not in his early thirties, but at just 27 years old.

⚽ **Buy players with personal problems (like Burns, or the gambler Stan Bowles) at a discount. Then help them deal with their problems.**

Clough, a drinker, and Taylor, a gambler, had empathy with troubled footballers. While negotiating with a new player they would ask him a stock question, 'to which we usually know the answer', wrote Taylor. It was: 'Let's hear your vice before you sign. Is it women, booze, drugs or gambling?'

Clough and Taylor thought that once they knew the vice, they could help the player manage it. Taylor says he told Bowles, who joined Forest in 1979 (and, as it happens, failed there): 'Any problem in your private life must be brought to us; you may not like that but we'll prove to you that our way of management is good for all of us.' After a player confided a problem, wrote Taylor, 'if we couldn't find an answer, we would turn to experts: we have sought advice for our players from clergymen, doctors and local councillors.' Taking much the same approach, Wenger helped Tony Adams and Paul Merson combat their addictions.

All this might sound obvious, but the usual attitude in football is, 'We paid a lot of money for you, now get on with it,' as if mental illness, addictions or homesickness should not exist above a certain level of income.

RELOCATION, RELOCATION, RELOCATION: THE RICE KRISPIES PROBLEM

Clough and Taylor understood that many transfers failed because of a player's problems off the pitch. In a surprising number of cases, these problems are the product of the transfer itself. Moving to a job in another city is always stressful; moving to another country even more so. Yet clubs who pay millions of pounds for foreign players are often unwilling to spend a few thousand more to help the players settle in their new home. Instead the clubs typically tell them: 'Here's a plane ticket, come over, and play brilliantly from day one.' The player fails to adjust to the new country, underperforms, and his transfer fee is wasted. 'Relocation', as the industry of relocation consultants call it, is one of the biggest inefficiencies in the transfer market.

All the inefficiencies surrounding relocation could be assuaged. Most big businesses know how difficult relocation is, and do their best to smooth the passage. When a senior Microsoft executive moves countries, a 'relocation consultant' helps his family find schools, a house, and learn the social rules of the new country. If Luther Blissett had been working for Microsoft, a relocation consultant could have found him Rice Krispies. An expensive relocation might cost £15,000, or 0.1 per cent of a largish transfer fee, but in football, the most globalised industry of all, spending anything at all on relocation is regarded as a waste of money.

Boudewijn Zenden, who has played in four countries, for clubs including Liverpool and Barcelona, told us at his latest stop, Marseille:

It's the weirdest thing ever that you can actually buy a player for 20 mil, and you don't do anything to make him feel at home. I think the first thing you should do is get him a mobile phone and a house. Get him a school for the kids, get something for his missus, get a teacher in for both of them straight away, because obviously everything goes with the language. Do they need anything for other family members? Do they need a driving licence? Do they need a visa? Do they need a new passport? Sometimes even at the biggest clubs it's really badly organised.

Milan: best club ever. AC Milan is organised in a way you can't believe. Anything is done for you. You arrive, you get your house, it's fully furnished, you get five cars to choose from, you know the sky's the limit. They really say: we'll take care of everything else, you make sure you play really well. Whereas unfortunately in a lot of clubs, you have to get after it yourself

… Sometimes you get to a club and you've got people actually at the club who take profit from players.

In football, bad relocations are the norm, like Chelsea signing cosmopolitan Ruud Gullit in 1996 and sticking him in a hotel in Slough, or Ian Rush coming back from two bad years in Italy marvelling, 'It was like another country.' Many players down the decades would have understood that phrase. But perhaps the great failed relocation, one that a Spanish relocation consultant still cites in her presentations, was Nicolas Anelka's to Real Madrid in 1999.

Half an hour of conversation with Anelka is enough to confirm that he is self-absorbed, scared of other people, and not someone who makes contact easily. Nor does he appear to be good at languages, because after a decade in England he still speaks very mediocre English. Anelka is the sort of expatriate who really needs a relocation consultant.

Real had spent £22 million buying him from Arsenal. They then spent nothing on helping him adjust. On day one the shy, awkward 20-year-old reported at the club, and found that there was nobody to show him around. He hadn't even been assigned a locker in the changing-room. Several times that first morning he would take a locker that seemed to be unused, only for another player to walk in and claim it.

Anelka doesn't seem to have talked about his problems to anyone at Real. Nor did anyone at the club ask him. Instead he talked to *France Football,* a magazine that he treated as his newspaper of record, like a 1950s prime minister talking to *The Times.* 'I am alone against the rest of the team,' he revealed midway through the season. He claimed to possess a video showing his teammates looking gloomy after he had scored his first goal for Real after six months at the club. He had tried to give this video to the coach, but the coach hadn't wanted to see it. Also, the other black Francophone players had told Anelka that the other players wouldn't pass to him. Madrid ended up giving him a 45-day ban, essentially for being maladjusted.

Paranoid though Anelka may have been, he had a point. The other players really didn't like him. And they never got to know him, because nobody at the club ever seems to have bothered to introduce him to anyone. As he said later, all Real had told him was, 'Look after yourself.' The club seemed to have taken the strangely materialistic view that Anelka's salary should determine his behaviour. But even in materialistic terms, that was foolish. If you pay £22 million for an immature young employee, it is bad management to make him look after himself. Wenger at Arsenal knew that, and he had Anelka on the pitch scoring goals.

Even a footballer with a normal personality can find emigration tricky. Tyrone Mears, an English defender who moved to Marseille, where his best relocation consultant was his teammate Zenden, says: 'Sometimes it's not a problem of the player adapting. A lot of the times it's the family adapting.' Perhaps the player's girl-friend is unhappy because she can't find a job in the new town. Or perhaps she's pregnant and doesn't know how to negotiate the local hospital, or perhaps she can't find Rice Krispies. ('Or beans on toast,' adds Zenden, when told about the Blissett drama.) The club doesn't care. It is paying her boyfriend well. He simply has to perform.

There may never have been a football club with an HR department. There are a few relocation consultants in football, but they are never called that, and they usually aren't hired by clubs. Instead they work either for players' agents, or for sportswear companies. If Nike or Adidas is paying a player to wear its boots, it needs him to succeed. If the player moves to a foreign club, the sportswear company – knowing that the club probably won't bother – sometimes sends a minder to live in that town and look after him.

The minder gives the player occasional presents, acts as his secretary, friend and shrink, and remembers his wife's birthday.

The minder of a young midfielder who was struggling in his first weeks at Milan said that his main task, when the player came home from training frustrated, lonely and confused by Italy, was to take him out to dinner. At dinner the player would grumble and say, 'Tomorrow I'm going to tell the coach what I really think of him,' and the minder would say, 'That might not be such a brilliant idea. Here, have some more *linguine alle vongole*.' To most players, this sort of thing comes as a bonus in a stressful life. To a few, it is essential.

However, these minders are clearly not enough. Too many players still flop abroad. Clubs often anticipate this by avoiding footballers who seem particularly ill-equipped to adjust. For instance, on average Brazilians are the world's best footballers. Yet historically English clubs rarely buy them, because Brazilians don't speak English, don't like cold weather, and don't tend to understand the core traditions of English football, like drinking 20 pints of beer in a night. Few Brazilians adjust easily to English football.

English clubs have traditionally bought Scandinavians instead. On average, Scandinavians are worse footballers than Brazilians, but they are very familiar with English, cold weather and 20 pints of beer. Scandinavians adapted to England, and so the clubs bought them. But the clubs were missing a great opportunity. Anyone who bought a great Brazilian player and hired a good relocation consultant to help him adjust would be on to a winner. Yet few clubs did. Years used to go by without any English club buying a Brazilian.

Gradually, the football business is becoming less stupid. A few years ago Ajax Amsterdam hired a woman to help foreign players settle in. She found that some of their problems were absurdly easy to solve. When Steven Pienaar and another young South African footballer joined Ajax, they were teenagers, had never lived on their own before, and suddenly found themselves sharing an apartment in a cold country at the other end of the earth. Inevitably, they put their music speakers on the bare floor and turned the music on. Inevitably, the neighbours complained. The South Africans had a miserable time in their building, until the woman from Ajax came round to see what was wrong, and suggested they put their speakers on a table instead. They did. The noise diminished, their lives got easier, and that might just have helped their football. Ajax has since appointed a full-time employee to help with relocation. Zenden says of clubs in general:

> For any foreign player, or even a player who comes in new, they could get one man who's actually there to take care of every-thing. But then again, sometimes players are a bit – I don't want to say abusive, but they might take profit of the situa-tion. They might call in the middle of the night, just to say there's no milk in the fridge. You know how they are sometimes.

Most clubs still don't believe in relocation. Didier Drogba in his autobiography recounts joining Chelsea from Olympique Marseille in 2004 for £24 million. He writes: 'I plunged into problems linked to my situation as an expatriate. Chelsea didn't necessarily help me.'

Nobody at the club could help him find a school for his chil-dren. All Chelsea did to get him a house was put him in touch with an estate agent who tried to flog him one for £10 million. For 'weeks of irritation' the Drogba family lived in a hotel while Drogba, who at that point barely spoke English, went house-hunting after training.

All Chelsea's expensive foreign signings had much the same experience, Drogba writes. 'We often laughed about it with Gallas, Makelele, Kezman, Geremi. 'You too, you're still living in a hotel?' After all these worries, I didn't feel like integrating [at Chelsea] or multiplying my efforts.'

At a recent conference in Rome, relocation consultants liter-ally queued to tell their horror stories about football. Almost all of them had tried to get into the sport and been rebuffed. A Danish relocator had been told by FC Copenhagen that her services weren't required because the players' wives always helped each other settle. Many clubs had never even heard of relocation. Moreover, they had never hired relocation consultants before, so given the logic of football, not hiring relocation consultants must be the right thing to do. One Swedish relocator surmised: 'I guess it comes down to the fact that they see the players as merchandise.'

The only relocation consultants who had penetrated football happened to have a friend inside a club or, in the case of one Greek woman, had married a club owner. She had told her husband: 'All these guys would be happier if you find out what their needs are, and address their needs.'

Another relocator had entered a German club as a language teacher and worked her way up. She said, 'I was their mother, their nurse, their real estate agent, their cleaning lady, their everything. They didn't have a car, they didn't speak the language.' Did her work help the players play better? 'Absolutely.' The club was happy for her to work as an amateur, but as soon as she founded a relocation company, it didn't want her any more. She had become threatening.

THE NICEST TOWN IN EUROPE:
HOW TO BUY AND SELL LIKE OLYMPIQUE LYON

If you had to locate the middle-class European dream anywhere, it would be in Lyon. It's a town the size of Leeds, about two thirds of the way down France, nestled between rivers just west of the Alps. On a warm January afternoon, drinking a coffee outside in the eighteenth-century Place Bellecour where the buildings are as pretty as the women, you think: nice. Here's a wealthy town where you can have a good job, nice weather, and a big house near the mountains.

Lyon also has some of the best restaurants in Europe, known locally as *bouchons,* or 'corks'. Even at the town's football stadium you can have a wonderful three-course pre-game meal consisting largely of intestines or head cheese, unless you prefer to eat at the local-boy Paul Bocuse's brasserie across the road and totter into the ground just before kick-off. And then you can watch some of the best football in Europe too.

Until about 2000 Lyon was known as the birthplace of cinema and *nouvelle cuisine,* but not as a football town. It was just too bourgeois. If for some reason you wanted football, you drove 55 kilometres (35 miles) down the motorway to gritty proletarian Saint-Étienne. In 1987 Olympique Lyon, or 'OL', or *'Les Gones'* ('The Kids'), were playing in France's second division on an annual budget of under £2 million. They were like any old backwater provincial club in Europe. Today they rule French football, and proclaim that it is only a matter of time before they win the Champions League. Their ascent is in large part a story of the international transfer market. Better than any other club in Europe today, Lyon have worked out how to play the market.

In 1987 Jean-Michel Aulas, a local software entrepreneur with the stark grooved features of a Roman emperor, became club president. Aulas had played fairly good handball as a young man, and had a season ticket at OL.

'I didn't know the world of football well,' he admits over a bottle of 'OL' mineral water in his office beside the stadium (which he aims to tear down and replace with a bigger one). Had he expected the transformation that he wrought? 'No.'

Aulas set out to improve the club step by step. 'We tried to abstract the factor "time",' he explains. 'Each year we fix as an aim to have sporting progress, and progress of our financial resources. It's like a cyclist riding: you can overtake the people in front of you.' Others in France prefer to liken Aulas to *'un bulldozer'*.

In 1987 even the local Lyonnais didn't care much about *Les Gones*. You could live in Lyon without knowing that football existed. The club barely had a personality, whereas Saint-Étienne were the 'miners' club' that had suffered tragic defeats on great European nights in the 1970s. Saint-Étienne's president at the time said that when it came to football, Lyon was a suburb of Saint-Étienne, a remark that still rankles. At one derby after Lyon's domination began, the *Gones* fans unfurled a banner that told the Saint-Étienne supporters: 'We invented cinema when your fathers were dying in the mines.'

Aulas appointed the local boy Raymond Domenech as his first coach. In Domenech's first season, OL finished top of the second division without losing a game. Straight after that they qualified for Europe. Aulas says: 'At a stroke the credibility was total. The project was en route.'

It turned out that the second city in France, even if it was a bit bourgeois, was just hungry enough for a decent football club. The Lyonnais were willing to buy match tickets if things went well; but if things went badly, they weren't immediately waving white hand-kerchiefs in the stands and demanding that the president or manager or half the team be got rid of. Nor did the French press track the club's doings hour by hour. It's much easier to build for the long term in a place like that than in a 'football city' like Marseille or Newcastle. Moreover, footballers were happy to move to a town that is hardly a hardship posting. Almost nothing they get up to in Lyon makes it into the gossip press. Another of Lyon's advantages: the locals had money. 'It allowed us to have not just a 'popular clientele', but also a 'business clientele', says Aulas.

Talking about money is something of a taboo in France. It is considered a grubby and private topic. Socially, you're never supposed to ask anyone a question that might reveal how much somebody has got. Football, to most French fans, is not supposed to be about money. They find the notion of a well-run football club humourless, practically American.

It therefore irritates them that Aulas talks about it so unabashedly. He might have invented the word 'moneyball'.

Aulas's theme is that over time, the more money a club makes, the more matches it will win, and the more matches it wins, the more money it will make. In the short term you can lose a match, but in the long term there is a rationality even to football. (And to baseball. According to Michael Lewis's *Moneyball*, Billy Beane believes that winning 'is simply a matter of figuring out the odds, and exploiting the laws of probability ... To get worked up over plays, or even games, is as unproductive as a casino manager worrying over the outcomes of individual pulls of the slot machines.')

Aulas thinks that rationality in football works more or less like this: if you buy good players for less than they are worth, you will win more games. You will then have more money to buy better players for less than they are worth. The better players will win you more matches, and that will attract more fans (and thus more money), because Aulas spotted early that most football fans everywhere are much more like shoppers than like religious believers: if they can get a better experience somewhere new, they will go there. He told us, 'We sold 110,000 replica shirts last season. This season we are already at 200,000. I think Olympique Lyon has become by far the most beloved club in France.'

Polls suggest he is right: in a 2008 survey of European supporters by the market research company Sport+Markt, Lyon emerged as the country's most popular club, just ahead of Olympique Marseille. This popularity was a new phenomon. In 2002, when Lyon first became champions of France, the overriding French emotion towards the club had still been: 'Whatever.' The editor of *France Football* magazine complained around that time that when Lyon won the title, his magazine didn't sell. But from 2002 to 2008 the club won the title every year – the longest period of domination by any club in any of Europe's five biggest national leagues ever – and many French fans began to care about them.

With more fans, Lyon make more money. On match days nowadays you can get a haircut at an official OL salon, drink an OL Beaujolais at an OL café, book your holiday at an OL travel agency, and take an OL taxi to the game – and many people do. Lyon use that money to buy better players.

Olympique Lyon now survive the winter in the Champions League almost every season, which makes it one of the 16 best clubs in Europe. Aulas says it is only a matter of time before they win the Champions League. 'We know it will happen, we don't know *when* it will happen. It's a necessary step to achieve a growth in merchandising.'

The cup with the big ears would cap perhaps the most remarkable rise in football history. And for all Aulas's 'OL mineral water', what made it possible was the transfer market. On that warm winter's afternoon in Lyon, Aulas told us, 'We will invest better than Chelsea, Arsenal or Real Madrid. We will make different strategic choices. For instance, we won't try to have the best team on paper in terms of brand. We will have the best team relative to our investment.' Here are Lyon's rules of the transfer market:

⚽ Use the wisdom of crowds.

When Lyon are thinking of signing a player, a group of men sit down to debate the transfer. Aulas is there, and so is Bernard Lacombe, once a bull-like centre-forward for Lyon and France, and for most of the last 20 years the club's 'technical director'. Lacombe is known for having the best pair of eyes in French football. He coached Lyon from 1997 to 2000, but Aulas clearly figured out that if you have someone with his knack for spotting the right transfer, you want to keep him at the club for ever rather than make his job contingent on four lost matches. The same went for Peter Taylor at Forest.

Whoever happens to be Lyon's head coach of the moment sits in on the meeting too, and so will four or five other coaches. 'We have a group that gives its advice,' Aulas explains. 'In England the manager often does it alone. In France it's often the technical director.'

Like Lyon, the Oakland A's also sidelined their manager. Like Lyon, the A's understood that he was merely 'a middle manager' obsessed with the very short term. The A's let him watch baseball's annual draft. They didn't let him say a word about it.

Lyon's method for choosing players is so obvious and smart that it's surprising all clubs don't use it. The theory of the 'wisdom of crowds' says that if you aggregate many different opinions from a diverse group of people, you are much more likely to arrive at the best opinion than if you just listen to one specialist. For instance, if you ask a diverse crowd to guess the weight of an ox, the average of their guesses will be very nearly right. If you ask a diverse set of gamblers to bet on, say, the outcome of a presidential election, the average of their bets is likely to be right too. (Gambling markets have proved excellent predictors of all sorts of outcomes.) The wisdom of crowds fails when the components of the crowd are not diverse enough. This is often the case in American sports. But in European football, opinions tend to come from many different countries, and that helps ensure diversity.

Clough and Taylor at least were a crowd of two. However, the typical decision-making model in English football is not 'wisdom of crowds', but short-term dictatorship. At most clubs the manager is treated as a sort of divinely inspired monarch who gets to decide everything until he is sacked. Then the next manager clears out his predecessor's signings at a discount. Lyon, notes a rival French club president with envy, never have expensive signings rotting on the bench. They never have revolutions at all. They understand that their coach is only a 'temp'. OL won their seven consecutive titles with four different coaches – Jacques Santini, Paul Le Guen, Gerard Houllier and Alain Perrin – none of whom, judging by their records in Britain, is exactly a Hegelian world-historical individual. When a coach leaves Lyon, not much changes. No matter who happens to be sitting on the bench, the team always play much the same brand of attacking football (by French standards).

Emmanuel Hembert grew up in Lyon supporting OL when they were still in the second division. Now, as head of the sports practice of the management consultancy A.T. Kearney, he is always citing the club as an example to his clients in football. 'A big secret of a successful club is stability,' explains Hembert over coffee in Paris. 'In Lyon, the stability is not with the coach, but with the sports director, Lacombe.'

⚽ **The best time to buy a player is when he is in his early twenties.**

Aulas says, 'We buy young players with potential who are considered the best in their country, between 20 and 22 years old.' It's almost as if he had read *Moneyball*. The book keeps banging on about a truth discovered by Bill James, who wrote: 'College players are a better investment than high-school players by a huge, huge, laughably huge margin.'

Baseball clubs traditionally preferred to draft high-school players. But how good you are at 17 or 18 is a poor predictor of how good you will become as an adult. By definition, when a player is that young there is still too little information to judge him. Billy Beane himself had been probably the hottest baseball prospect in the US at 17, but he was already declining in his senior year at school, and he then failed in the major leagues. Watching the 2002 draft as the A's general manager, he 'punches his fist in the air' each time rival teams draft schoolboys.

It's the same in soccer, where brilliant teenagers tend to disappear soon afterwards. Here are a few recent winners of the Golden Ball for best player at the Under-17s' World Cup: Philip Osundo of Nigeria, William de Oliveira of Brazil, Nii Lamptey of Ghana, the Scottish goalkeeper James Will, and Mohammed Al Kathiri of Oman. Once upon a time they must all have been brilliant, but none of them made it as adults. (Will ended up a

policeman in the Scottish Highlands playing for his village team.)
The most famous case of a teenager who flames is the American Freddy Adu, who at 14 was the next Pelé and Maradona.

Only a handful of world-class players in each generation, most
of them creators or goalscorers – Pelé, Maradona, Wayne Rooney
– reach the top before they are 18. Most footballers get there
considerably later. You can be confident of their potential only
when they are more mature.

Beane knows that by the time players are in college – which
tends to put them in Lyon's magical age range of 20 to 22 – you
have a pretty good idea of what they will become. There is lots of
information about them. They are old enough to be nearly fully
formed, but too young to be expensive stars.

Lyon always try to avoid paying a premium for a star player's
'name'. Here, again, they are lucky to be a club from a quiet town.
Their placid supporters and local media don't demand stars. By
contrast, the former chairman of a club in a much more raucous
French city recalls: 'I ran [the club] with the mission to create a
spectacle. It wasn't to build a project for 20 years to come.' A
team from a big city tends to need big stars.

Soccer being barely distinguishable from American baseball,
the same split between big and small towns operates in that
sport too. 'Big-market teams', like the Boston Red Sox and the
New York Yankees, hunt players with names. Their media and fans
demand it. In *Moneyball*, Michael Lewis calls this the pathology
of 'many foolish teams that thought all their questions could be
answered by a single player'. (It's a pathology that may sound
strangely familiar to European soccer fans.) By contrast the
Oakland A's, as a small-market team, were free to forego stars.
As Lewis writes: 'Billy may not care for the Oakland press but it is
really very tame next to the Boston press, and it certainly has no
effect on his behavior, other than to infuriate him once a week or
so. Oakland A's fans, too, were apathetic compared to the mani-
acs in Fenway Park or Yankee Stadium.'

Happy is the club that has no need of heroes. Lyon were free to buy young unknowns like Michael Essien or Mahamadou Diarra just because they were good. And unknowns accept modest salaries. According to the French sports newspaper *L'Equipe,* in the 2007–08 season Lyon spent only 31 per cent of its budget on players' pay. The average in the English Premier League was about double that. Like Clough's Forest, Lyon perform the magic trick of winning things without paying silly salaries.

Here are a few more of Lyon's secrets:

⚽ Try not to buy centre-forwards.

Centre-forward is the most overpriced position in the transfer market. (Goalkeeper is the most underpriced, even though keepers have longer careers than outfield players; in baseball, the most overpriced position is pitcher.) Admittedly Lyon 'announced' itself to football by buying the Brazilian centre-forward Sonny Anderson for £12 million in 1999, but the club have scrimped on the position since. Houllier left OL in 2007 grumbling that even after the club sold Florent Malouda and Eric Abidal for a combined total of £23 million, Aulas still wouldn't buy him a centre-forward.

⚽ Help your foreign signings relocate.

All sorts of great Brazilians have passed through Lyon: Sonny Anderson, the current club captain Cris, the future internationals Juninho and Fred, and the world champion Edmilson. Most were barely known when they joined the club. Aulas explains the secret: 'Ten years ago we sent one of our old players, Marcelo, to Brazil. He was an extraordinary man, because he was both an engineer and a professional footballer. He was captain of Lyon for five years. Then he became an agent, but he works quasi-exclusively for OL. He indicates all market opportunities to us.' As a judge of players, Marcelo is clearly in the Lacombe/Peter Taylor class.

Marcelo says he only scouts 'serious boys'. Or as the former president of a rival French club says: 'They don't select players just for their quality but for their ability to adapt. I can't see Lyon recruiting an Anelka or a Ronaldinho.'

After Lyon signs the serious boys, it makes sure they settle. Drogba notes enviously: 'At Lyon, a translator takes care of the Brazilians, helps them to find a house, get their bearings, tries to reduce as much as possible the negative effects of moving … Even at a place of the calibre of Chelsea, that didn't exist.'

Lyon's 'translator', who works full-time for the club, sorts out the players' homesickness, bank accounts, *nouvelle cuisine*, etc. Other people at the club teach the newcomers Lyon's culture: no stars or show-offs. By concentrating on Brazilians, the club can offer them a tailor-made relocation service. Almost all the other foreign players Lyon buys are French-speakers.

⚽ **Sell any player if another club offers more than he is worth.** This is what Aulas means when he says, 'Buying and selling players is not an activity for improving the football performance. It's a trading activity, in which we produce gross margin. If an offer for a player is greatly superior to his market value, you must not keep him.' The ghost of Peter Taylor would approve.

Like Clough and Taylor, and like Billy Beane, at Lyon they never get sentimental about players. In the club's annual accounts, it books each player for a certain transfer value. (Beane says: 'Know exactly what every player in baseball is worth to you. You can put a dollar figure on it.')

The club knows that sooner or later its best players will attract somebody else's attention. Because it expects to sell them, it replaces them even before they go. That avoids a transition period or a panic purchase after the player's departure. Aulas explains: 'We will replace the player in the squad six months or a year before. So when Michael Essien goes [to Chelsea for £24 million], we already have a certain number of players who are ready to replace him. Then, when the opportunity to buy Tiago arises, for 25 per cent of the price of Essien, you take him.'

Before Essien's transfer, Aulas spent weeks proclaiming that the Ghanaian was 'untransferable'. He always says that when he is about to transfer a player, because it drives up the price. In his words: 'Every international at Lyon is untransferable. Until the offer surpasses by far the amount we had expected.'

As a free service to clubs, here are the 12 main secrets of the transfer market in full:

1. A new manager wastes money on transfers; don't let him.
2. Use the wisdom of crowds.
3. Stars of recent World Cups or European championships are overvalued; ignore them.
4. Certain nationalities are overvalued.
5. Older players are overvalued.
6. Centre-forwards are overvalued; goalkeepers are undervalued.
7. Gentlemen prefer blonds; identify and abandon 'sight-based prejudices'.
8. The best time to buy a player is when he is in his early twenties.
9. Sell any player when another club offers more than he is worth.
10. Replace your best players even before you sell them.
11. Buy players with personal problems, and then help them deal with their problems.
12. Help your players relocate.

Alternatively, clubs could just stick with the conventional wisdom.

THE WORST BUSINESS IN THE WORLD: WHY FOOTBALL CLUBS DON'T (AND SHOULDN'T) MAKE MONEY

A man we know once tried to do business with a revered institution of English football. 'I can do business with stupid people,' he said afterwards, 'and I can do business with crooks. But I can't do business with stupid people who want to be crooks.'

It was a decent summary of the football business, if you can call football a business. People often do. William McGregor, the Scottish draper who founded the Football League in 1888, was probably the first person to say 'Football is a big business', but the phrase has since become one of the game's great clichés.

In fact McGregor was wrong. Football is neither big business nor good business. It arguably isn't even business at all.

'BIG BUSINESS'

Few people have heard of a British company called BBA Aviation.
It started out in 1879 making conveyor belts in Dundee, but over
time it morphed into a supplier to the aeroplane industry. Mostly
it now helps fuel, clean, repair and maintain planes. This is
pretty unglamorous work, and BBA is an unglamorous company.
It's in the FTSE 250, meaning that it ranks as one of the
250 biggest companies on the London stock market. In 2008 it
had revenues of £1.15 billion, and profits of £66 million. BBA,
whose headquarters are on a quiet street in Mayfair, is not big
business. For comparison: in 2008 the biggest company on
the London market, Royal Dutch Shell, had revenues that were
282 times bigger.

But compared to any football club, BBA is a behemoth. Every
year the business advisor Deloitte ranks the richest clubs on
earth in its 'Football Money League'. In 2009 Real Madrid led the
league with revenues of £325 million. That's a handy sum, but
less than a third of BBA's revenues, and almost exactly one thou-
sandth the size of Shell's. Second in the Football Money League
were Manchester United with a paltry £288 million.

It's worth noting that the Money League ranks clubs according
to how much they sell. When business analysts judge normal
companies they usually focus on profits, or the company's value
if it were sold in the market. However, neither of those methods
works with football clubs. Because hardly any clubs are quoted
on the stock market nowadays, for extremely good reasons, it is
hard to work out their value. We can certainly say that not even
Real nor United would make it into the 'FTSE 500' of the 500
most valuable companies on the London stock market.

And if Deloitte ranked clubs by their profits, the results would
be embarrassing. Not only do most clubs make losses and fail to
pay any dividends to their shareholders, but many of the 'bigger'
clubs would rank near the bottom of the list. Deloitte reported in

2008 that the three most profitable clubs in the Premier League were Watford, Reading and Arsenal, while the three least profitable were Chelsea, Manchester United and Newcastle.

Whichever way you measure it, no football club is a big business. Real and United are dwarfed by BBA Aviation. As for all the rest, the author Alex Fynn noted in the 1990s that the average Premier League club had about the same turnover as a supermarket – not a chain of supermarkets, but one single out-of-town Tesco's. True, football clubs have grown since then: by 2008 the average club in the Premier League had a turnover of £75 million, compared with £50 million for the average Tesco supermarket. However, since Tesco has 600 supermarkets/superstores, the average takings of the 20 largest are probably still much larger than those of the average club. And unlike most clubs, Tesco actually makes a profit.

A good way to visualise the size of the football industry is to visit UEFA's HQ in the Swiss town of Nyon. The building has a lovely view of Lake Geneva, but it looks like the offices of a small insurance company. Football is small business.

This feels like a contradiction. We all know that football is huge. Some of the most famous people on earth are footballers, and the most watched TV programme in history is generally the most recent World Cup final. Nonetheless football clubs are puny businesses. This is partly a problem of what economists call appropriability: football clubs can't make money out of (can't appropriate) more than a tiny share of our love of football.

It may be that season tickets are expensive, and replica shirts overpriced, but buying these things once a year represents the extravagant extreme of football fanaticism. Most football is watched not from £1,000-seats in the stadium but on TV – sometimes at the price of a subscription, often at the price of watching a few adverts, or for the price of a couple of pints in the pub. Compare the cost of watching a game in a pub with the cost of eating out, or watching a movie, let alone going on holiday.

Worse still, football generates little income from repeat showing of matches, transfers to DVD, or re-runs on ITV4. And watching football (even on TV) is only a tiny part of the fan's engagement with the game. There are newspaper reports to be read, internet sites to be trawled, and a growing array of computer games to keep up with. Then there is the football banter that passes time at the dinner table, work, or the bus stop. All this entertainment is made possible by football clubs, but they cannot appropriate a penny of the value we attach to it. Chelsea cannot charge us for talking or reading or thinking about Chelsea. As the Dutch international Demy de Zeeuw says: 'There are complaints that we [footballers] earn too much, but the whole world earns money from your success as a footballer: newspapers, television, companies.' In fact the world earns more from football than the football industry itself does.

BAD BUSINESS

Football is not merely a small business, it's also a bad one. Anyone who spends any time inside football soon discovers that just as oil is part of the oil business, stupidity is part of the football business.

This becomes obvious when people in football encounter people in other industries. Generally, the football people get exploited, because people in other industries understand business better. In 1997 Peter Kenyon, then chief executive of the sportswear company Umbro, invited a few guests to watch a European game at Chelsea, the club he would end up running a few years later. After the game, Kenyon took his guests out for dinner. Over curry he reminisced about how the sportswear industry used to treat football clubs. In the 1970s, he said, big English clubs used to *pay* companies like Umbro to supply their kit. It was obviously great advertising for the kit-makers to have some of England's best footballers running around in their clothes, but the clubs had not yet figured that out. And so sportswear companies used to get paid to advertise themselves.

Ricky George saw the ignorance of football in those days from point-blank range. In 1972, when George scored the legendary goal for non-league Hereford that knocked Newcastle out of the FA Cup, he was working for Adidas as a 'soccer PR'. His job was to represent Adidas to England players, former world champions like Bobby Moore, Bobby Charlton and Gordon Banks. There was little need to persuade them to choose Adidas. Most of them wore the three stripes for free anyway.

George says: 'It is quite a fascinating thing if you compare it with today. There were no great sponsorship deals going on. All that happened is that you would give the players boots. But even then, at the beginning of every season the clubs would go to their local sports retailer and just buy 20, 30 pairs of boots and hand them out. For a company like Adidas, it was the cheapest type of PR you could imagine.'

Only on special occasions did George have to pay players. 'When it came to a big international, and the game was going to be televised, my job was to go to the team hotel, hang around there, make myself known, and a couple of hours before the game I would go into the players' rooms and paint the white stripes on their boots with luminous paint so it was more visible. My bosses used to be keenly watching the television to make sure the stripes were visible, and if they weren't I would be in for a bollocking.'

For this service, an England player would receive £75 per match – not a princely sum even in 1972. George recalls: 'Bobby [Moore], the most charming of people, didn't take the money on the day of the game. He just used to say to me, "Let it build up for a few games, and I'll ring you when I need it." And that's what he did.' Then the most famous defender of the era would pocket a cumulative few hundred quid for having advertised an international brand to a cumulative audience of tens of millions.

Only in the late 1980s did English football clubs discover that some people were willing to buy replicas of their team shirts. That made it plain even to them that their kit must have some value. They had already stopped paying sportswear companies for the stuff; now they started to charge them.

Gradually over time, football clubs have found new ways of making money. However, the ideas almost never came from the clubs themselves. Whether it was branded kit, or the Pools, or television, it was usually people in other industries who first saw there might be profits to be made. It was Rupert Murdoch who went to English clubs and suggested putting them on satellite TV; the clubs would never have thought of going to him. In fact, the clubs often fought against new money-making schemes. Until 1982 they refused to allow any league games to be shown live on TV, fearing that that might deter fans from coming to the stadium. It took another decade for clubs to grasp that games on TV meant both free money and free advertising.

It took them even longer to realise how much football was worth to people like Murdoch. In 1992 he began paying about £60 million a season for the television rights to the new Premier League. Now the league gets about 10 times as much a season from television. 'I've been screwed by television,' admitted Sir John Hall, then the Newcastle chairman, one rowdy night at Trinity College Dublin in 1995. 'But I'll tell you one thing: I won't be screwed again.'

Or take the renovating of English stadiums in the early 1990s. It was an obvious business idea. Tesco doesn't receive customers in sheds built in the Victorian era and gone to seed since. It is forever doing up its stores. Yet football clubs never seem to have thought of spending money on their grounds until the Taylor Report of 1990 forced them to. They did up their stadiums, and bingo: more customers came.

All this proves how much like consumers football fans are. It's not that they come running when a team do well; rather, it seems that football can quickly become popular across a whole country. All teams then benefit, but particularly those that build nice new stadiums where spectators feel comfortable and safe. That would explain why the three English clubs whose crowds grew fastest over the 1990s were Manchester United, Sunderland and Newcastle. (The club that lost most spectators was Sheffield Wednesday, which shed 8,953 from its average gate during the decade.) In other leagues, clubs such as Ajax and Celtic also drew huge new crowds to their new grounds – in Ajax's case, even though their football spontaneously combusted. There is such a close link between building a nice ground and drawing more spectators that the traditional fans' chant of 'Where were you when you were shit?' should be revised to 'Where were you when your ground was shit?'

Yet like almost all good business ideas in football, the Taylor Report was imposed on the game from outside. Football clubs are classic late adopters of new ideas. Several years after the internet emerged, Liverpool, a club with millions of fans around the world, still did not have a website. No wonder that from 1992 through to May 2008, even before the financial crisis struck, 40 of England's 92 professional clubs had been involved in insolvency proceedings, some of them more than once.

HOW THE TRIBE CHOOSES ITS CHIEFS

Rather than stack up endless examples of the dimness of football clubs, let's take one contemporary case study: how clubs hire their key employee, the manager. English fans are still asking themselves how Steve McClaren ever got to be appointed England manager, but in fact it is unfair to single him out. The profusion of fantasy football leagues, in which office workers masquerade as coaches, indicates the widely held suspicion that any fool could do as well as the people who actually get the jobs. The incompetence of football managers may have something to do with the nonsensical and illegal methods by which they are typically recruited.

Football 'is a sad business', says Bjørn Johansson, who runs a headhunting firm in Zurich. Like his colleagues in headhunting, Johansson is never consulted by clubs seeking managers. Instead, this is how a club typically chooses its man:

⚽ **The new manager is hired in a mad rush.**

In a panel at the International Football Arena conference in Zurich in 2006, Johansson explained that in 'normal' business 'an average search process takes four to five months'. In football, a club usually finds a coach within a couple of days of sacking his predecessor. 'Hesitation is regarded as weak leadership,' explained another panellist in Zurich, Ilja Kaenzig, then general manager of the German club Hannover 96. Brian Barwick, the Football Association's former chief executive, has noted that McClaren's recruitment 'took from beginning to end nine weeks', yet the media accused the FA of being 'sluggish'. If only it had been more sluggish.

A rare slow hire in football became perhaps the most inspired choice of the last two decades: Arsenal's appointment of Arsène Wenger in 1996. Wenger, working in Japan, was not free immediately. Arsenal waited for him, operating under caretaker managers for weeks, and were inevitably accused of being sluggish. Similarly, in 1990 Manchester United's chairman Martin Edwards was derided as sluggish when he refused to sack his losing manager Alex Ferguson. Edwards thought that, in the long term, Ferguson might improve.

⚽ **The new manager is interviewed only very cursorily.**

In 'normal' business, a wannabe chief executive writes a business plan, gives a presentation and undergoes several interviews. In football, a club calls an agent's mobile and offers the job.

⚽ **The new manager is always a man.**

The entire industry discriminates illegally against women. He is also almost always white, with a conservative haircut, aged between 35 and 60, and a former professional footballer. Clubs know that if they choose someone with that profile, then even if the appointment turns out to be terrible they won't be blamed too much, because at least they will have failed in the traditional way. As the old business saying went: 'Nobody ever got fired for buying IBM.'

There is no evidence that having been a good player (or being white and of conservative appearance) is an advantage for a football manager. Arrigo Sacchi, coach of the great Milan from 1987 to 1991, who couldn't play football himself, explained: 'You don't have to have been a horse to be a jockey.' Playing and coaching are different skill-sets. Match for match, the most successful coach in soccer's history is probably José Mourinho, who barely ever kicked a ball for money. When Milan's coach Carlo Ancelotti noted Mourinho's modest record as a player, the Portuguese replied: 'I don't see the connection. My dentist is the best in the world, and yet he's never had particularly bad toothache.' Asked why failed players often became good coaches, Mourinho said: 'More time to study.'

The problem with ex-professionals may be precisely their experience. Having been steeped in the game for decades, they just *know* what to do: how to train, who to buy, how to talk to their players. They don't need to investigate whether these inherited prejudices are in fact correct. Rare is the ex-pro who realises, like Billy Beane at the Oakland A's, that he needs to jettison what he learnt along the way. Michael Lewis writes in *Moneyball:* 'Billy had played pro ball, and regarded it as an experience he needed to overcome if he wanted to do his job well. "A reformed alcoholic," is how he described himself.'

⚽ **In British football, managers traditionally didn't need professional qualifications.**

Only in 2003 did UEFA insist that new managers in the Premier League must have passed the 'Pro Licence' course. In England's lower divisions this remains unnecessary. Yet Sue Bridgewater, an associate professor at Warwick Business School, showed that managers with the Pro Licence won significantly more matches than managers without it. She also showed that experienced managers outperformed novices. That qualifications and experience are useful is understood in every industry except football, where a manager is expected to work the magic he acquired as a superhero player.

⚽ **The new manager is often under-qualified even if he has qualifications.**

Chris Brady, a business-school professor, teaches finance and accounting on the Pro Licence course. He says his entire module takes half a day. No wonder some English managers mismanage money: they don't understand it. Clubs are ceasing to entrust their finances to managers, giving them instead to more qualified executives like Hannover 96's Ilja Kaenzig, who guarantee stability by staying longer than the club manager's average two-year tenure. That at least is the theory: the week after that conference in Zurich, Hannover released Kaenzig.

⚽ **The new manager is appointed either because he is able to start work immediately (often as a result of having just been sacked), or because he has achieved good results over his career, or, failing that, because he achieved good results in the weeks preceding the appointment.**

McClaren became England manager only because his team, Middlesbrough, reached the UEFA Cup final in 2006 and avoided relegation just as the FA was deciding who to pick. By the time

Middlesbrough were tonked 4–0 by Seville in the final, McClaren already had the job.

His period under review was so short as to be a random walk. The same went for the main candidates to manage England in 1996: Bryan Robson, Frank Clark, Gerry Francis and the eventual choice Glenn Hoddle. Today none of them works as a manager (Francis and Clark haven't for many years), none had his last job in the Premier League, and none will probably work at that high a level again. They were in the frame in 1996 because they had had good results recently and were English – another illegal consideration in hiring.

⚽ **The new manager is generally chosen not for his alleged managerial skills, but because his name, appearance and skills at public relations are expected to impress the club's fans, players and the media.**

That is why no club hires a woman – stupid fans and players would object – and why it was so brave of Milan to appoint the unknown Sacchi, and Arsenal the unknown Wenger. Tony Adams, Arsenal's then captain, doubted the obscure foreigner at first sight. In his autobiography *Addicted*, the player recalls thinking: 'What does this Frenchman know about football? He wears glasses and looks more like a schoolteacher. He's not going to be as good as George. Does he even speak English properly?'

A manager must above all look like a manager. Clubs would rather use traditional methods to appoint incompetents than risk doing anything that looks odd.

BAD STAFF

The most obvious reason why football is such an incompetent business is that football clubs tend to hire incompetent staff. The manager is only the start of it. Years ago one of us requested an interview with the chairman of an English club quoted on the stock market. The press officer asked me to send a fax (a 1980s technology revered by football clubs). I sent it. She said she never got it. On request I sent three more faxes to different officials. She said none arrived. This is quite a common experience for football journalists. Because football clubs are the only businesses that get daily publicity without trying to, they treat journalists as humble supplicants instead of as unpaid marketers of the club's brand. The media often retaliate by being mean. This is not very clever of the clubs, because almost all their fans follow them through the media rather than by going to the stadium.

A month after all the faxes, I was granted permission to send my request by e-mail. When I arrived at the club for the interview, I met the press officer. She was beautiful. Of course she was. Traditionally, football clubs recruit the women on their office staff for their looks, and the men because they played professional football or are somebody's mate.

If football clubs wanted to, they could recruit excellent executives. Professors at business schools report that many of their MBA students, who might be paying £30,000 a year in tuition fees, dream of working in football for a pitiful salary. Often the students beg clubs to let them work for free as summer interns. The clubs seldom want them. If you work for a football club, your goal is to keep working there, not to be shown up by some overeducated young thing who has actually learnt something about business.

In part this is because much of the traditionally working-class football industry distrusts education. In part, says Emmanuel Hembert of A.T. Kearney, it is because many clubs are dominated by a vain owner-manager. Hembert says: 'Lots of them invested for ego reasons, which is never a good thing in business. They prefer not to have strong people around them, except the coach. They really pay low salaries.'

Historically only Manchester United recruited respected executives from normal industries (such as Peter Kenyon from Umbro), though now a few other big clubs like Barcelona are starting to do so too.

Baseball appears to be quite as incompetent. In *Moneyball* Lewis asks why, among baseball executives and scouts, 'there really is no level of incompetence that won't be tolerated'. He thinks the main reason 'is that baseball has structured itself less as a business than as a social club ... There are many ways to embarrass the Club, but being bad at your job isn't one of them. The greatest offense a Club member can commit is not ineptitude but disloyalty.' Club members – and this applies in soccer as much as in baseball – are selected for clubbability. Clever outsiders are not clubbable, because they talk funny, and go around pointing out the things that people inside the Club are doing wrong. 'It wasn't as simple as the unease of jocks in the presence of nerds,' writes Lewis – but that unease did have a lot to do with it.

The staff of football clubs tend not merely to be incompetent, they are also often novices. This is because staff turnover is rapid. Whenever a new owner arrives, he generally brings in his cronies. The departing staff rarely join a new club, because that is considered disloyal (Kenyon, an exception, was persecuted for moving from United for Chelsea), even though footballers change clubs all the time. So football executives are always having to rein-vent the wheel.

Worse, the media and fans often make it impossible for clubs to make sensible decisions. They are always hassling the club to do something immediately. If the team loses three games, fans start chanting for the club to sack the coach, buy a new player, in short, tear up the plans it might have made a month ago. 'Consumer activism in this industry is extreme,' warns A.T. Kearney in its report *Playing for Profits.* Hembert says: 'As soon as you sign a player for £10 million, you blow up your business plan. Commercial employees have to fight for £100,000 of spending here or there, but then suddenly the club spends £10 million.'

Or more. Sven Goran Eriksson once flew into Zurich to tell the International Football Arena a 'good story' about his time managing Lazio.

'The chairman I had was very good,' Eriksson recalled for an audience of mostly Swiss businessmen. 'If I wanted a player, he would try to get that player. One day I phoned him up and I said: "Vieri".'

Christian Vieri was then playing for Atletico Madrid. Eriksson and Lazio's chairman Sergio Cragnotti flew to Spain to bid for him. Atletico told them Vieri would cost 50 billion Italian lire. At the time, in 1998, that was about £17 million. Eriksson reminisced: 'That was the biggest sum in the world. No player had been involved for that.'

He says the talks then went more or less as follows:

Cragnotti: 'That's a lot of money.'
Eriksson: 'I know.'

Atletico said they might accept some Lazio players in part-payment for Vieri.

Cragnotti: 'Can we do that?'
Eriksson: 'No, we can't give away these players.'
Cragnotti: 'What shall we do then?'
Eriksson: 'Buy him.'
Cragnotti: 'OK.'

Eriksson recalled in Zurich: 'He didn't even try to pay 49. He just paid 50.'

Nine months after Vieri joined Lazio, Inter Milan wanted to buy him. Once again, Eriksson reports the conversation:

Cragnotti: 'What shall I ask for him?'
Eriksson: 'Ask for double. Ask 100.'
Cragnotti: 'I can't do that.'

Eriksson recalled: 'So he asked 90. And he got 90. That's good business.' (Or the ultimate example of the greater-fool principle.)

Someone in the audience in Zurich asked Eriksson whether such behaviour was healthy. After all, Lazio ran out of money in 2002 when Cragnotti's food company Cirio went belly-up. Cragnotti later spent time in prison, which even by the standards of Italian football is going a bit far.

Eriksson replied, 'It's not healthy. And if you see Lazio, it was not healthy. But we won the league. And we won the Cup-Winners' Cup. We won everything.'

The point is that football clubs, prompted by media and fans, are always making financially irrational decisions in an instant. They would like to think long-term, but because they are in the news every day they end up fixating on the short term. An executive with an American entertainment company tells a story about his long-arranged business meeting with Real Madrid. His company was hoping to build a relationship with the club. But on the day of the meeting, Real ritually sacked their manager. The usual chaos ensued. Two of the club officials scheduled to attend the meeting with the American executive did not show up. That's football.

SAFER THAN THE BANK OF ENGLAND: WHY FOOTBALL CLUBS ALMOST NEVER DISAPPEAR

On 15 September 2008, the investment bank Lehman Brothers collapsed, followed almost immediately by the world's stock markets.

Any football club on earth was a midget next to Lehman. In the year to September 2007, the bank had income of $59 billion (148 times Manchester United's at the time), profits of $6 billion (50 times Manchester United's) and was valued by the stock market at $34 billion. If United's shares had still been traded on the market, they would probably have been worth less than 5 per cent of Lehman's. Yet Lehman no longer exists while United very much do.

Over the last decade, people worried a lot more about the survival of football clubs than of banks. Yet it was many of the world's largest banks that disappeared. The public perception that football clubs are inherently unstable businesses is wrong. Despite being incompetently run, they are some of the most stable businesses on earth.

First, some facts. In 1923 the Football League consisted of 88 teams spread over four divisions. In the 2007–08 season:

- ⚽ 85 of these clubs still existed (97 per cent).
- ⚽ 75 remained in the top four divisions (85 per cent).
- ⚽ An actual majority, 48 clubs, were in the same division as they had been in 1923.
- ⚽ Only nine teams still in the top four divisions were two or more divisions away from where they had been in 1923 (poor Notts County had sunk from first to fourth tier).

So almost every professional club in England had survived the Great Depression, the Second World War, recessions, corrupt chairmen and appalling managers. It is a history of remarkable stability. For comparison, the economic historian Les Hannah made a list of the top 100 companies in 1912, and researched what had become of them by 1995. Nearly half the companies – 49 – had ceased to exist. Five of these had gone bankrupt, six were nationalised, and 37 were taken over by other firms. Even among the businesses that survived, many had gone into new sectors or moved to new locations.

What made these non-football businesses so unstable was, above all, competition. There is such a thing as brand loyalty, but when a better product turns up most people will switch sooner or later. So normal businesses keep having to innovate or die. They face endless pitfalls: competitors pull ahead, consumers' tastes change, new technologies make entire industries obsolete, cheap goods arrive from abroad, government interferes, recessions hit, companies over-invest and go bust, or they simply get unlucky. By contrast, football clubs are immune from almost all these effects:

- ⚽ A club that fails to keep up with the competition might get relegated, but it can always survive at a lower level.
- ⚽ Some fans lose interest, but clubs have geographical roots. A bad team might find its catchment area shrinking, but not disappearing completely.
- ⚽ The 'technology' of football can never become obsolete because the technology is the game itself. At worst football might become less popular.
- ⚽ Foreign rivals cannot enter the market and supply football at a lower price. The rules of football protect domestic clubs by forbidding foreign competitors from joining their league. English clubs as a whole could fall behind foreign competitors and lose their best players, but foreign clubs have financial problems and incompetent management of their own.
- ⚽ The government is not about to nationalise football.
- ⚽ Clubs often over-invest, but this almost never destroys the club, only the wealth of the investor. At worst, the club gets relegated.
- ⚽ A club's income might decline in a recession, but it can always live with a lower income.

In most industries a bad business goes bankrupt, but football clubs almost never do. The 40 English clubs that entered insolvency proceedings through May 2008 cut deals with their creditors (usually the players and the taxman) and moved on. Yes, Aldershot FC went bankrupt in 1992, but supporters simply started a new club almost identical to the old one. The 'new' Aldershot Town AFC has a badge that shows a phoenix rising from the ashes. In Italy Fiorentina went bust in 2002, and got relegated to the Italian fourth division, but within a couple of years they were back at the top, the bankruptcy forgotten. No big football club disappears under its debts. If West Ham or (imagine) Liverpool fell into administration, they too would be guaranteed to be reborn under new ownership. No matter how much money clubs waste, someone will always bail them out. This is what is known in finance as 'moral hazard': when you know you will be saved however much money you lose, you are free to lose money. Football clubs are incompetent because they can be. The professional investors who briefly bought club shares in the 1990s got out as soon as they discovered this.

Even the current economic crisis is unlikely to destroy any clubs. A glance at past crises shows how resilient they are. You would have expected the Great Depression to pose something of a threat to English clubs. After all, the Depression bit deepest in the north of England, where most professional clubs were based, and all romantic rhetoric aside, you would have thought that when people cannot afford to buy bread they would stop going to football matches.

Crowds in the Football League did indeed fall 12 per cent between 1929 and 1931. However, by 1932 they were growing again, even though the British economy was not. And clubs helped each other through the hard times. When Orient hit trouble in 1931, Arsenal wrote them a cheque for £3,450 to tide them over. Clubs know they cannot operate without opponents, and so, unlike in most businesses, the collapse of a rival is not a cause for celebration.

The Depression culled only a couple of clubs. Merthyr Town, after failing to be re-elected to the Football League in 1930, folded a few years later, victims of economic hardship in the Valleys (as well as competition from far more popular rugby union). Wigan Borough went bankrupt a few games into the 1931–32 season. They left the league, and their remaining fixtures were never played. Aldershot were elected to replace them, and 60 years later, in another recession, they became only the second English club in history to withdraw from the league with fixtures unplayed.

During the 'Thatcher recession', crowds in the Football League fell by nearly a quarter between 1979–80 and 1982–83. Many clubs struggled, and several survived only thanks to a 'sub' – financial support – from the players' union, which didn't want to see employers go bust. Charlton and Bristol Rovers had to move grounds because they could not pay the rent. However, nobody 'did an Accrington Stanley' and resigned from the league.

Most stricken clubs instead 'do a Leeds': cut their wages, get relegated and compete at a lower level. Imagine if other businesses could do this. Suppose that Ford could sack skilled workers, and hire unskilled ones to produce worse cars; or that British Airways could replace all their pilots with people who weren't as well qualified to fly planes. The government would stop it, and in any case, consumers would not put up with rubbish products. Football clubs, unlike most businesses, survive crises because some of their customers stick with them no matter how lousy the product. Calling this brand loyalty is not quite respectful enough of the sentiment involved. To quote Rogan Taylor, the Liverpool fan and Liverpool University professor: 'Football is more than just a business. No one has their ashes scattered down the aisle at Tesco.'

NOT BUSINESSES AT ALL

When business people look at football, they are often astonished at how unbusinesslike the clubs are. Every now and then one of them takes over a club and promises to run it 'like a business'. Alan Sugar, who had made his money in computers, became chairman of Tottenham Hotspur in 1991. His brilliant wheeze was to make Spurs live within their means. Never would he fork out 50 billion lire for a Vieri. After Newcastle bought Alan Shearer for

£15 million in 1996, Sugar remarked, 'I've slapped myself around the face a couple of times but I still can't believe it.'

He more or less kept his word. In the 10 years that he ran Spurs, they lived within their means. But most of their fans hated it. The only thing Spurs won in that decade was a solitary League Cup. They spent most of their time in mid-table of the Premier League, falling far behind Arsenal. Nor did they even make much money: about £2 million a year in profits in Sugar's first six years, which was much less than Arsenal and not very good for a company their size. Sugar's Spurs disappointed both on and off the field, and they also illustrated a paradox: when business people try to run a football club as a business, then not only does the football suffer, but so does the business.

Other businessmen pursue a different strategy from Sugar's. They assume that if they can get their clubs to win prizes, profits will inevitably follow. But they too are wrong. Even the best teams seldom generate profits. We plotted the league positions and profits of all the clubs that have played in the Premier League from its inaugural season of 1992–93 until the 2006–07 season:

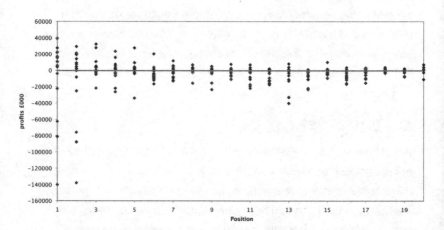

Pre-tax profits and position in the Premier League 1992–03 to 2006–07.

The chart shows how spectacularly unprofitable the football business is. Each point on the chart represents the combination of profit and position for a club in a particular year. One obvious point to note is that most of the dots fall below zero on the profits axis: these clubs were making losses. But the chart also shows that there was barely any connection between finishing high and making money. While there is some suggestion that a few clubs at the top of the table make more money than other clubs, the chart also shows that other clubs in these positions can make huge losses. Manchester United's profitability is clearly the exception. In the 13 years before being taken over by the Glazer family the club generated over £250 million in pre-tax profits while also winning eight league titles. Indeed, other American owners might never have bothered buying into English football without United's example. But no other club could replicate their success.

For most English clubs, our chart shows that there is not even a connection between changing league position and changing profits. In 45 per cent of all cases, when a club changed its league position, its profits moved in the opposite direction: either higher position, lower profits or lower position, higher profits. Only 55 per cent of the time did profits and position move in the same direction. Had there been no correlation at all between winning and making profits, that figure would have been much the same, namely 50 per cent. Clearly, winning games is not the route to making money. As Francisco Pérez Cutiño notes in his MBA paper, it's not that winning matches can help a club make profits; rather, the effect works the other way around: if a club finds new revenues, that can help it win matches.

It is in fact almost impossible to run a football club like a profit-making business. This is because there will always be rival owners – the Cragnottis, the Abramoviches, or the Gaddhafis, who own a chunk of Juventus – who don't care about profits and will spend whatever it takes in the hope of winning prizes. All other club owners are forced to keep up with them. If one owner won't pay large transfer fees and salaries, somebody else will, and that somebody else will get the best players and win prizes. The consequence is that the biggest slice of money that football makes gets handed over to the best players. As A.T. Kearney says, you could even argue that football clubs are nothing more than vessels for transporting football's income to footballers. 'The players are completely free to move,' explains Hembert. 'They are a key factor in winning, and also in the ego, in pleasing the fans. And they all have pretty savvy agents who are able to maximise their bargaining power.'

It means that even the cautious Sugar type cannot make decent profits in football. In fact, because his team will win fewer matches than its free-spending rivals, some fans will desert him. That will eat further into his profits. From 1991 to 1998 average attendances in the Premier League rose 29 per cent, but Tottenham's crowds fell 5 per cent.

Running a football club to make money looks like a lost cause. Nor, it might be argued, should anyone attempt it. Most of a club's customers (its fans) and employees (its players and coaches) and even usually its owners would say that the club exists to play good football and win things, not to turn profits. That's why a report by the Commission on Industrial Relations in 1974 quoted an anonymous club chairman as saying: 'Any club management which allows the club to make a profit is behaving foolishly.' In the not so distant past the FA used to forbid club owners to profit from their investment. Traditionally, football clubs have behaved more like charitable trusts than like businesses.

Making profits deprives a club of money that it could spend on the team. One reason why Bundesliga clubs rarely do well in the Champions League any more is precisely that they make profits. In the 2006–07 season, they spent an average of just 45 per cent of their revenues on players' salaries. That's not the way to win things, unless you happen to be Olympique Lyon.

The business of football is football. Almost all football clubs that are not Manchester United should ditch the fantasy of making profits. But that doesn't mean that they should continue to be badly run. The weight of money that now washes through football demands a more businesslike approach to managing cash. Bungs might have been no big deal when transfer fees were measured in the hundreds of thousands of pounds, but become a problem when they run into the tens of millions.

Football clubs need to know what they are. They shouldn't kid themselves that they are BBA Aviation. Rather, they are like the British Museum: public-spirited organisations that aim to serve the community while remaining reasonably solvent. It sounds like a modest goal, but few of them achieve even that.

NEED NOT APPLY: DOES ENGLISH FOOTBALL DISCRIMINATE AGAINST BLACK PEOPLE?

In 1991 Ron Noades, chairman of Crystal Palace, popped up on Channel Four talking about blacks.

'The problem with black players,' explained Noades, whose heavily black side had just finished third in the old first division, 'is they've great pace, great athletes, love to play with the ball in front of them … When it's behind them it's chaos. I don't think too many of them can read the game. When you're getting into the mid-winter you need a few of the hard white men to carry the athletic black players through.'

Noades's interview was one of the last flourishes of unashamed, overt racism in British football. Through the 1980s racism had been more or less taken for granted in the game. Fans threw bananas at black players. Pundits such as Emlyn Hughes explained the curious absence of black players at Liverpool and

Everton by saying, 'They haven't got the bottle.' The writer Dave Hill summed up the stereotypes:

> 'No bottle' is a particular favourite, lack of concentration another. 'You don't want too many of them in your defence,' one backroom bod told me, 'they cave in under pressure.' Then there is the curious conviction that blacks are susceptible to the cold and won't go out when it rains.

It's clear that English football in those days was shot through with racism: prejudice based on skin colour. But what we want to know is whether that racism translated into discrimination: unfair *treatment* of people. People like Noades may have been prejudiced against black players, but did they make it harder for these players to get jobs in football? The black striker Garth Crooks, who played in the 1980s, thought they did: 'I always felt I had to be 15 per cent better than the white person to get the same chance,' he said.

Yet the notion of discrimination against blacks clashes with something we think we know about football: that on the field at least, the game is ruthlessly fair. In football good players of whatever colour perform better than bad ones. Fans and chairmen and managers may walk around with Noadesesque fantasies in their heads, but when a black player plays well, everyone can see it. Nick Hornby writes in *Fever Pitch*, in his famous riff on Gus Caesar: 'One of the great things about sport is its cruel clarity; there is no such thing, for example, as a bad one-hundred-metre runner, or a hopeless centre-half who got lucky; in sport, you get found out. Nor is there such a thing as an unknown genius striker starving in a garret somewhere.'

In short, it would seem that in football there is no room for ideologies. You have to be right, and results on the field will tell you very quickly if you are. So would clubs really discriminate against blacks at the cost of winning matches? After all, even Ron

Noades employed black players. (He knew something about football too: after leaving Palace he bought Brentford, appointed himself manager, won promotion and was voted manager of the year in Division Two.) In fact, the very success of blacks on the field might be taken as evidence that the opportunities were there.

It's also often hard to prove objectively that discrimination exists. How can you show that you failed to get the job because of prejudice, rather than just because you weren't good enough? Liverpool and Everton might argue that they employed white players in the 1980s simply because the whites were better.

Luckily, there is no need to get into a 'he said, she said' argument. We have data to prove that English football discriminated against black players. We can show when this particular kind of discrimination ended. And we can predict that the new forms of discrimination that pervade English football today will be harder to shift.

The first black person to set foot in the British Isles was probably a soldier in Julius Caesar's invading army, in 55 BC. The 'indigenous' English themselves only arrived about 400 years later, during the collapse of the Roman empire.

Much later, under Victoria, Britain's own empire ruled a large share of the world's black people. A few of the better educated or entrepreneurial ones made their way from the Raj, the Caribbean or Africa to Britain. Arthur Wharton, born in 1865 in the Gold Coast (now Ghana), became the world's first black professional footballer. As well as keeping goal for Preston, he set the world record of 10 seconds for the 100-yard sprint.

But until the 1950s most Britons had probably never seen a black person. Unlike Americans, they never developed any kind of relationship with blacks, whether positive or negative. Then, after the Second World War, hundreds of thousands of colonial immigrants began arriving. The influx was small enough – less than

5 per cent of Britain's total population, spread over a quarter of a century – to pose little threat to the concepts of Englishness, Scottishness or Welshness. Nonetheless, the signs went up in the windows of bedsits: 'No Coloureds'.

One of the authors of this book, Stefan Szymanski, is the son of an immigrant from Poland who had escaped to London in 1940 and joined the British army to fight the Nazis. Stefan remembers his father telling him about looking for lodgings in London in the early 1950s, and finding signs in the windows saying 'Rooms to let – no Poles, no Hungarians'. Not only was this kind of discrimination legal, but Stefan's father accepted it. In his mind, he was the immigrant, and it was his job to fit in. Luckily for him (and for Stefan) he was an educated man, able to find a reasonable job and make a reasonable living. He was also a racist. This might sound harsh, but by today's standards most adults seemed to be racist in the 1970s, when Stefan was growing up. In the popular comedy series of the time, *Till Death Us Do Part*, the hero Alf Garnett was a ludicrously prejudiced East Ender who favoured labels like 'Coon', 'Nig-nog', 'Darky', 'Paki' and 'the Jews up at Spurs' (Garnett supported West Ham). Not only were these words used on the BBC, but they were accompanied by canned laughter.

Admittedly, the joke of the series was ultimately on Garnett, who was regularly exposed to the falsity of his own prejudices. But Stefan used to argue that these labels were offensive. His father took this as evidence of a lack of sense of humour.

It was against this 1970s background of instinctive racism that black players began arriving in English football. Most were children of immigrants, like Garth Crooks (born in Stoke), Chris Kamara (Middlesbrough) or Vince Hilaire (Forest Hill). That didn't stop them being treated to monkey noises and bananas. (As Hornby noted in *Fever Pitch*, 'There may well be attractive, articulate and elegant racists, but they certainly never come to football matches.') For a while, neo-Nazi parties even imagined that they could lead a revolution from the football terraces.

Given the abuse the early black players received, it would have been easy for them to give up on football. It was thinkable that they would be driven out of the game. Instead they stayed, played and triumphed. In 1978, when Viv Anderson became the first black player to be capped for England, it became apparent that children of Caribbean migrants might have something of a role to play in English football. Still, even after John Barnes scored his solo goal to beat Brazil at the Maracanã in 1984, the FA's chairman was harangued by England fans on the flight back home: 'You fucking wanker, you prefer sambos to us.'

As late as 1993 you could still witness the following scene: a crowd of people in a pub in the City of London is watching England–Holland on TV. Every time Barnes gets the ball, one man – in shirtsleeves and a tie, just out of his City office – makes monkey noises. Every time, his workmates laugh. If anyone had complained, let alone gone off to find a policeman and asked him to arrest the man, the response would have been: 'Where's your sense of humour?' (Hornby's line on this sort of problem: 'I wish I were enormous and of a violent disposition, so that I could deal with any problem that arises near me in a fashion commensurate with the anger I feel.')

Whenever people reminisce about the good old days, when ordinary working people could afford to go to football matches, it's worth scanning the photographs of the cloth-capped masses standing on the terraces for the faces you *don't* see: blacks, Asians, women. It's true that today's all-seater grounds in the Premier League exclude poor people. However, the terraces before the 1990s probably excluded rather more varieties of people. In the 1970s and 1980s, when football grew scary, the violence forced out even many older white men.

In the late 1980s Stefan Szymanski began thinking about the economics of football. He was then working for the Centre for Business Strategy at London Business School. Everyone in the

Centre was an economist, and therefore tempted to think that markets, more or less, 'worked'. The theory was that any business person who came up with a brilliant innovation – inventing the telephone, say – would not keep his advantage for long, because others would imitate him and compete.

But the economists were interested in the few companies that stayed successful despite competition. Clearly there must be something to learn from them. Stefan suggested looking for these paragons in football. It was evidently a highly competitive industry, and yet some clubs managed to dominate for years on end. How did they manage to stay ahead for so long?

Stefan enlisted the support of Ron Smith, who had taught him when he was writing his PhD. Smith, as well as being an expert on Marxist economics and the economics of defence, is a well-known econometrician. Econometrics is essentially the art of finding statistical methods to extract information from data; or, as a lawyer friend of Stefan's likes to put it, taking the data down into the basement and torturing it until it confesses. Studying the accounts of football clubs, Stefan and Smith could see how much each club spent on salaries. The two discovered that this spending alone explained almost all the variation in positions in the English Football League. We've already seen that when Stefan analysed the accounts of 40 clubs for the period 1978–97, he found that their wage spending accounted for 92 per cent of the variation in their league positions.

Clearly the market in players' pay was highly efficient: the better a player was, the more he earned. And this made sense, because football is one of the few markets that indisputably meet the conditions in which competition can work efficiently: there are large numbers of buyers and sellers, all of whom have plenty of information about the quality of the players being bought and sold. If a player got paid less than he was worth, he could move to another club. If he got paid more, he would soon find himself being sold off again.

But what about the variation in league position that remained unexplained after adjusting for players' pay? If buying talent was generally enough to win titles – as Jack Walker at Blackburn Rovers and Roman Abramovich at Chelsea would soon demonstrate – what else accounted for a team's success? If it was something that was easy to copy – a new tactic, for instance – then other teams would copy it, and the advantage would disappear. That got Stefan thinking about discrimination. What if owners were simply not willing to copy the secret of others' success, because they didn't want to hire the kinds of players that brought that success? He began to search for discrimination against black players.

In most industries, there is a way to demonstrate that discrimination exists. Suppose you could construct a sample of all applicants for a job, and also of all their relevant qualifications. If you then found that a much larger proportion of relevantly qualified white applicants received job offers than relevantly qualified black applicants, you could reasonably infer the presence of discrimination. For example, if 50 per cent of white applicants with a first-class honours degree in philosophy got job offers from university philosophy departments, but only 10 per cent of equally high-achieving black applicants did, then you should suspect discrimination.

This is essentially how economists have tried to identify job discrimination. The method also works for wage discrimination. If equivalently qualified blacks (or women, or left-handers, or whoever) get lower wages for equivalent jobs, then there is probably discrimination going on. Researchers have put together databases of thousands of workers, each identified by dozens of relevant qualifications, to test whether discrimination exists. When it comes to ethnic minorities and women, the evidence usually shows that it does.

The problem is that there are few measurable qualifications that make someone a great footballer. When a company is accused of racism, it often says that while the black (or purple, or

female) candidates may possess some of the relevant characteristics, there are other, less quantifiable characteristics that
they don't have. Intellectually this point is hard to overturn.
Hundreds of cases of racial discrimination have been fought out
in American courts, and evidence based on the kinds of studies
we have mentioned has often run into trouble.

Happily, there is another way to test for discrimination in football. Once again, it relies on evidence from the market. As a
general rule, the best way to find out what people are up to is to
see how they behave when faced with a price. Don't know if you
prefer Coke to Pepsi? Well, let's see what you choose when they
both cost the same. (Most people choose Coke.) Don't know if
you prefer watching the FA Cup or the league? Let's see what you
do when tickets cost the same. Do managers prefer white players to blacks? Well, let's see how they spend their clubs' money.

If clubs discriminate, then they will prefer to hire a white player
to an equivalently talented black player. If they do that, then
blacks will find it harder to get jobs as professional footballers.
The blacks will then be willing to accept lower wages than equivalently talented whites. After all, when demand for what we sell is
lower, we tend to lower our asking price. So black players become
cheaper than white players.

If black players are being discriminated against, that creates
an economic opportunity for unprejudiced clubs. By hiring black
players they can do just as well in the league as an equivalently
talented (but more expensive) team of whites.

That means that a simple experiment will reveal whether
discrimination exists: *If teams with more black players achieve
higher average league positions for a given sum of wage spending, then the teams with fewer black players must have been
discriminating.*

Otherwise, the 'whiter' teams would have seen that black players were good value for money, and would have tried to hire them.
Then black players' wages would have risen due to increased

competition for their services, and the relative advantage of hiring black players would have disappeared.

Note that the argument is not that some teams hire more black players than others. That could happen for many reasons. Rather, we can infer discrimination if (a) some teams have more black players than others and (b) those same teams outperform their competitors for a given level of wage spending.

After Stefan figured this out, he had the luck of running into just the right person. Around that time, he was also researching the relationship between the pay of senior executives in FTSE 100 companies and the performance of their companies. (Very unlike footballers' wages, there turned out to be almost no correlation between the pay of senior executives and the performance of a company's share price, until share options became common in the 1990s.) Stefan was interviewed for the BBC *Panorama* programme by the political journalist Michael Crick. Over time he and Crick got talking about football.

Crick is a famously thorough researcher. Book reviewers delight in finding errors, no matter how trivial, but they never succeed with Crick's political biographies. And as it happens, Crick supports Manchester United. In 1989 he wrote a fascinating history of the club with David Smith, describing how United packaged their legend for commercial gain. About this time Crick became interested in whether football clubs discriminated in their hiring. Everyone knew of the suspicious cases of the day, chiefly Liverpool and Everton.

Crick began collecting data from the 1970s onwards to see which clubs had hired black players. This was no easy task. How do you decide who is 'black'? Crick took a commonsense approach. He started with the old Rothmans Football Yearbooks, which published a photograph of every league team. From this he made a judgement as to which players 'looked black'. He then followed up by asking clubs and supporters' clubs to fill any gaps. It took him months to come up with a list of players who, to most fans, would have appeared to be black. This sounds arbitrary, but it is precisely what was required. Prejudice is based on appearances. For example, several years after Crick did his research, it emerged that Ryan Giggs's father was black. Giggs even spoke publicly about his pride in his African ancestry. However, until that point, most people would not have considered Giggs a black player. He didn't *look* black, and for that reason he would have been unlikely to face discrimination. So Crick was right not to count Giggs as black.

When Crick told Stefan about his list of black players, it was a cinch to create a test for discrimination. All that was necessary was to count how many times each black player had played for his club in a given season. It would then be clear which teams hired a larger share of black players.

Stefan then matched this data with figures on each team's league position, and its spending on wages. If there were no discrimination in the market, then wages alone would almost entirely explain league performance. Everything else would just be random noise – 'luck'. But if black players were systematically being paid less than equally talented white players, then logically the teams which hired an above average proportion of black players would do systematically better than their wage bill alone would predict.

Back in the 1970s, there were very few black players in English football. Combining our data on wages with Crick's database had given us a sample of 39 out of the 92 professional league teams. In the 1973–74 season only two of these clubs had fielded any black players at all. By 1983–84, there were still 20 teams in our sample that did not a field a black player all season. However, at this point there seems to have been a major breakthrough. By 1989 every team in the sample had fielded at least one black player at some point during these years. By 1992, when the Premier League was founded, only five teams in the sample did not field a black player that season. This implied that about 90 per cent of clubs were putting blacks in the first team. Attitudes were changing. Bananas left the game. When Noades voiced his theories on black players in 1991, he was widely mocked.

It is interesting to look at the characteristics of the black players in the English game in these years. For purposes of comparison, Stefan constructed a random sample of an equal number of white players with similar age profiles. Almost all the black players (89 per cent) were born in Britain, not very different from the white players (95 per cent). However, the blacks were more likely to have been born in the South (46 per cent compared to only 26 per cent of white players) than the North (22 per cent of blacks, compared to 54 per cent of whites). Most of the black players were strikers (58 per cent) compared to only 33 per cent of white players. There were no black goalkeepers at the time. Noades would have noted the fact that black players seemed under-represented in defence. But then strikers always carry a premium in relation to defenders in the market: it takes more talent to score than to stop other people from scoring.

Certain facts about the sample stood out: the careers of the black players averaged more than six years, compared to less than four for the whites. And 36 per cent of the blacks had represented their country, compared to only 23 per cent of the whites. On this evidence, it looked suspiciously as if the black players were better than the whites.

The proof came when Stefan deployed the economist's favourite tool, the regression analysis. He used it to isolate the distinct effects of wages and the share of black players on each club's league performance. What he found was discrimination. The data showed that clubs with more black players really did have a better record in the league than clubs with fewer blacks, after allowing for wage spending. If two teams had identical annual wage budgets, the team with more blacks would finish higher in the league.

The test implied that black players were systematically better value for money than whites. Certain teams of the 1980s such as Arsenal, Noades's Palace and Ron Atkinson's West Bromwich Albion (this was years before Atkinson called Marcel Desailly 'a fucking lazy thick nigger' on air) benefited from fielding blacks.

The clubs with fewer blacks were not suffering from a lack of information. Anyone who knew football could judge fairly easily how good a player was just by watching him play. So the only credible reason why clubs would deny themselves the opportunity to hire these players was prejudice. Clubs didn't like the look of black players, or they thought their fans wouldn't, either simply because of skin hue, or because they perceived weaknesses that were just not there. By testing the behaviour of managers against the market, it proved possible to uncover evidence of discrimination.

In football, you can judge someone's performance only against other competitors. This means that I lose nothing by being inefficient if my competitors are inefficient in the same way as me. I can go on hiring mediocre players as long as other clubs do so too. As long as all clubs refused to hire talented black players, the cost of discriminating was low. What the data showed was that by the beginning of the 1980s, so many teams were hiring talented blacks that the cost of discriminating had become quite high. Teams that refused to field black players were overpaying for white players and losing more matches as a consequence. Yet some level of discrimination persisted. Even by the end of the 1980s, an all-white team such as Everton would cost around 5 per cent more than an equally good team that fielded merely an average proportion of black players. As Dave Hill wrote in the fanzine *When Saturday Comes* in 1989: 'Half a century after Jesse Owens, a quarter of a century after Martin Luther King, and 21 years after two American sprinters gave the Black Power salute from the Olympic medal rostrum, some of these dickheads don't even know what a black person is.'

But by the time he wrote that, precisely because football is so competitive, more and more clubs had begun to hire black players. In 1995 even Everton signed the Nigerian Daniel Amokachi. The economic forces of competition drove white men to ditch their prejudices.

Quite soon, so many clubs were hiring blacks that black players came to be statistically over-represented in football. Only about 1.6 per cent of people in the British census of 1991 described themselves as black. Yet in the early 1990s, about 10 per cent of all players in the Football League were black. By the end of the decade, after the influx of foreign players, the share was nearer 20 per cent.

So did clubs learn to overcome their prejudices? A few years after Stefan ran his first test for discrimination, he badgered some students who were looking for undergraduate projects into compiling a list of black players for another six seasons. That took the dataset up to the 1998–99 season. Once again Stefan merged the data with figures on wages and league performances. Now he could run the regression to the end of the 1990s. For these six additional years, there was no evidence that the share of black players in a team had any effect on team performance, after allowing for the team's wage bill. In other words, by then, black players were on average paid what they were worth – judged, at least, by their contribution to winning football matches.

Perhaps the best witness to the acceptance of blacks in football is Lilian Thuram. A black man born on the Caribbean island of Guadeloupe, and raised in a poor suburb of Paris, he played professionally from 1991 to 2008 and became France's most capped player. Thuram is also a French intellectual, possibly the only footballer ever to have spoken the words, 'There's an interesting young ethnographer at the Musée de l'Homme ...'

He is acutely sensitive to racism. He now runs an anti-racism foundation. Nonetheless, he feels football is innocent of the sin.

Over late-night pasta in an Italian restaurant in Barcelona, he explains: 'In football it's harder to have discrimination, because we are judged on very specific performances. There are not really subjective criteria. Sincerely, I've never met a racist person in football. Maybe they were there, but I didn't see it.'

In fact, he adds: 'In sport, prejudices favour the blacks. In the popular imagination, the black is in his place in sport. For example, recently in Barcelona, the fitness coach said about Abidal [a black French defender]: "He's an athlete of the black race." It's not because he stays behind after training to run. No, it's because he's black.'

So by the 1990s discrimination against black players had disappeared. Gradually they came to feel at home in the industry. Here is a scene from inside the marble halls of Highbury, after a game in 1995: Arsenal's black Dutch winger Glenn Helder is introducing his black teammate Ian Wright (one of Ron Noades's ex-players) to some Dutch people. Then Helder says, 'Ian, show these guys what I taught you.' A look of intense concentration appears on Wright's face, and he begins jumping up and down and shouting in Dutch: 'Buzz off! Dirty ape! Dirty ape!' He and Helder then collapse laughing. There was still racism in football, but by then blacks could mock it from the inner sanctums of the game's Establishment.

The story of racism in American sports followed much the same arc. Right through the Second World War, baseball and basketball had segregated blacks into 'negro leagues'. In 1947 Branch Rickey of the Brooklyn Dodgers broke an unwritten rule among baseball owners and hired the black infielder Jackie Robinson to play for his team. Robinson eventually became an American hero. However, the co-star of his story was economics. The Dodgers had less money than their crosstown neighbours the New York Yankees. If Rickey wanted a winning team, he had to tap talent that the other owners overlooked. Racism provided him with an opportunity.

Of course, discrimination against black players persisted in American sports long after Robinson. Lawrence Kahn, an economist at Cornell University, surveyed the data and found little evidence that before the 1990s baseball teams were withholding jobs or pay from blacks. But he did think they were giving black players unduly short careers, and only using them in certain positions. In basketball, Kahn did find wage discrimination. When he repeated his study in 2000, he discovered, like Stefan the second time around, that discrimination was fading.

NEW FOOTBALL, NEW DISCRIMINATION

Trevor Phillips points a finger at his own shaven black head: 'Excuse me, here I am: bullseye!' The son of an early Caribbean immigrant, Phillips was raised in London, and has supported Chelsea for nearly 50 years. But in the 1970s, when darts-throwing was the favourite sport of the Shed Stand, he didn't go to matches. His head felt like too obvious a target. Hardly any black people went to Chelsea then. 'Now I can take my daughters,' he marvels.

But as head of the Commission for Equalities and Human Rights, Phillips doesn't think football has slain discrimination yet. One snowy morning in Norwich, he identifies two surviving types of discrimination in British football:

The big stain still on the game – entirely apart from the fact of loads of black players on the field and none in the dugout – is the absence of Asian footballers. I now think we have three pro footballers who are British Asians [this was in 2005]. Well, you know, it's a start. But there are people playing out there on the parks on Sunday mornings, who come from Asian communities, and you think to yourself: why aren't some of them getting in at least in the lower leagues? Why don't we see any Asian footballers in the Conference, for

God's sake? Can't be that hard to get into the Conference.
And we don't know the answer to that.

In the census of 2001, 4 per cent of respondents in England (not Britain) defined themselves as being of Indian, Pakistani or Bangladeshi origin. Large numbers of these people play football. It's possible that some of them discourage their children from becoming professional footballers. However, it's also likely that English clubs now discriminate against Asians just as they used to discriminate against blacks.

You might think that this new form of discrimination would disappear fast; that just as competition pushed clubs into buying black players, it will push them into hiring Asians.

However, the British Asians may have a harder time getting into football than the blacks did, because English football has changed since the early 1990s. There is no longer much room in the Premier League for Englishmen of any colour. Of the 498 players who started matches in the Premier League in the 2007–08 season, only 170 were English. If 4 per cent of the English population is of South Asian origin, then even if there were no discrimination, you would expect to find only seven British Asians in the Premier League.

However, the vast majority of British Asian hopefuls, like most English footballers in general, will be looking for jobs in the lower divisions – and there, discrimination is more likely to persist. Small clubs are probably freer than big clubs to ignore talent, because they have fewer demanding fans to worry about, because their rewards for success are modest, and because the cost of rejecting a halfway decent local Asian lad is smaller than that of rejecting an England international. In the 2008–09 season, there were only seven British Asian players in all of English professional football. If few British Asians get jobs in the lower divisions, then few of these players will eventually rise to the Premier League. It would therefore be surprising to see even as many as seven British Asians in the top flight any time soon.

The other surviving form of discrimination that Phillips noted will be even harder to shift: the prejudice against black managers. This will continue because the market in football managers is much less efficient than the market in footballers.

Like discrimination against black players, discrimination against black managers first became visible in American sports. As early as 1969 Jackie Robinson, who had become quite rebellious as he grew older, refused to attend Old Timers' Day at Yankee Stadium, in protest at baseball's shunning of black coaches and managers.

The issue only hit Britain when the first generation of black players began to retire (it being an item of faith in football that only ex-players have what it takes to become managers). In the 1990s Luther Blissett applied for 22 jobs as a manager. The former England international did not get a single interview. Stella Orakwue, who recounts his story in her 1998 book *Pitch Invaders*, concludes: 'I feel a British black managing a Premiership team could be a very long way off.' Indeed, it was not until 2008, ten years after she wrote this, that Blackburn gave Paul Ince a chance for a few months. Even after Ince's appointment, John Barnes, who himself had struggled to get work as a manager in Britain, said: 'I believe the situation for black managers is like it was for black players back in the 1970s.'

True, the black managers Ruud Gullit and Jean Tigana have worked in the Premier League. But as Orakwue points out, the crucial point is that they were foreigners. They were perceived in Britain first of all as Dutch or French, and only secondarily as black. Gullit was cast as a typical sophisticated Dutch manager, not as an untried 'black' one.

You would think that, given this discrimination, unprejudiced clubs could clean up by hiring the best black (or female) managers on low salaries. Tranmere Rovers, say, could probably take its pick of the world's black managers. It could get the best female manager in history. Yet it probably won't. That's because the market in football managers is so different from the market in players. Markets tend to work when they are transparent – when you can see who is doing what and place a value on it. That is pre-eminently true of footballers, who do their work in public. When you can't see what people do, it's very hard to assign a value to their work. Efficient markets punish discrimination in plain view of everyone, and so discrimination tends to get rooted out. Inefficient markets can maintain discrimination almost indefinitely.

Black players became accepted because the market in players is transparent. It is pretty obvious who can play and who can't, who's 'got bottle' and who hasn't. The market in players' salaries, as we have seen, is so efficient that it explains 92 per cent of the variation in clubs' league positions.

But the market in managers doesn't work nearly as well. Only a few managers, for example Brian Clough or Bill Shankly, consistently perform better with their teams than the players' wage bill suggests that they should. It's hard to identify what it is that these men do better than others, because if it were easy, everyone would copy them. Most other managers simply do not matter very much, and do not last very long in the job. They appear to add so little value that it is tempting to think that they could be replaced by their secretaries, or their chairmen, or by stuffed teddy bears, without the club's league position changing. Even Alex Ferguson, who has won more prizes than anyone else in the history of football, has probably only performed about as well as the manager of the world's richest club should. Perhaps his unique accomplishment is not winning, but keeping all the interest groups in the club united behind him for so long. If you manage to stay manager of the world's richest club for nearly 25 years in an era when the rich are getting ever richer, you are guaranteed to stack up prizes.

It would be interesting to see what would happen if a club stopped hiring managers, and allowed an online survey of registered fans to pick the team. We suspect the club would perform decently, perhaps even better than its rivals, because it would be harnessing the wisdom of crowds. And it could use the money it saved on managers to up those crucial players' wages.

None of this is good news for black managers. Because it is so hard to measure a manager's performance, it will never become painfully obvious that clubs are undervaluing black managers. That means clubs can continue to choose their managers on the basis of appearances. Any club appointing someone who is not a white male ex-player with a conservative haircut must worry about looking foolish if their choice fails. Hiring a black manager feels risky, because as Barnes says, 'Black guys haven't proved themselves as managers.' White guys have – or at least some of them appear to have.

At last, footballers get more or less the jobs that they deserve. If only other professions were as fair.

THE ECONOMIST'S FEAR OF THE PENALTY KICK: ARE PENALTIES COSMICALLY UNFAIR, OR ONLY IF YOU ARE NICOLAS ANELKA?

A famous football manager stands up from the table. He's going to pretend he is Chelsea's captain John Terry, about to take the crucial penalty in the Champions League final in Moscow.

The manager performs the part with *Schadenfreude*; he is no friend of Chelsea. He adjusts his face into a mask of tension. He tells us what Terry is thinking: 'If I score, we win the Champions League.' And then, terrifyingly: 'But first I have to score.'

The manager begins pulling at the arm of his suit jacket: he is mimicking Terry pulling at his captain's armband. Terry is telling himself (the manager explains), 'I am captain, I am strong, I will score.'

Still pulling rhythmically at his suit, the manager looks up. He is eyeing an imaginary, grotesquely large Edwin van der Sar who is guarding a goal a very long 12 yards away. Terry intends to hit the ball to Van der Sar's left. We now know that a Basque economist told Chelsea that the Dutch keeper tended to dive right against right-footed kickers. Terry runs up – and here the manager, cackling, falls on his backside.

Van der Sar did indeed dive right, as the Basque economist had foreseen, but Terry slipped on the wet grass, and his shot into the left-hand corner missed by inches.

'This really is football,' the manager concludes. A player hits the post, the ball goes out, and Chelsea's coach, Avram Grant, is sacked even though he is exactly the same manager as if the ball had gone in. By one estimate, Terry's penalty cost Chelsea £85 million.

The penalty is probably the single thing in football that economists have most to say about. The penalty feels cosmically unfair; economists say otherwise. Penalties are often dismissed as a lottery; economists tell both kicker and goalkeeper exactly what to do. (Indeed, if only Nicolas Anelka had followed the economist's advice, Chelsea would have won the final.) And best of all, penalties may be the best way in the known world of understanding game theory.

DIABOLICAL: ARE PENALTIES REALLY UNFAIR?

At first sight, the penalty looks like the most unfair device in all of sport. First of all, it may be impossible for a referee to judge most penalty appeals correctly, given the pace of modern football, the tangles of legs and ball, and the levels of deception by players. When the Canadian writer Adam Gopnik watched the World Cup of 1998 on TV for the *New Yorker* magazine, he as an outsider to football immediately focused on this problem. The 'more customary method of getting a penalty', he wrote,

... is to walk into the 'area' with the ball, get breathed on hard, and then immediately collapse ... arms and legs splayed out, while you twist in agony and beg for morphine, and your teammates smite their foreheads at the tragic waste of a young life. The referee buys this more often than you might think. Afterward the postgame did-he-fall-or-was-he-pushed argument can go on for hours.

Or decades. The fan at home is often unsure whether it really should have been a penalty even after watching several replays.

And the referee's misjudgements matter, because the penalty probably has more impact than any other refereeing decision in sport. An umpire in baseball or cricket might wrongly call a strike or an lbw, but there are 54 outs in a baseball match, and 40 wickets to fall in a Test match, and so no individual decision tends to make all that much difference. Referees in rugby and American football blunder too, but because these games are higher-scoring than soccer, individual calls rarely change outcomes here either. In any case, officials in all these sports can now consult instant replays.

But football referees cannot. And since important football matches usually hinge on one goal, the penalty usually decides the match. As Gopnik says, the penalty 'creates an enormous disproportion between the foul and the reward'.

No wonder the penalty drives managers crazy. As Arsène Wenger lamented at the end of the 2007–08 season: 'Every big game I've seen this year has been decided, offside or not offside, penalty or not penalty.' Indeed, it's now a standard tactic for managers in England, after their team has lost, to devote the post-match press conference to a penalty given or not given. It's a ritual song of lament, which goes like this:

The penalty completely changed the outcome of the game. We were clearly winning/drawing but lost because of the (diabolical, unjust) penalty.

The manager knows that most newspapers prefer covering personality clashes to tactics, and so the 'match' reports will be devoted to the press conference rather than his team's losing performance. Meanwhile, the winning manager, when asked about the penalty, recites:

> It made no difference whatever to the outcome of the game. We were clearly winning and would inevitably have done so without the (entirely just) penalty.

These two ritual managerial chants amount to two different hypotheses about how penalties affect football matches. The first manager is claiming that randomly awarded penalties distort results. The second manager is saying penalties make no difference. On occasion, either manager might be right. But taken over the long term, one of them must be more right than the other. So which is it: do penalties change results, or don't they? We have the data to answer this question.

Our guru is Dr Tunde Buraimo. One of the growing band of sports econometricians – the British equivalent of baseball's sabermetricians – Tunde works, appropriately, in the ancient heartland of professional football at the University of Central Lancashire in Preston. As the saying goes, the plural of 'anecdote' is 'data', and Tunde prefers to work with tens of thousands of pieces of evidence rather than a few random recollections. To help us with our book, he examined 1,520 Premier League games played over four years, from the 2002–03 season until 2005–06. For each game he knew the pattern of scoring and, crucially, which team was expected to win given the pre-match betting odds.

Our test of the two rival hypotheses about penalties is simple. We asked Tunde to divide the games into two groups:

1. Games in which penalties were awarded.
2. Games in which they were not.

We then asked him to compare how often the home team won when there was a penalty, and how often when there wasn't. This is what he found:

PENALTY AWARDED IN MATCH?

Result	No	Yes	Total
Home win	577	142	719
	46.76%	49.65%	47.30%
Away win	336	80	416
	27.23%	27.97%	27.37%
Draw	321	64	385
	26.01%	22.38%	25.33%
Total	1,234	286	1,520
	100.00%	100.00%	100.00%

Look at the last column first. Taking all games in the database, 47.3 per cent ended in home wins, 27.37 per cent in away wins, and 25.33 per cent in draws. These frequencies reflect the intrinsic advantage of home teams. Now imagine that the first manager is right: penalties change the outcome of the game. How will they do that? It might be that they always favour home teams (because referees are cowards) in which case we would expect the percentage of home wins to be greater when penalties are given. Alternatively, it might be that penalties favour away teams (perhaps enabling a team under the cosh to get off the hook). If so, the proportion of away wins (or draws) would rise with penalties.

But in fact, as the first two columns show, the percentages for all results barely change whether a penalty is given or not. The percentage of home wins is about three percentage points higher when there is a penalty (up from 46.75 per cent to 49.65 per cent) and the percentage of draws is commensurately lower (down to 22.38 per cent from 26.01 per cent). The percentage of away wins remains almost identical (27.97 per cent against

27.23 per cent) with or without penalties. So in games with penalties, there are slightly more home wins and slightly fewer draws.

It's tempting to read significance into this: to think that the rise in home wins when there is a penalty is big enough to show that penalties favour the home team. However, statisticians warn against this kind of intuitive analysis. The absolute number of home wins when there were penalties in the game was 70. Had the frequency of home wins been the same as in games when there no penalty, the number of home wins would have been 66. So the difference (four extra home wins) is too small to be considered statistically significant. The rise is likely due to chance.

It would have been a different matter had the number of home wins when there was penalty exceeded 78 (or 55 per cent of the games concerned). Then, the increase would have met the standard generally used by statisticians for confidence that there was a statistically reliable difference in outcomes depending on the award of a penalty. As it is, though, the data suggests that the award of a penalty does not affect either home wins, away wins or draws.

But perhaps penalties have a different effect on match results. Perhaps they help favourites (if refs favour the big team). Or do they help underdogs (if penalties truly are given randomly, they should help the worse team more than the better one)? Tunde tested these hypotheses too:

	0	1	Total
Favourite win	633	147	780
	51.30%	51.40%	51.32%
Underdog win	254	67	321
	20.58%	23.43%	21.12%
Draw	347	72	419
	28.12%	25.17%	27.57%
Total	1,234	286	1,520
	100.00%	100.00%	100.00%

It's obvious even to the naked eye that penalties have no impact at all on whether the favourite wins: favourites win 51.3 per cent of games without a penalty, and 51.4 per cent with a penalty. It's true that underdogs win nearly 3 per cent more often when there is a penalty than when there is not, but once again the tests demonstrate that this fact has no statistical significance. We can put the increase down to chance. Match results appear to be the same with or without penalties. Penalties do not matter.

Now, this is a statistical statement that requires a very precise interpretation. Penalties do matter in that they often change the outcome of some individual games. Clearly, a team that scores from a penalty is more likely to win, and so, whatever a manager says, a converted penalty will affect the evolution of almost any game.

However, *on average*, taken over a large sample of games, a penalty does not make it any more likely that home teams or away teams or favourites or underdogs win. If penalties were abolished tomorrow, the pattern of football results would be exactly the same.

This sounds counterintuitive. After all, we argued that penalties look like the most unfair device in sport. They are often wrongly awarded, they cause a lot of goals, and many of these goals decide matches. So surely penalties should make results less fair?

To explain why penalties don't change the pattern of match results, we need to consult Graham Taylor. The retired manager is now remembered as the turnip whose long-ball game cost England qualification for the World Cup of 1994. However, the long-ball game had previously served Taylor very well at Watford and Aston Villa. No wonder, because it rested on one crucial insight into football: that you will only score goals if you get possession in the opposition's final third of the pitch.

Much the same insight applies to penalties: in practice you will only get them if you have possession (or at least a decent chance of winning possession) in the opponent's penalty area. Many a penalty is wrongly given. But it is almost always a reward for deep territorial penetration. That makes it, on average, a marker of the balance of power in the game. That's why good teams get proportionately more penalties than bad teams, and why home teams get more than away teams. On average, a penalty is given with the grain of a game.

RIGHT, LEFT, OR LET VAN DER SAR DECIDE FOR YOU? GAME THEORY IN BERLIN AND MOSCOW

The next question is how to take them. Economists may have no idea when house prices will crash, but they do know something about this one.

A surprising number of economists have thought hard about the humble penalty kick. Even Steve Levitt, author of *Freakonomics* and winner of perhaps the most important prize in economics (the Clark Medal, which some insiders think outranks the Nobel), once co-wrote a little-known paper on penalties. Probably only a trio of economists would have watched videos of 459 penalties taken in the French and Italian leagues. 'Testing Mixed-Strategy Equilibria When Players Are Heterogeneous: The Case of Penalty Kicks in Soccer' is one of those you might have missed, but it always won Levitt handshakes from European economists. Here's an American who *gets it*, they must have thought. Levitt, P.-A. Chiappori and T. Groseclose explain that they wrote the paper because 'testing game theory in the real world may provide unique insights'. Economists revere the penalty as a real-life example of game theory.

Game theory was developed in the 1940s by the likes of John von Neumann, a brilliant mathematician who also helped create the architecture of the modern computer. It is the study of what happens when people find themselves in situations exactly like a penalty-taker facing a goalkeeper: when what I should do depends on what you do, and what you should do depends on what I do.

The American government used game theory extensively during the Cold War, to plan its interactions with the Soviet Union, and to try to predict Soviet moves. (It is said that game-theoretic advice was given during the Cuban Missile Crisis to consider questions like, 'If we bomb Cuba, then the Russians will seize West Berlin, then we'll have to attack Russian troops, then they'll use nuclear bombs and then ...') Today economists use game theory all the time, particularly to plan government policies or analyse business strategy. Game theory even plays a big role in research on biology.

The key to game theory is the analysis of how the strategies of different actors interact. In a penalty kick, for instance, the kicker and the keeper must each choose a strategy: where to kick the ball, and where to dive. But each person's strategy depends on what he thinks the other person will do.

Sometimes in game theory, what's best for the actors is if they both do the same thing – going to the same restaurant to meet for dinner, for instance. Situations of this kind are known as co-ordination or co-operative games. But the penalty kick is a non-cooperative game: the actors succeed by achieving their objectives independently of others. In fact, the penalty is a 'zero-sum game': any gain for one player is exactly offset by the loss to the other side (+1 goal for me is −1 goal for you).

The issue of game theory behind the penalty was best put in 'The Longest Penalty Ever', a short story by the Argentine writer Osvaldo Soriano. A match in the Argentine provinces has to be abandoned seconds before time when a bent referee, who has just awarded a penalty, is knocked out by an irate player. The league court decides that the last 20 seconds of the game – the penalty kick, in effect – will be played the next Sunday. That gives everyone a week to prepare for the penalty.

At dinner a few nights before the penalty, 'Gato Díaz', the keeper who has to stop it, muses about the kicker:

'Constante kicks to the right.'

'Always,' said the president of the club.

'But he knows that I know.'

'Then we're fucked.'

'Yeah, but I know that he knows,' said el Gato.

'Then dive to the left and be ready,' said someone at the table.

'No. He knows that I know that he knows,' said Gato Díaz,
and he got up to go to bed.

Game theorists try to work out strategies for players in different types of games, and try to predict which strategy each player will pursue. Sometimes the prediction is easy. Consider the game in which each player has only two choices: either 'Develop a nuclear bomb' or 'Don't develop a nuclear bomb'. To make a prediction, you have to know what the pay-off is to each player depending on the game's outcome. Imagine the players are India and Pakistan (but it could be Israel and Iran, or any other pair of hostile nations). Initially Pakistan does not know if India will or won't develop a bomb, so it figures:

IF INDIA HAS NO BOMB

(a) We don't get a bomb: we can live alongside each other, but there will always be incidents

(b) We get a bomb: India will have to treat us with respect

IF INDIA HAS A BOMB

(c) We don't get a bomb: we can't resist anything India does

(d) We get a bomb: India will have to treat us with respect

Plainly, if you are Pakistan, you will end up developing the bomb, whether India has the bomb or not. Likewise, India will choose the same strategy, and will develop the bomb whether Pakistan does or doesn't. So the *equilibrium* of this game is for both nations to acquire a bomb. This is the gloomy logic of an arms race. The logic of a football match is much the same, and there are many examples of arms races in football, from inflation of players' wages to illegal doping.

PIECES OF PAPER IN STUTTGART, MUNICH, BERLIN AND MOSCOW

The problem for experienced penalty-takers and goalkeepers is that, over time, they build up track records. People come to spot any habits they might have – always shooting left, or always diving right, for instance. Levitt and his colleagues observed 'one goalie in the sample who jumps left on all eight kicks that he faces (only two of eight kicks against him go to the left, suggesting that his proclivity for jumping left is not lost on the kickers).'

There have probably always been people in the game tracking the past behaviour of kickers and keepers. Back in the 1970s, a Dutch manager named Jan Reker began to build up an archive of index cards on thousands of players. One thing he noted was where the player hit his penalties. The Dutch keeper Hans van Breukelen would often call Reker before an international match for a briefing.

Nobody paid much attention to this relationship until 1988. That May, Van Breukelen's PSV reached the European Cup final against Benfica. Before the match in Stuttgart, the keeper phoned Reker. Inevitably, the game went to a penalty shootout. At first Reker's index cards didn't seem to be helping much – Benfica's first five penalties all went in – but Van Breukelen saved the sixth kick from Veloso, and PSV were European champions. A month later, so were Holland. They were leading the USSR 2–0 in the final in Munich when a silly charge by Van Breukelen conceded a penalty. But using Reker's database, he saved Igor Belanov's weak kick.

In Berlin in 2006, the World Cup quarter-final between Germany and Argentina also went to penalties. Jens Lehmann, the German keeper, emerged with a crib sheet tucked into his sock. On a little page of hotel notepaper ('Schlosshotel, Grunewald', it said), the German keeper's trainer Andreas Köpke had jotted down the proclivities of some potential Argentine penalty-takers:

1. Riquelme   left
2. Crespo   long run-up/right
                    short run-up/left
3. Heinze   left low
4. Ayala   2 [His shirt number, presumably given for fear
                    that Lehmann would not recognise him] waits
                    long time, long run-up, right
5. Messi   left
6. Aimar   16, waits long time, left
7. Rodriquez   18, left

Apparently the Germans had a database of 13,000 kicks. The crib sheet might just have tipped the balance. Of the seven Argentines on the list, only Ayala and Rodriquez actually took penalties. However, Ayala stuck exactly to Lehmann's plan: he took a long run-up, the keeper waited a long time, and when Ayala dutifully shot to Lehmann's right, the keeper saved. Rodriquez also did his best to oblige. He put the ball in Lehmann's left-hand corner as predicted, but hit it so well that the keeper couldn't reach it.

By the time of Argentina's fourth penalty, Germany were leading 4–2. If Lehmann could save Esteban Cambiasso's kick, the Germans would maintain their record of never losing a penalty shootout in a World Cup. Lehmann consulted his crib sheet. Sönke Wortmann, the German film director, who was following the German team for a fly-on-the-wall documentary, reports what happened next:

> Lehmann could find no indication on his note of how Cambiasso would shoot. And yet the piece of paper did its job, because Lehmann stood looking at it for a long time. Köpke

had written it in pencil, the note was crumpled and the writing almost illegible.

Wortmann says that as Cambiasso prepared to take his kick, he must have been thinking: 'What do they know?' The Germans knew nothing. But Cambiasso was psyched out nonetheless. Lehmann saved his shot, and afterwards there was a mass punch-up on the pitch.

Both Van Breukelen's and Lehmann's stories have been told before. What is not publicly known is that Chelsea received an excellent crib sheet before the Champions League final in Moscow in 2008.

In 1995 the Basque economist Ignacio Palacios Huerta, who was then a graduate student at the University of Chicago, began recording the way penalties were taken. His paper, 'Professionals play Minimax', was published in 2003.

One friend of Ignacio's who knew about his research was a professor of economics and mathematics at an Israeli university. It so happened that this man was also a friend of Avram Grant. When Grant's Chelsea reached the final in Moscow in 2008, the professor realised that Ignacio's research might help Grant. He put the two men in touch. Ignacio then sent Grant a report that made four points about Manchester United and penalties:

1. Van der Sar tended to dive to the kicker's 'natural side' more often than most keepers did. This meant that when facing a right-footed kicker, Van der Sar would usually dive to his own right, and when facing a left-footed kicker, to his own left. So Chelsea's right-footed penalty-takers would have a better chance if they shot to their 'unnatural side', Van der Sar's left.

2. Ignacio emphasised in his report 'that the vast majority of the penalties that Van der Sar stops are those kicked to a mid-height (say, between 1 and 1.5 metres), and hence that

penalties against him should be kicked just on the ground or high up.'

3. Cristiano Ronaldo was another special case. Ignacio wrote: 'Ronaldo often stops in the run-up to the ball. If he stops, he is likely (85%) to kick to the right-hand side of the goalkeeper.'

   Ignacio added that Ronaldo seemed able to change his mind about where to put the ball at the very last instant. That meant it was crucial for the opposing keeper not to move early. When a keeper moved early, Ronaldo always scored.

4. The team that wins the toss before the shootout gets to choose whether or not to go first. But this is a no-brainer: they should always go first. Teams going first win 60 per cent of the time, presumably because there is too much pressure on the team going second – that of always having to score to save the game.

Ignacio doesn't know how his research was used, but watching the shootout on TV, he was certain it was. Indeed, once you know the content of Ignacio's note, it's fascinating to study the shootout on YouTube. The Chelsea players seem to have followed his advice almost to the letter – except for poor Anelka.

United's captain Rio Ferdinand won the toss, and turned to the bench to ask what to do. Terry tried to influence him by offering to go first. Unsurprisingly, Ferdinand ignored him. United went first, meaning that they were now likely to win. Carlos Tevez scored from the first kick.

Michael Ballack hit Chelsea's first penalty high into the net to Van der Sar's left. Juliano Belletti scored low to Van der Sar's left. Ignacio had recommended that Chelsea's right-footed kickers choose that side. But at this early stage, he still couldn't be sure that Chelsea were being guided by his report.

He told us later: 'Interestingly, my wife had been quite sceptical about the whole thing as I was preparing the report for coach

Grant, not even interested in looking at it. But then the game went into extra time, and then into a penalty shootout. Well, still sceptical.'

At this point Cristiano Ronaldo stepped up to take his kick for United. Watching on TV, Ignacio told his wife the precise advice he had given Chelsea in his report: Chelsea's keeper shouldn't move early, and if Cristiano paused in his run-up, he would most probably hit the ball to the keeper's right.

To Ignacio's delight, Chelsea's keeper Petr Cech stayed motionless – 'not even blinking', in the Spanish football phrase. Then, exactly as Ignacio had recommended, Cech dived to his right and duly saved Ronaldo's shot. Ignacio recalled later: 'After that, I started to believe that they were following the advice quite closely.' As for his wife, 'I think she was a bit shocked.'

What's astonishing – though it seems to have passed unnoticed at the time – is what happened after that. Chelsea's next four penalty-takers, Frank Lampard, Ashley Cole, John Terry and Salomon Kalou, *all* hit the ball to Van der Sar's left, just as Ballack and Belletti had done. In other words, the first six Chelsea kicks went to the same corner.

Ashley Cole was the only one of the six who partly disregarded Ignacio's advice. Cole was left-footed, so when he hit the ball to Van der Sar's left, he was shooting to his own 'natural side' – the side that Ignacio had said Van der Sar tended to choose. Indeed, the Dutchman chose correctly on Cole's kick, and very nearly saved the shot, but it was well struck, low (as Ignacio had recommended), and it just wriggled out of the keeper's grip. But all Chelsea's right-footed penalty-takers had obeyed Ignacio to the letter and kicked the ball to their 'unnatural side', Van der Sar's left.

So far, Ignacio's advice had worked very well. Much as the economist had predicted, Van der Sar had dived to his natural side four times out of six. He hadn't saved a single penalty. Five of Chelsea's six kicks had gone in, while Terry's, as the whole world knows, flew out off the post with Van der Sar in the wrong corner.

But after six kicks, Van der Sar figured out that Chelsea were pursuing a strategy. Admittedly he didn't quite get their strategy right. Wrongly but understandably, he seems to have decided that their strategy was to put all their kicks to his left. After all, that's where every kick he had faced up to the point had gone.

As Anelka prepared to take Chelsea's seventh penalty, the gangling keeper, standing on the goal-line, extended his arms to either side of him. Then, in what must have been a chilling moment for Anelka, the Dutchman pointed with his left hand to the left corner. 'That's where you're all putting it, isn't it?' he seemed to be saying. (This is where books fall short as a medium. We urge you to watch the shootout on YouTube.)

Now Anelka had a terrible dilemma. This was game theory in its rawest form. Van der Sar had come pretty close to divining Chelsea's strategy: Ignacio had indeed advised right-footed kickers like Anelka to put the ball to Van der Sar's left side.

So Anelka knew that Van der Sar knew that Anelka knew that Van der Sar tended to dive right against right-footers. What was Anelka to do? He decided to avoid the left corner, where he had presumably planned to put the ball. Instead he kicked to Van der Sar's right. That might have been fine, except that he hit the ball at mid-height – exactly the level that Ignacio had warned against. Watching the kick on TV, Ignacio was 'very upset'. Perhaps Anelka was all at sea because Van der Sar had pressured him to change his plans at the last moment. Van der Sar saved the shot. Alex Ferguson said afterwards: 'That wasn't an accident, his penalty save. We knew exactly where certain players were putting the ball.' Anelka's decision to ignore Ignacio's advice probably cost Chelsea the Champions League.

RANDOMISATION: FRANCK RIBÉRY CRACKS GAME THEORY

Crib sheets like Lehmann's might just work on penalty shootouts. Many of the players who take kicks in a shootout aren't regular penalty-takers. (David Batty's penalty against Argentina in France 98 was the first he had ever taken as a professional.) These inferior penalty-takers are not skilled or steady-headed enough to be able to vary their strategy. Quite likely, they will just aim for their favourite corner, hoping that their lack of a track record means the other side won't know their preference.

But that is not how a good penalty-taker – his team's regular man – thinks.

Suppose the good kicker always chose the same corner for his penalty (game theorists call this a 'pure strategy'). It would be easy to oppose: if the kicker always kicks left then the goalkeeper knows what to do. Pure strategies don't work for penalty-taking. As Levitt and Co. found: 'There are no kickers in our sample with at least four kicks who always kick in one direction.' Take that, Jens Lehmann.

Even a more complicated pure strategy does not work. For example, suppose the kicker always shoots in the opposite corner to the one he chose last time. Then a future opponent studying this player would discover the sequence – left, right, left, right, left, right – and with a bit of thought, guess what comes next. The essence of good penalty-taking is unpredictability: a good penalty-taker will be one whose next penalty cannot be predicted with certainty from his history of penalty-taking.

This is a particular kind of unpredictability. It does not mean that the kicker should go left half of the time and right half of the time. After all, most kickers have a natural side, and favouring that side gives them a higher chance of scoring. But even if you naturally shoot to the keeper's right, as most right-footed kickers do, sometimes you have to shoot to his left, just to keep him honest.

In fact, if a kicker knows his chances of scoring for either corner of the net (depending also on which way the goalkeeper dives), he can choose the proportion of kicks to his natural side that maximises the probability of scoring. A right-footed kicker won't put 100 per cent of his kicks to his natural 'right' side, because that would give the goalkeeper certainty. Even a small change, like kicking right only 99 per cent of the time, would raise the chances of scoring considerably by creating uncertainty in the goalkeeper's mind.

Kicking to the left half the time would leave the keeper very uncertain. However, it would also entail the kicker hitting many poor shots to his unnatural side. So the kicker does best by hitting somewhere over half his kicks to his natural right side.

Likewise, we can calculate the proportion of times a goalkeeper should dive left or right. (Note that we are assuming the goalkeeper cannot know which way the ball is going before he decides which way to dive.) Kickers and keepers who mix it up like this are pursuing what game theorists call 'mixed strategies'.

Mixed strategies are peculiar because they require the actor to incorporate randomness into decision-making. Should I go to the pub or the cinema? A mixed strategy requires me to toss a coin, which sounds odd, since one might expect that I prefer one to the other. With a mixed strategy, you let the coin make the decision for you.

Game theorists have wondered for years whether people in the real world follow mixed strategies. They have found in tests that people tend not to use mixed strategies even when it is profitable for them to do so. In fact, our behaviour seems to fall short of mixed play in a very specific way: in most cases, our sequence of choices is predictable, because people tend to do the opposite of what they have done in the past. For instance, they choose first left, then right, then left, then right, left, right, left, right, confusing *change* with *randomness*. These guinea pigs would not make good penalty-takers.

Eventually, game theorists began to test mixed strategies in the natural laboratory of penalty-taking. Years before Ignacio Palacios Huerta advised Chelsea, he collected a database of 1,417 penalties taken between 1995 and 2000. First, he calculated the proportion of successful kicks based on whether the kicker went to his natural side (left or right). The success rate was 95 per cent if the kicker went to his natural side and the goalkeeper went to the opposite side (the remaining 5 per cent of kicks missed the goal). The success rate was 92 per cent if the kicker went to his 'unnatural' side and the goalkeeper went to his natural side. Obviously the kicker's success rates were lower if the keeper chose correctly: a scoring rate of 70 per cent if both keeper and kicker went to the kicker's natural side, and 58 per cent if both went to the other side.

Using these figures, Ignacio calculated the optimal mixed-strategy choices for each player. To maximise his chances of scoring, an imaginary penalty-taker would have to hit 61.5 per cent of his kicks to his natural side, and 38.5 per cent to the other side.

In reality, the penalty-takers Ignacio observed got pretty close to this: they hit 60 per cent to their natural side, and 40 per cent the other way.

A keeper's best strategy (if he insists on diving rather than standing still) was to dive to the kicker's natural side 58 per cent of the time and to the other side 42 per cent of the time. The actual figures, Ignacio found, were scarily close: 57.7 per cent and 42.3 per cent. Levitt's team, using a different database of penalties, found that keepers went to the right 57 per cent of the time. So, it looks as if keepers as well as penalty-takers really do follow mixed strategies.

But what we most want to know are the choices of individual kickers and goalkeepers, not the overall averages. Ignacio studied

22 kickers and 20 goalkeepers, each of whom was involved in more than 30 penalties in his database. Again, Ignacio calculated the success rates depending upon the side the kicker and goalkeeper chose, and calculated the frequencies in each direction that would maximise the chances of success for kickers and keepers.

In real life, the actual frequencies the players observed were indistinguishable from the best mixed-strategy choices in over 95 per cent of cases. We can say with a high degree of confidence that penalty-takers and goalkeepers really do use mixed strategies. Levitt's paper found the same thing: except for the bizarre keeper who always dived left, almost all the other kickers and keepers played mixed strategies.

Finally Ignacio tested the most important question of all: are footballers capable of constructing a truly random sequence in their penalty-taking decisions, as the mixed-strategy theory requires? Careful statistical testing showed that indeed they are. In other words, it is impossible to predict which way a regular penalty-taker will kick on the basis of his history of kicks. Each time he chooses his corner without any reference to what he did the last time.

Randomisation of penalties is a completely logical theory that against all odds turns out to be true in practice. As long as the penalty-taker is a pro, rather than some terrified Southgateian innocent roped in for a job that he doesn't understand, lists like Lehmann's are useless.

All this shows the extraordinary amount of subconscious thought that goes into playing top-level football. Previous studies in game theory had shown that people could construct random sequences if the problem was first explained to them in some detail. Nobody is suggesting that footballers have sat at home ginning up on mixed-strategy equilibria. Rather, the best players intuitively grasp the truth of the theory and are able to execute it. That is what makes them good players.

Franck Ribéry is the designated penalty-taker for Bayern Munich and France. Needless to say, the scar-faced little playmaker places his kicks according to a randomised mixed strategy. But more than that, one of his former managers explains, even once Ribéry has embarked on his jagged hither-and-thither run-up, *he himself* does not know which corner he will choose. When the born economist Arsène Wenger was told this, he gushed with admiration.

Good footballer as Ribéry is, he might do even better as a game theorist.

THE SUBURBAN NEWSAGENT'S: CITY SIZES AND FOOTBALL PRIZES

The scene: the VIP room at the Athens Olympic Stadium, a couple of hours before the Champions League final of 2007 between Milan and Liverpool kicks off. Michel Platini and Franz Beckenbauer are being buttonholed every couple of yards by other middle-aged men in expensive suits. There is a crush at the buffet, and another across the room, where a familiar silver cup with 'big ears' stands on a dais. You queue up, assume a conquering pose beside the Champions League trophy, and grin. Nice young ladies from UEFA slip the snap into a frame for you.

An Englishman watching the scene, a football official, confides that he first got this close to the cup 30 years ago. Where? In Bramcote, a suburb of Nottingham. One of Brian Clough's brothers ran the local post office-cum-newsagent's, and Clough himself would sometimes pop in and serve customers, or just stand behind the counter reading the papers. One Sunday morning when the future official went in with his grandfather, there was the European Cup freshly won by Forest, plonked on top of a pile of *Nottingham Evening Post*s. Behind it stood Brian Clough, holding an open newspaper in front of his face. He neither moved nor spoke, but he knew the boy would remember the scene for ever. The official remembers: 'I was too young and shy to speak to the man, which I regret to this day.'

It's odd to think of the game's biggest club trophy ending up in a place like Bramcote (population 7,318). Yet it's not that exceptional. Provincial towns like Nottingham, Glasgow, Dortmund, Birmingham or Rotterdam have all won European Cups, while the seven biggest metropolitan areas in Europe – Istanbul, Paris, Moscow, London, St Petersburg, Berlin and Athens – never have. This points to an odd connection between city size, capital cities and footballing success. Here's why Arsenal and Chelsea haven't won the Champions League (but may soon).

GENERAL FRANCO'S TRANSISTOR RADIO: THE ERA OF TOTALITARIAN FOOTBALL

The best measure of success in club football is a simple list: the names of the clubs that have won the European Cup since the competition began in 1956. Study this list, and you'll see that the history of the European Cup breaks down into three periods.

The first, from 1956 through the late 1960s, is dominated by the capital cities of Fascist regimes. Of the first 11 European Cups, eight were won either by Real Madrid (favourite club of General Franco) or Benfica (from the capital of the Portuguese dictator Salazar). Seven of the losing teams in the first 16 finals also came from Fascist capitals: Real, Benfica and, in 1971, Panathinaikos from the Athens of the colonels' regime.

But by the start of the 1970s, the dominance of Fascist capitals was eroding. Fascist governments seldom outlast their leaders, and Portugal's had entered a twilight after Salazar died in 1970. Meanwhile everyone was waiting for Franco to go too.

Yet even after Fascism disappeared, teams from Europe's remaining dictatorial capitals continued to thrive. Steaua

Bucharest, run by Nicolae Ceaucescu's son Valentin, won the cup in 1986. Red Star Belgrade triumphed in 1991 just as Yugoslavia was breaking into pieces. The same phenomenon was at work in the communist countries as in the Fascist capitals before them. Dictators send resources to the capital because that is where they and their bureaucrats and soldiers and secret policemen live. So the dictators do up the main buildings, boost the local economy, and help the football club. That's totalitarian football.

A communist takeover of Britain could have done wonders for a capital side like Arsenal. Just look at the triumphs of Dynamo Berlin, founded in the former East Germany with the express purpose of keeping the league title in the capital. The club president until the Berlin Wall fell was Erich Mielke, feared octogenarian chief of the East German secret police, the Stasi. Mielke loved Dynamo. He made all the best East German players play for it. He also talked to referees, and Dynamo won lots of matches with penalties in the 95th minute. Dynamo were popularly known as '*Die Elf Schweine*' (The 11 Pigs), but they did win the East German league title every year from 1979 to 1988. This was possibly Europe's most extreme case of politicians rigging the football market.

Dynamo never got far in the European Cup, but General Franco's local team did. The general made a point of catching Real Madrid's games on the radio, taking a transistor along with him if he was out partridge-shooting, writes Jimmy Burns in his *When Beckham Went to Spain*. It wasn't so much that Franco fixed referees or gave Real money. Rather, he helped the club indirectly, by centralising Spain's power and resources. And he believed that Real's European Cups helped him. Fernando María Castiella, foreign minister under Franco, called Real Madrid 'the best embassy we have ever had'.

DOWN AND OUT, PARIS AND LONDON:
THE FAILURE OF DEMOCRATIC CAPITALS

Totalitarian capitals got off to a great start in the European Cup. But for the first 41 years of the trophy's life, the democratic capitals of Europe never won it.

There is only one caveat: Amsterdam is nominally the Dutch capital, and Ajax of that city won the European Cup four times. However, Amsterdam really is only nominally the capital. The government, Queen Beatrix and the embassies are all in The Hague, a city that often does not even have a team in the Dutch premier division. The Hague's only professional club, ADO, traditionally play their games in front of a couple of thousand people, a large proportion of whom are nuts. Little happens on the pitch beyond the occasional smoke-bomb or plague of rabbits. This is the curse of the democratic capital.

Instead of western capitals, provincial western European cities have dominated the competition. The rule of the provinces holds true even in the most obsessively centralised countries. Teams from five provincial British cities have won the European Cup, but never one from London. Olympique Marseille won the cup in 1993, but Paris St Germain never have. Porto have won it twice since Portugal went democratic, while the Lisbon clubs have been winless since 1962. Clubs from Milan and Turin win all the time, but never one from Rome. The cup has gone to Munich and Hamburg, but never to Bonn or Berlin. For many years, in fact, neither of those cities even had a team in the Bundesliga. Hertha Berlin, the only big club in the current capital, have not been champions of Germany since the Weimar Republic.

Capitals – especially London, Paris and Moscow – tend to have the greatest concentrations of national resources. It's therefore striking how badly their clubs seem to underperform. We can speculate about why this is. One reason might be that capital cities produce few great footballers. The great Italians Riva, Zoff,

Rossi, Baggio, Del Piero and Cannavaro are all provincials, while Vieri actually came from Australia; Matthäus and Klinsmann grew up in very small towns indeed; in England most of best players were born around Newcastle or the north-west, and in Spain most come from the Basque country. In Holland they overwhelmingly come from Amsterdam. The Hague's best-known footballers, Dick Advocaat and Martin Jol, gained their fame chiefly as managers.

Maybe it's because there are very few places to kick about in the average capital. In Paris people have to trek out to the Bois de Boulogne, or play on the tiny patches of grass in front of Les Invalides, where every good shot disappears into traffic. In London, except on Hackney Marshes, most football is five-a-side, and even then some teams end up playing under the Westway. Islington has one million inhabitants but only one proper grass pitch, the Arsenal ground. Berliners used to play on the patch of grass in front of the Reichstag, though when the capital moved back there that became impossible. When one of us, Simon, played his football in Berlin, his team had to travel out to Spandau for their home matches. Maybe the citizens of capital cities don't have the time or space for football.

But perhaps the main reason why teams from democratic capital cities are not up to much is psychological. In capital cities, no football club can matter all that much. There was an instructive sight, some time in the late 1990s, of a group of visiting fans from an English provincial town wandering down London's Baker Street yelling their club songs at passers-by. In their minds, they were shaming the Londoners, invading the city for a day, making all the noise. But the Londoners they were shouting at – many of them foreigners anyway – didn't care or even understand the point they were making.

Capitals simply have less to prove than provincial cities. They have bigger sources of pride than their football teams. Londoners don't go around singing songs about their city, and they don't believe that a prize for Arsenal or Chelsea would enhance

London's status. Roman Abramovich and David Dein brought trophies to Chelsea and Arsenal, but neither could ever have been voted mayor of London. Football matters even less in Paris, where it's possible to spend a lifetime without ever knowing that football exists. Paris St Germain, whose ground is not even entirely within the city's Périphérique ring road, are hardly going to become the main focus of Parisian pride.

London, Paris and Moscow don't need to win the Champions League. It is a different type of city where a football club can mean everything: the provincial industrial town. These are the places that have ousted the Fascist capitals as rulers of European football.

DARK SATANIC MILLS: WHY FACTORY TOWNS BECAME FOOTBALL TOWNS

In 1878 a football club started up just by the newish railway line in Manchester. Because the players worked at the Newton Heath carriage works of the Lancashire and Yorkshire Railway Company, their team was called Newton Heath. They played in work clogs against other works teams.

Of course we know that Newton Heath became Manchester United. What matters here are the club's origins, well recounted in Jim White's *Manchester United: The Biography*. White describes the L&YR's workers, 'sucked in from all over the country to service the growing need for locomotives and carriages'. Life in Manchester then was neither fun nor healthy, he writes. 'In the middle of the nineteenth century the average male life expectancy in Little Ireland, the notorious part of Manchester ... was as low as seventeen.' This was still the same brutal Manchester where a few decades before Karl Marx's pal Friedrich Engels had run his father's factory; the industrial city so awful it inspired communism.

Industrial Manchester had grown like no other city on earth. In 1800 it had been a tranquil little place of 84,000 inhabitants, so insignificant that as late as 1832 it did not even have an MP. It was the Industrial Revolution that changed everything. Workers poured in from English villages, from Ireland, and feeble economies everywhere. By 1900 Manchester was the sixth biggest city in Europe, with 1.25 million inhabitants, more than Moscow at the time. Inevitably, most 'Mancunians' were rootless migrants. Unmoored in their new home, many of them embraced the local football clubs. Football must have given them something of the sense of the community that they had previously known in their villages.

The same thing happened in Britain's other new industrial cities: the migrants attached themselves to football clubs with a fervour unknown in more established towns. When the Football League was founded in 1888, six of the 12 founding members came from industrial Lancashire, while the other six were from the industrial Midlands. Montague Shearman wrote for the Badminton Library that year: 'No words of ours can adequately describe the present popularity [of football] which, though great in the metropolis, is infinitely greater in the large provincial towns … it is no rare thing in the north and midlands for 10,000 people to pay money to watch an ordinary club match, or for half as many again to assemble for a "Cup Tie".' It helped that workers in the textile industry in the north-west began to get Saturdays off in the 1890s, a luxury that workers elsewhere in Britain did not enjoy.

By 1892, all 28 English professional clubs were from the north or the Midlands. Football was as northern a game as rugby league. The champions in the Victorian era came from northern industrial towns like Preston, Sheffield or Sunderland, then still among the richest spots on earth. When these places became too poor and small to support successful clubs, the league title merely migrated to larger northern cities.

The legacy of the Industrial Revolution still shapes English fandom. Today the combined population of Greater Merseyside, Greater Manchester and Lancashire county is less than

5.5 million, or a little over 10 per cent of the English population. Nonetheless, in 2008–09 a third of all clubs in the Premier League were based in this region. Their advantage: more than a century of brand-building. Manchester United became arguably the most popular club on earth partly because Manchester had been the first industrial city on earth. The club is only the biggest local footballing relic of that era. The 43 professional clubs within 150 kilometres (90 miles) of Manchester probably represent the greatest football density on earth.

Almost all Europe's best football cities have a profile like Manchester's. They were once new industrial centres that sucked in hapless villagers. The newcomers cast around for something to belong to, and settled on football. Supporting the club helped them make a place for themselves in the city. So clubs mattered more here, and grew bigger, than in capital cities or ancient cathedral towns with old-established hierarchies.

The market research company Sport+Markt has been studying fandom since 1994. In 2008 it asked 9,600 people interested in football, spread over 16 European countries, to name their 'preferred' club. This was the top 20:

	Club	Estimated number of fans (in millions)		Club	Estimated number of fans (in millions)
1	Barcelona	44.2	11	CSKA Moscow	11.1
2	Real Madrid	41.9	12	Inter Milan	10.3
3	Manchester United	37.6	13	Olympique Lyon	9.4
4	Chelsea	25.6	14	Olympique Marseille	9.4
5	Zenit St Petersburg	23.9	15	Galatasaray	9.0
6	Liverpool	23.0	16	Spartak Moscow	8.1
7	Arsenal	21.3	17	Fenerbahce	7.3
8	AC Milan	21.0	18	Wisła Kraków	6.5
9	Bayern Munich	19.8	19	Ajax Amsterdam	6.5
10	Juventus	17.5	20	Dynamo Moscow	5.7

It would be wrong to treat the results as at all precise. The figures differed significantly from those in Sport+Markt's survey of the previous year. In that one year Chelsea, for instance, had supposedly gained almost six million fans. Enormous numbers of people change their answers to the question, 'Which is your preferred team?' depending on who just won the league or where David Beckham happens to be playing. However, the survey does tell us something. Few would dispute that this top 20 includes most of Europe's best-supported clubs. And there is something remarkable about this list: the biggest clubs are not in the biggest cities. They are in the formerly industrial ones.

Of course some teams from capitals are popular. They would be, given that London, Paris, Rome and Moscow are by far the largest cities in their countries. Clubs in capitals have unparalleled catchment areas, even given the profusion of local teams. But in none of the seven largest European countries surveyed does the best-supported club come from a capital city. Here is the favourite team of each large country, according to Sport+Markt:

BEST-SUPPORTED CLUB

England	Manchester United
France	Olympique Lyon
Germany	Bayern Munich
Italy	AC Milan
Poland	Wisla Krakow
Russia	Zenit St Petersburg
Spain	Barcelona

In six out of seven countries, the number one team comes from a provincial town with a strong industrial history. The sole exception is France, where Lyon is a provincial town but was mostly bypassed by the Industrial Revolution. We saw how the club's popularity has come from nowhere since just 2002, thanks to their brilliant gaming of the transfer market under president Jean-Michel Aulas.

Taken together, the provincial industrial towns in Sport+Markt's top 20 dominate European football. Between them they won 26 out of 46 European Cups from 1963 to 2008. The smaller industrial or port cities Glasgow, Nottingham, Birmingham, Porto, Dortmund, Eindhoven and Rotterdam have won another nine between them. And all these cities have a story much like Manchester's, although their growth spurts happened later. Peasants arrived from the countryside, leaving all their roots behind. Needing something to belong to in their new cities, they chose football. That's why in all these places, the football clubs arose soon after the factories.

In most of the cities on Sport+Markt's list, the industrial migrants arrived in a whoosh in the late nineteenth century. Munich had 100,000 inhabitants in 1852, and five times as many by 1901. Barcelona's population trebled in the same period to 533,000 people. Turin, for centuries a quiet Piedmontese town, began acquiring factories in the 1870s. Milan surged with the new railways that followed Italian reunification.

Once the local merchants had grown wealthy and discovered English ways, they founded football clubs: Juventus in 1897, Barcelona and AC Milan two years later, Bayern in 1900. The clubs then grew with their cities. Newly industrial Milan, for instance, sucked in so many migrants that it could eventually support two of the three most popular teams in the country.

The second stage of the football boom in the continent's industrial cities happened after the war. The 1950s and 1960s were the years of Italy's 'economic miracle', when flocks of poor southern Italian peasants took the 'train of the sun' north. Many of these people ended up in Turin making cars for Fiat. The historian Paul Ginsborg writes: 'So great and persistent was the flow from the South, that by the end of the sixties Turin had become the third largest "southern" city in Italy, after Naples and Palermo.' The migrants found jobs, but not enough schools or hospitals or apartments. Often there was so little space that housemates had to take turns sleeping. Amid such dislocation, football mattered all the more. Goffredo Fofi, author of a study of southern immigration to Turin in the 1960s, said that 'during a Juventus–Palermo match, there were many enthusiastic immigrant Sicilian fans whose sons, by now, like every respectable FIAT worker, backed the home team.'

It's one of the flukes of history that this mass migration to Turin began soon after the Superga air disaster of 1949 had decimated the city's previous most popular team, Torino. The migrants arrived soon after Juve had established itself as the local top dog, and they helped make it a global top dog. For a start, they transmitted the passion to their relatives down south.

Barcelona experienced the same sort of growth spurt at about the same time as Turin. In the 1950s and 1960s perhaps 1.5 million Spaniards moved to the Barcelona area. Entire villages in the country's interior were left almost empty. On wastelands outside Barcelona, self-built shantytowns sprang up – the sort of thing you might now see on the outskirts of Jakarta – packed with peasants who had left behind everything they knew. Many were illiterate, and hardly any spoke the local language, Catalan. A lot of them attached themselves to Barça. In Spain's new Manchester, it was the quickest way to belong.

The link between industry and football is almost universal across Europe. The largest average crowds in all of continental Europe in the 2008–09 season have been at Borussia Dortmund (average: 72,400), one of many clubs in the industrial Ruhr region. In France, too, it is the industrial cities that have historically loved their clubs best. The country's few traditional hotbeds of football are the mining towns of Lens and Saint-Étienne, and the port of Marseilles.

All these industrial cities were products of a particular era. In all of them the Industrial Revolution ended, often painfully. But besides the empty docks and factory buildings, the other legacy of industrialisation was beloved football clubs. The quirk of a particular era gave Manchester United, Barcelona, Juventus, Bayern Munich and the Milan clubs enough fans to dominate first their own countries, and then Europe.

If Sport+Markt had polled the popularity of football clubs in Turkey, it would have found the universal principle holding there too. The country's capital of football is not the capital city, Ankara, but the new industrial powerhouse Istanbul. The city is home to all three of Turkey's most popular clubs: Galatasaray, Fenerbahce, and Besiktas.

It's true that Istanbul, like St Petersburg, was once the seat of government, but both cities lost that role more than 80 years ago, long before football amounted to anything in their countries. Even as late as 1950, Istanbul was a sleepy place with barely a million inhabitants. Then it became possibly the last big European city to experience an Industrial Revolution. Migrants were sucked in from all over Anatolia. Between 1980 and 1985 alone, Istanbul's population doubled. Today it is the largest city in Europe with nearly 12 million inhabitants. The rootless peasants needed somehow to belong in their new home, and so they attached themselves to one of the city's great clubs. Often, these were their strongest loyalties in Istanbul.

Admittedly almost all cities in Europe have some experience of industrialisation. But very few have had as much as Manchester, Turin, Milan, Istanbul or Barcelona. These were the European cities with the most flux, the fewest longstanding hierarchies, the weakest ties between people and place. Here, there were emotional gaps to fill. This becomes obvious when we contrast the industrial cities with old towns that have a traditional upperclass streak. In England, Oxford, Cambridge, Cheltenham, Canterbury, York and Bath are all decent-sized places, with somewhere between 100,000 and 150,000 inhabitants each. Many industrial towns of that size or even smaller – Middlesbrough, Reading, Ipswich, Blackburn, Watford, Burnley – have serious football traditions. Yet Oxford, Cambridge, Bath, Canterbury, York and Cheltenham between them currently have just one team in the Football League: Cheltenham Town, which joined it only in 1999. In towns like these, with settled hierarchies, people simply didn't need football clubs to root themselves.

Oxford's face to the world is the university. In industrial cities it is the football club. The clubs of Barcelona, Newcastle and Marseille are the pride of their cities, a symbolic two fingers up at the capital. When Barcelona win something, the president of Catalonia traditionally hoists himself up on the balcony of his palace on the Plaça Sant Jaume, and shouts at the crowds below: 'Barça wins, Catalonia wins!'

These provincial clubs have armies of fans, players who will bleed for the club, and backing from local plutocrats. Bernard Tapie put money into Olympique Marseille, the Agnelli family into Juventus, and Sir John Hall into Newcastle because they wanted to be kings of their town. Local fans and sponsors invest in these clubs partly because they feel civic pride is at stake. In the Middle Ages they would have built a cathedral instead.

Usually, provincial cities such as these only have one major club, which often becomes the only thing that many outsiders know about the place. For instance, there must be many Manchester United fans around the world who don't know that Manchester is a city in England. True, most provincial cities have two teams that compete for top-dog status: United and City in Manchester, Inter and AC Milan in Milan, Torino and Juventus in Turin, United and Wednesday in Sheffield, Celtic and Rangers in Glasgow, Forest and County in Nottingham, Everton and Liverpool, Bayern and 1860 in Munich, Barça and Espanyol in Barcelona. Many of these rivalries have something to do with religion and/or politics. But usually one team struggles. Manchester City, Torino and 1860 Munich have all spent long phases in the lower divisions. Everton last won the league in 1987. FC Amsterdam went bust. Mid-sized provincial cities are simply not big enough to sustain two big clubs for long. In the end, one club pulls ahead.

'THEY MOVED THE HIGHWAY':
THE RISE AND FALL OF SMALL TOWNS

Provincial industrial towns began to dominate the European Cup in the late 1960s. But their rule breaks down into two main periods. The first, from 1970 to 1981, is the small-town era, when clubs from some very modest places won the European Cup.

Here they are, with the populations not just of the cities themselves but of their entire metropolitan areas, including people in all the local dormitory towns:

Club	Year(s) they won it	Metropolitan area
Feyenoord Rotterdam	1970	1 million
Ajax Amsterdam	1971–1973	1 million
Bayern Munich	1974–1976	2.9 million
Liverpool	1977–1978, 1981	1.4 million
Nottingham Forest	1979–1980	470,000

Note that we are estimating the size of these places very generously, going way beyond the city borders. The figure for Liverpool, for instance, includes all of Merseyside.

The rule of the small is even more striking when you consider some of the losing teams in European Cup finals in this era. In a remarkable four-year period from 1976 to 1979, the towns of Saint-Étienne, Mönchengladbach, Bruges and Malmö all had teams in the final.

Club	Size of town	Size of total metropolitan area
Saint-Étienne	175,000	320,000
Mönchengladbach	260,000	260,000
Bruges	115,000	270,000
Malmö	240,000	600,000

Perhaps the emblematic small-town team of the 1970s are Borussia Mönchengladbach, whose rise and fall encapsulates the story of all these towns.

In that decade Gladbach won five German titles and reached four European finals. The Bökelberg stadium, perched on a hill among the gardens of smart houses, saw the best years of Gunter Netzer, Rainer Bonhof and Alan Simonsen. Fans drove in from neighbouring Holland and Belgium, as well as from the town's British army barracks. Decades later, a German marketing company showed that the knee-jerk response of the country's fans to the word 'counterattack' was still 'Gladbach'.

It was a cosy little club: Berti Vogts spent his whole career here, and when Netzer later played in Zurich he often used to drive up, sometimes to scout players for Spanish clubs, but often just to eat sausages in the canteen.

Like David Cassidy, Gladbach would have done well to combust spontaneously at the end of the Seventies. In 1980 they lost their last UEFA Cup final to Eintracht Frankfurt, and the decades since have been disappointing. There was the spell in 1998, for instance, when they just couldn't stop getting thrashed. 'We can only get better,' announced Gladbach's coach, Friedel Rausch, just before his team lost 8–2 to Bayer Leverkusen. 'I feel I can solve our problems,' he said afterwards. When Gladbach lost their next match 7–1 to Wolfsburg, Rausch was sacked. Gladbach have spent most of the decade since in Germany's second division.

This upsets leftist, educated 40-somethings all over Germany, who still dislike Bayern, revere the socialist Netzer, and on Monday mornings check the Gladbach result first. But there is nothing to be done. The glory days cannot come back, because what did for Gladbach was the modern era.

In the words of Norman Bates in Hitchcock's *Psycho*: 'They moved the highway.' In the 1970s Gladbach's coach Hennes Weisweiler was able to build a team of boys from the local towns.

The part-Dutch Bonhof came from nearby Emmerich, Vogts was an orphan from Neuss-Büttgen, and Hacki Wimmer, who did Netzer's dirty work, spent decades after his playing career running his parents' stationery shop just down the road in Aachen.

These stars stayed at Gladbach for years because there was little more money to be earned anywhere else in football, because most rich clubs were only allowed a couple of foreign players, and because their own club could generally stop them leaving. In short, there were market restraints. That's why Gladbach, Nottingham Forest, Bruges and Saint-Étienne could thrive in the 1970s. Even then big cities had bigger resources, but they had limited freedom, or limited desire, to use them.

The beginning of the end for small towns was the day in February 1979 when Trevor Francis became football's first 'million-pound man'. In fact, Clough agreed a fee of only £999,999 to bring him from Birmingham to Forest, but there were taxes on top. Three months later Francis headed the goal (against Malmö) that gave Forest the European Cup. But the swelling of the football economy that he embodied would eventually do for small clubs like Forest.

In the 1980s TV contracts grew, and Italy opened its borders to foreigners. Later clubs around Europe began redoing their stadiums, which allowed the ones with lots of fans to make more money. After the European Court of Justice's 'Bosman ruling' in 1995, big clubs could easily sign the best players from any country in the European Union. Around the same time, the clubs with most fans began earning much more from their television rights. Big clubs everywhere got bigger. Bayern Munich, previously Gladbach's main rivals, mushroomed into 'FC Hollywood'.

After that, clubs like Gladbach could no longer keep their best players. Lothar Matthäus made his debut for 'Die Fohlen' (The Foals) at the end of the golden era, but when he was only 23 he graduated to Bayern. The next great white hope, the local lad

Sebastian Deisler, left Gladbach for Hertha aged 19 in 1999, as soon he distantly began to resemble Netzer. Small towns couldn't afford the new football.

'THAT'S NOT COCAINE, IT'S SAFFRON': THE DEMISE OF THE CATHEDRAL CITIES

Wandering around Florence, you can still imagine it as the centre of the universe. It is the effect of the great cathedral, the endless Michelangelos, and all the tourists paying seven euros for an orange juice. A Medici ruler returning from the dead, as in one of Florence's umpteen paintings of the Day of Judgement, might feel his city had won the battle of prestige among European city-states.

But he would be wrong. These days a mid-sized city in Europe derives its status less from its cathedral than from its football club. Here towns the size of Florence (600,000 people in its metropolitan area) have slipped up.

Fiorentina's last flurry came in 1999, when they beat Arsenal in a Champions League match at Wembley thanks to a goal by Gabriel Batistuta, with Giovanni Trapattoni sitting on their bench. In those days the biggest problems facing 'Trap' were his players' insistence on busing the 150 metres from changing rooms to training ground, and the Brazilian Edmondo's ritual late return from the Rio carnival. But those days will never return. In the Champions League, the mid-sized cities are now finished.

Fiorentina's demise can be dated to the day in July 2001 that the Italian police raided the home of their owner, the Italian film baron Vittorio Cecchi Gori. What happened was exactly what should happen when police raid a film baron's home, as if Cecchi Gori had read up on Jackie Collins beforehand.

The police broke into his apartment in the Palazzo Borghese in Rome, but then took 90 minutes to find him. This was because his bedroom door was concealed inside a mirrored wall. Only after the Filipina maid had pointed this out did they enter the bedroom to find Cecchi Gori asleep with his girlfriend, Valeria Marini, a Caprice-like figure who calls herself a singer–actress but in fact can do neither.

The police told Cecchi Gori to open his safe. Donning his silk dressing-gown, he did so. When the police remarked on the stash of cocaine stored inside, Cecchi Gori replied nonchalantly: 'Cocaine? That's not cocaine, it's saffron!'

Meanwhile his business empire was untangling. It should be said that he acquired the empire only by inheritance from his father Mario, who before dying in 1993 had warned his old business partner, Silvio Berlusconi: 'Take care of Vittorio, he is so impulsive and naive.'

Vittorio's problem was that he wanted to be Berlusconi. He bought commercial TV channels (a failure), pumped fortunes into his football team (no titles), dabbled in politics (getting no further than senator), but might have been OK had he not got caught in a divorce expected to be so expensive that it alone could have funded Fiorentina for years. Cecchi Gori remained admirably upbeat even after all this, leaning out of the window of his Mercedes limousine on Rome's Via Veneto to shout '*La dolce vita*!' to friends. However, he ruined Fiorentina.

It was hard to work out which bit of Cecchi Gori's empire owed what to which, but it was clear that he had borrowed tens of millions of pounds from the club. After everything went wrong, he tried the traditional Italian remedy of putting his 82-year-old mother in charge, but even she could not save Fiorentina. A fax from a Colombian bank offering to pay off the club's entire debt proved, amazingly, to be a forgery.

In 2002 Fiorentina went bankrupt, slipping into Italy's fourth division, where they had to visit Tuscan village teams most of whose players were Fiorentina fans. Now they are back in Serie A, but the days of Trap, Batistuta and 'The Animal' Edmondo won't return. Florence is just too small now.

Florence is typical. Mid-sized European cities (between 150,000 and a million inhabitants) have all but dropped off the map of European football. They can no longer afford to compete with clubs from bigger places. In early 2004 it was the turn of Parma, whose owners, the dairy company Parmalat, turned out to have mislaid 10 billion euros. Leeds United are the great English example. In Spain Deportivo La Coruña, pride of a mid-sized Galician city, suddenly discovered that their debt had hit the strictly notional figure of 178 million euros. Valencia followed a few years later. These clubs fell short because they had hardly any supporters outside their own city walls. Other mid-sized cities – Glasgow, Amsterdam, Nottingham – have retreated with less fanfare, but they too must know they will never again produce a European champion. Even Newcastle is slowly beginning to emerge from denial.

The third period of the European Cup began in 1982, and hasn't ended yet: rule by sturdy provincial city. There were still a few undersized winners: Porto and Liverpool twice each, and Eindhoven, Marseille and Dortmund. However, these towns are not exactly midgets. Four of the five are from agglomerations of 1.2 million inhabitants or more. Only Eindhoven has just 210,000 people, and a metropolitan area – if you draw it very generously – of only 750,000. In general, European champions were getting bigger. In modern times, the race has usually gone to the rich.

The swelling of the football economy – the bigger TV contracts, the new stadiums, the freer movement of players and so on – favoured the most popular clubs. For historical reasons, these tended to be the ones in big provincial cities. Their teams came to dominate the Champions League in a sort of endless loop. Every club that has won the trophy since 1998 had won it at least once before. Most had won it several times before. Are their fans growing blasé? When you have won the thing nine times, the buzz probably starts to fade.

The new dominant clubs aren't from the mega-cities of Moscow, London, Paris or Istanbul, but from urban areas with two to four million inhabitants: Milan, Manchester, Munich and Madrid. These M-cities are big enough to produce the required fan base, yet provincial enough to generate a yearning for global recognition.

Strangely, one of these cities, Madrid, is a democratic capital. How could Real break the golden rule of the Champions League and win the trophy in 1998, 2000 and 2002? Because they had built their mammoth stadium, brand and support in the days when Madrid was the capital of a dictatorship. Spain may have gone social democratic, but Real's players still enter the Santiago Bernabeu in those white 'meringue' shirts as if it were 1955. The club's global standing is a relic of the Fascist era.

GEORGE ZIPF COMES TO LONDON: THE FUTURE METROPOLITAN ERA?

George Kingsley Zipf is an almost forgotten Harvard linguist. Born in 1902, he died in 1950 just as he was starting to make a name, and Zipf is now known only for having formulated a law that explains almost everything. Among other things, Zipf's law tells us that London or Moscow should start winning Champions Leagues soon.

Consider the following: if you rank every American city by the size of its population, the difference in population between two consecutive cities is simply the ratio of their ranks. So if you compare cities number one and two, city two has half (or ½) the population of city one. If you compare cities number two and three, city three has two thirds (⅔) the population of city two. City 100 has 99/100ths the population of city 99, and so on down the list. Statistically speaking, the fit of this relationship is almost as perfect as it is possible to be.

This is a particularly elegant example of a more general relationship known as Zipf's law, and it applies to a lot more than city sizes. For instance, it is also true of the frequency with which words are used in English. 'The' is the most commonly used word in the language, 'of' is second, and so 'of' is used about half (½) as often as 'the'. All in all, Zipf's law has been called possibly 'the most accurate regularity in economics'.

Zipf's law also works for European cities, though not quite as neatly. City sizes in most European countries are more closely bunched, and so the second city is closer to the first city's size than in the US, the third closer to the second, and so on.

Why might this be? Zipf's law must have something to do with migration. People will always try to migrate to where the money is. In the US, with its open markets and very high mobility of labour, they generally do. But in Europe, political and cultural barriers have limited migration. That might explain why city sizes are more compressed here. Nonetheless, Kwok Tong Soo from the London School of Economics has shown that if you measure European metropolitan districts, Zipf's law works well in eight out of nine European countries (Denmark, France, Germany, Greece, Netherlands, Norway, Switzerland and Britain).

For a long time nobody could understand why Zipf's law should hold for so many different phenomena. Now, though, economists and scientists are starting to generate models of growth in which the natural outcome of a process is distribution obeying Zipf's Law. Recently, the MIT economist Xavier Gabaix came up with an explanation for why Zipf's law applies to city sizes. He said Zipf's law emerges when all cities grow at the same rate, regardless of their size and their history, but subject to random variation. This implies that common factors drive the growth of cities within a country, while the differences in growth are due to a series of random events ('shocks' in the economic jargon), like for instance bombing during the war, which in principle could occur anywhere. A story as simple as this is enough to explain the city sizes predicted by Zipf's law.

Two consequences of Zipf's law are crucial to football. First, giants – whether giant cities, giant football clubs, or giants of any other kind – are rare. That is because becoming a giant requires a long sequence of positive shocks, like tossing a coin 50 times and coming up 'heads' every time. It can happen, but it is rare. Second, once a city becomes a giant, it is unlikely to shrink into the middle ranks unless it experiences a long series of repeated misfortunes (50 'tails' in a row). By contrast, small cities are unlikely ever to become giants. In other words, the hierarchy of cities, which has established itself over centuries, probably won't change much in the foreseeable future.

This 'law of proportionate growth' has some other consequences. What's true for cities is also true for many other social phenomena. For example, if your kid is behind at school, don't worry: he or she will almost certainly catch up, since all children tend to learn at the same rate, plus or minus a few shocks. Likewise, if you think your brilliant six-year-old footballer is going to become another Beckham or Rooney, don't. More likely the boy had a few positive shocks in his early years, which will cancel out. Rooneys and Beckhams almost never happen. The distribution of talent is thus a bit like the distribution of city sizes: a few great talents stand out at the top, the Maradonas and Ronaldinhos, but as you go down the list the differences become smaller and smaller.

This brings us back to European cities: there are only a few giants, chiefly Moscow, Istanbul, Paris and London. You would expect these giant cities to produce the biggest clubs, and yet none of them has ever won a Champions League.

But soon they might. Football is changing. It is becoming more of a free market, as Fascist dictators no longer interfere, and the best players are free to move clubs almost as they like. Inevitably, the best players are starting to move to the biggest markets, as happens in American baseball. And so you would expect dominance in European football to move too: after rule by dictatorial capitals, mid-sized provincial towns, and big provincial cities, now London and possibly Moscow and Paris should get in on the act at last.

Moscow might, because it is Europe's last large, non-democratic capital. Russia's resources are being sent to the centre, and with all that oil and gas under the soil, that's a lot of resources. Paris might, because it has nearly 12 million inhabitants and only one top-division football club, Paris St Germain, who surely cannot be appallingly run for ever.

London might do it, because even after the implosion of the City, London has the largest local economy in Europe. London already supports two of Europe's biggest teams, and could probably cope with more. This represents quite a change. In the early 1990s, London rather resembled Moscow *circa* 1973. Tired people in grey clothes waited on packed platforms for 1950s Tube trains. Coffee was an exotic drink that barely existed. Eating a meal outside was forbidden. The city centre was almost uninhabited, and closed at 11pm anyway. There was a sense of permanent decline.

Nor had London ever been even the footballing capital of Britain. Only in 1931 did a southern club – Arsenal – first win the league. Even after that, though, the title generally went north.

But in the 1990s London transformed. Cheap flights from five airports took Londoners around Europe. Trains began running to Paris and Brussels. Today it is quicker to get there than to the shrinking northern cities of Liverpool and Manchester, and less of a culture shock when you arrive. London became a European city, detached from the rest of Britain. The geographer Daniel Dorling said Britain was starting to look like a city-state. Moreover, the city was starting to grow again. Greater London's population had been falling from the Second World War until the 1980s, but boom-time London changed that.

From the late 1990s until 2008, London offered a technicolour vista of raucous young people from all over the world dressed in weird youth-culture outfits chucking cash at each other. The Tube trains ceased to be antique curios. The place came to smell of money. All this started to give London footballing dominance.

At the same time as the city became fully international, so did the market in footballers. The best ones could now work wherever they wanted. Many of them – like many investment bankers and actors – chose London.

Black and foreign footballers liked living in a city where 95 per cent of inhabitants agree with the statement, 'It is a good thing that Britain is a multicultural society.' When Thierry Henry was spending his best years at Arsenal, he said: 'I love this open, cosmopolitan city. Whatever your race, you never feel people's gaze on you.' In a virtuous cycle, foreigners attract foreigners. The Frenchman Jacques Santini, Tottenham's manager for about five minutes, wanted to come to London because his son Sebastien already lived there – a classic example of chain migration.

Equally to the point, even in the current economic crisis a footballer can still earn a living in London. The capital's clubs have been coining it. In the first place, their customers can still afford to pay the highest ticket prices in global football. Arsenal charge £885 for their cheapest season ticket, which is a lot more than Barcelona charge for their most expensive. So many Londoners were happy to fork out this kind of money that Arsenal were able to build a new stadium with 60,000 seats, and sell it out. No club in London's history has drawn such a large regular crowd. For the 2007–08 season, the business advisory firm Deloitte ranked Arsenal and Chelsea among the world's six richest clubs.

What is more, even now, no other European city has as many investors. When Roman Abramovich decided to buy a football club, it was inevitable that he would end up owning Chelsea rather than, say, Blackburn. The word is that he chose it because it was the nearest club to his house on Eaton Square. Similarly, Muhammed Al Fayed, who lives on Park Lane, bought Fulham. Even Queens Park Rangers got bought up by the Indian Lakshmi Mittal, the world's fifth richest man, who of course lives round the corner in Kensington. Yes, other rich foreigners have bought

Manchester City and Aston Villa, but London is still a touch more appealing to billionaires.

The handful of the biggest provincial clubs – Manchester United, Liverpool, Bayern, Barcelona, the two Milan clubs – have built up such strong brands that they will remain at the top of European football. However, their new challengers will probably not be other provincial clubs but teams from London, Moscow and perhaps Paris.

At last, being in a giant capital city is becoming a strategic asset to a football club. When Arsenal and Chelsea finished in the top two spots in the Premier League in 2004, it was the first time in history that two London teams had achieved that feat. In 2005 they did it again. From 2006 to 2008, they figured in two out of three Champions League finals. Soon one of these clubs could become the first London team to be champions of Europe. Then the city will dominate every aspect of British life.

SECTION II

THE COMPETITIONS:
Inequality, a Pint at the Local, and a New Tradition

UNFAIR AND UNBALANCED: ARE MANCHESTER UNITED REALLY A PROBLEM?

Kevin Keegan has a knack for phrasing things. In May 2008, at the end of another hopeless season for his club Newcastle, he delivered a 13-minute monologue about the tedium of the Premier League.

'This league is in danger of becoming one of the most boring, but great leagues in the world,' he told a press conference. 'The top four next year will be the same as this year. No manager is going to say what I said 12 years ago, "Watch out, Alex, we are after your title." If they do, they will think they have been drinking something or they are on something.'

He was right about the top four of Manchester United, Chelsea, Arsenal and Liverpool staying the same in 2009. However, the main point about Keegan's monologue is that it phrased so well a new truism of football: that the game is becoming boring because the big clubs win everything.

However, this truism is not true. Fans may say that they wish football were fairer – the Champions League as well as the

Premier League – but the truth is that most of them don't. The majority of supporters prefer unequal leagues. In fact, if football were even less fair, it might become even more popular.

Football stole the idea for a league from baseball. Professional American baseball players had come up with the concept in 1871. The format worked because fans turned out to want a championship in which the winner had played all the other teams. Early championships had involved either irregular schedules, in which some teams may not have faced all the others, or the knockout cups beloved of English public schoolboys. The all-play-all format of a league has nothing romantic about it, but the winner can justly claim to be the best over a sustained period. No underdog who wins the FA Cup can say the same. Even some world champions can't.

William McGregor proposed the format for his new Football League in 1888, prompted by the musings of several journalists and inspired, according to some contemporaries, by league baseball. His public-school detractors pointed out the idea's American origins as a way of implying that he was only doing it for the money. Yet leagues spread around the world almost as quickly as football did. If cups are high drama, then a league is a soap opera in dozens of episodes with endless crises and some sort of suspense until the very last day. In sports where leagues have traditionally been weak, like rugby union or cricket, fans tend to focus on the national team, and don't follow the sport day-to-day.

The English league has always had strong and weak teams. However, for decades the differences between them had little to do with money. Football was not a free market. Players used to have little freedom to join rich clubs, which is why a small club like Stoke City could hang on to Stanley Matthews for so long. Little clubs were sometimes able to keep a set of good players together for a while. Though Liverpool won the English league from 1982 through 1984, the runners-up were first Ipswich, then Watford, then Southampton. This is no accident. Any rigid labour market will keep talent locked in place.

But we have seen that from the 1980s rich clubs got richer, mostly thanks to new stadiums and TV contracts. As players became freer to change teams, the best went where the money was. In 1995 the Bosman ruling became football's Big Bang: suddenly a European player could join any club in the European Union once his contract had ended. Rich clubs started to gain a monopoly on good players.

That made the rich clubs even richer. In 1992 all the teams in the English top division combined had a total income of £166 million. Over the next 15 years that figure grew by 15 per cent annually – nearly twice as fast as the growth of the British housing bubble in the same period – to reach £1.48 billion in 2007.

Meanwhile, in the same period the teams in the second tier of English football raised their revenues by a mere 13 per cent a year. Their total income went from £62 million to about £400 million.

Thanks to those two extra percentage points a year, the biggest clubs ran away from the rest. In 1991, remarkably, the English club with the highest income had been Tottenham, with £19 million. Hull City, with £1 million, had the lowest income in the second division. By 2007 the highest revenue of any club in English football was £212 million, and the lowest in the second tier was Burnley with £7 million. In other words, the ratio of biggest to smallest in these divisions had jumped from 19:1 to 30:1.

The rich put their money to use. Since the creation of the Premier League in 1992, the club with the highest revenues has usually won the title. Manchester United won 10 from 1993 through 2008, and Chelsea won two after Roman Abramovich arrived.

No wonder Keegan complained about tedium. Only four clubs in England had any hope of winning the title. The *Observer* remarked before the 2008–09 season that even though Everton had just finished fifth, you could get odds of 200–1 against their winning the title. Hull were at 10,000–1. The paper noted that fans of most clubs fantasised about finishing fourth; they could imagine nothing grander. Things were similar in the Champions League, where Liverpool and Chelsea flattened tiny foreign clubs like PSV Eindhoven and Bordeaux.

Perhaps the main critic of rule by big clubs is UEFA's president, Michel Platini. The Premier League's lobbyists need to portray the Frenchman as a dangerous enemy, given that nobody with any power in Britain opposes their product, and the old romantic does his best to oblige. Platini is always talking about helping the smaller clubs. Though a former superstar, he even manages to look like a friend of the little man. He is a touch chubby, his suit trousers are too long, and he has the friendly grin of a local grocer.

During an interview in UEFA's headquarters on Lake Geneva, Platini kept grumbling about big money in football. Abu Dhabi's takeover of Manchester City had upset him. Manchester City ought to be a local club, he said. 'Otherwise why should the club call itself Manchester? They should call themselves, I don't know, Coca-Cola.'

Platini has spent a lot of energy trying to limit the disproportionate buying power of English clubs. However, he has had almost no success. 'The English TV rights are very, very, very, very, very significant,' he mused to us. 'So the English league is the richest, so players go to the English league. How to even that out?'

Perhaps it's impossible to even out?

He paused, then admitted: 'Legally it's impossible. You can't stop the foreigners from coming. Financially it's impossible.'

Searching for a way to even things out, in the spring of 2009 Platini put a team of UEFA officials on a plane to the US. Like many others in European football, he had been impressed by the equality in American sports. Perhaps this was something that football could copy? Even Emilio Butragueño, sporting director of plucky little Real Madrid, told the BBC: 'You need uncertainty at the core of every competition … We may eventually have something similar to the [salary cap] system in the US, to give a chance to all the clubs.'

Andy Burnham, Britain's culture secretary, warned in 2008 that while the Premier League was 'the world's most successful domestic sporting competition', it risked becoming 'too predictable'. He told the *Guardian*: 'I keep referring to the NFL, which has equal sharing … In the US, the most free-market country in the world, they understand that equal distribution of money creates genuine competition.'

Indeed, the NFL of American football has been called 'the socialist league'. Its clubs share TV income equally. Moreover, 40 per cent of each game's gate receipts goes to the visiting team. In the famous slogan promoted by the league, 'On any given Sunday any team can beat any other team.' Baseball, basketball and the US's major league soccer also share far more of their income than European soccer does. Take the New York Yankees baseball cap, one of the most popular pieces of merchandise in all of sport. Outside of New York, the Yankees receive only one thirtieth of the profit on each cap sold, the same as every other team in baseball. It is as if each Premier League club got one twentieth of the profit every time Manchester United sold a shirt. That's the sort of thing Platini, Burnham and Keegan seem to dream of.

Yet their premise is wrong. There is almost no evidence to support their arguments for balance. The data show that, overall, football fans prefer unbalanced leagues.

If predictable results bored fans, then more of them would go to matches where the outcome was very uncertain. How to test whether fans really behave like that? Researchers have tried to gauge expected outcomes of games by using either pre-match betting odds, or the form of both teams over the previous half-dozen games. Studies of football, mostly in England, show mixed results. Some find that more balanced games attract more fans. Others find the reverse.

A moment's thought suggests why some unbalanced games might be very attractive. Often they involve strong home teams playing weak away teams (Manchester United v Stoke, say), in which case the home team typically has lots of fans who enjoy watching their heroes score lots of goals; or they are games between weak home teams and strong away teams (Stoke v Manchester United), in which local fans come to see the visiting stars or in the hope of seeing an upset.

The economists David Forrest of Salford Business School and Robert Simmons of Lancaster University have done some of the best work in this field. They found that a balanced game could sometimes increase attendance. However, they also carried out a simulation to show that if the English leagues became more balanced, they would attract *fewer* fans. That is because a balanced league, in which all teams were equally good, would turn into an almost interminable procession of home wins and away losses. By contrast, in real existing football, some of the most balanced games occur when a weak team plays at home against a strong team (again, Stoke v Manchester United).

Forrest and Simmons found that the people who care most about competitive balance are television viewers. Most fans at the ground are the hard core: they simply want to see their team. But TV viewers tend to be 'floating voters'. When the outcome of a game seems too predictable, they switch off. The two economists found that the closer a televised match was expected to be (measured by the form of both teams going into the game), the higher the viewing figures on Sky TV. Yet the size of this effect was modest. Forrest and Simmons said that even if the Premier League were perfectly balanced (in the sense that each team had an equal probability of winning each game) TV audiences would rise by only 6 per cent. That would be a small effect for such a revolutionary change.

Another way of looking at competitive balance is to view the league as a whole, rather than match by match. Do more spectators come when the title race is exciting than when one side runs away with it?

It turns out that a thrilling title race does little to improve attendances. Fans will watch their teams play in the league even when they haven't a hope of winning it (or else dozens of English clubs would not exist).

It is true that a game has to be significant to draw fans, but that significance need not have anything to do with winning the title. A study by Stephen Dobson and John Goddard showed that when a match matters more either for winning the league *or* for avoiding relegation then attendance tends to rise. Trying to qualify for Europe also gives meaning to matches. Most matches in the Premier League are significant for something or other. Given that they can be significant in many different ways, it is unclear why a more balanced league would create more significance. As the Premier League's chief executive Richard Scudamore said, responding to Keegan's lament: 'There are a lot of different tussles that go on in the Premier League, depending on whether you're at the top, in the middle or at the bottom, that make it interesting.'

There is a third way of looking at balance: the long term. Does the dominance of the same teams year in, year out turn fans off?

Let's compare a long period with dominance to a long period without dominance: the fairly 'equal' era in English football that ran from 1949 to 1968, and the 'unfair' era that began around 1989 and still continues.

In the first 20-year period, 11 different teams won the English league. The most frequent winner, Manchester United, won five titles in the period. The second period was far more predictable: only six teams won the title, one of whom (guess who) won it 10 times. And yet during the first, 'equal' period, total annual attendance in the first division fell from an all-time high of 18 million in 1949 to only 15 million in 1968 (and even that figure got a temporary boost from England winning the World Cup). During the second, 'unequal' period, total attendance rose from 8 million to 13 million, even though tickets became much more expensive and people had many more choices of how to spend their free time.

Anyone who says that the Premier League has become 'one of the most boring leagues in the world', a closed shop that shuts out smaller clubs from the lower divisions, has to explain why so many people now go to watch all levels of English league football. In the 2006–07 season, 29.5 million spectators paid to see professional matches in England, the highest number since 1970. The Premier League drew crowds matched globally only in Germany, even though, as Keegan said, everyone knew the top four finishers in advance. But more than half of those 29.5 million watched the Football League, the three divisions below the Premier League. All the clubs in the Championship have supposedly been doomed to irrelevance by Manchester United, and can only dream of clinging on at the bottom of the Premier League, yet their division that season had the fifth highest average crowd of any league in Europe.

Some of English football's critics have not digested these figures. When we pointed out to Platini that English stadiums are full nowadays, he replied: 'Not all. They're full at the teams that win.' Indeed, whenever rows of empty seats appear at struggling teams like Blackburn or Middlesbrough, it is back-page news, and regarded as ominous for the Premier League as a whole. Yet it's natural that some fans should desert disappointing teams, while others flock to exciting ones. Sunderland, Arsenal, Manchester United and other clubs have built bigger stadiums, and filled them. Not every English team has gained spectators since 1992, but most have.

Admittedly today's large crowds don't in themselves prove that dominance attracts fans. After all, many other things have changed since the more equal 1949–68 period. Crucially, the stadiums have improved. However, the rising attendances do make it hard to believe that dominance in itself significantly undermines interest. Indeed, pretty much every football league in Europe exhibits more dominance than the American major leagues, and yet fans still go.

There are good reasons why fans generally prefer inequality to balance. First, most fans in the stadium are fans of the home team, and so they do not really want a balanced outcome. Second, big teams have more fans than small ones, and so if Manchester United beat Stoke more people are happy than if Stoke win. Third, fans are surprisingly good at losing. Psychological studies show that they are skilled at transferring blame: 'We played well, but the referee was rubbish.' This means that fans will often stick with a team even if it always loses. It also explains why, the morning after England get knocked out of a World Cup, people don't collapse into depression but get on with their lives.

Fourth, dominant teams create a special interest of their own. In the 1990s, millions of people supported Manchester United, and millions of others despised them. In a way, both groups were following the club. United were the star of football's soap opera. Every other team's fans dreamt of beating them. Much of the meaning of supporting West Ham, for instance, derives from disliking Manchester United. Keegan thrillingly captured that national sentiment with his famous 'I will love it if we beat them! Love it!' monologue in 1996. Big bad United made the league more fun.

Strangely, it was the fanzine *When Saturday Comes* that put this best. *WSC* is, in large part, the journal of small clubs. It publishes moving and funny pieces by fans of Crewe or Swansea. Few of its readers have much sympathy with Manchester United (though some, inevitably, are United fans). Many have argued for a fairer league. One of the magazine's regular writers, Ian Plenderleith, is fairly typical in being a Lincoln City supporter. Yet in

September 2008 Plenderleith, who lives outside Washington DC, argued in *WSC* that American major league soccer, in which 'all teams started equal, with the same squad size, and the same amount of money to spread among its players' wages', was boring. The reason: 'No truly memorable teams have the space to develop.'

'MLS is crying out for a couple of big, successful teams,' Plenderleith admitted. 'Teams you can hate. Dynasties you really, really want to beat. Right now, as LA Galaxy coach Bruce Arena once memorably said: "It's a crapshoot."'

In short, the MLS lacks one of the joys of an unbalanced league: the David v Goliath match. And one reason why fans enjoy those encounters is that surprisingly often, given their respective budgets, David wins.

The economist Jack Hirshleifer called this phenomenon 'the paradox of power'. Imagine, he said, that there were two tribes, one large, one small. Each can devote its efforts to just two activities: farming and fighting. Each tribe produces its own food through farming, and steals the other tribe's food through fighting. Which tribe will devote a larger *share* of its efforts to fighting?

The answer is the small tribe. The best way to understand this is to imagine that the small tribe is very small indeed. It would then have to devote almost all its limited resources to either fighting or farming. If it chose farming, it would be vulnerable to attack. Everything it produced could be stolen. On the other hand, if the tribe devoted all its resources to fighting, it would have at least a chance of stealing some resources. So Hirshleifer concludes – and proves with a mathematical model – that smaller competitors will tend to devote a greater share of resources to competitive activities.

He found many real-world examples of the paradox of power. He liked citing Vietnam's defeat of the US, but one might also add the Afghan resistance to the Soviet Union in the 1980s, the Dutch resistance to the Spanish in the sixteenth century or the American resistance to the British in the War of Independence. In these cases the little guy actually defeated the big guy. In many other cases, the little guy was eventually defeated, but at much greater cost than might have been expected on the basis of their physical resources (the Spartans at Thermopylae, the Afrikaners in the Boer War, the Texans at the Alamo).

In football, as in war, the underdog tends to try harder. Big teams fight more big battles, and so each contest weighs a little less heavily than it does with their smaller rivals. Little teams understand that they may have few opportunities to compete at the highest level, and so they give it everything. They therefore probably win more often than you would predict on the basis of ability alone.

Fans enjoy unbalanced modern football. Yet the complaints about its imbalance continue. The curious thing is that these complaints are relatively new, a product of the last 15 years or so. Contrary to popular opinion, football was unbalanced in the past too, but before the 1990s fewer people complained.

It is a fantasy that in the past every team had a chance to win, just as it's a fantasy that football used to be more popular. (It is possible that more people are interested today than at any time in the past.) Europe as a whole has never been a very balanced footballing continent. In smaller countries, clubs from the capital tended to rule. Serie A was always dominated by Juventus, Milan and Inter, and the Primera Liga by Barcelona and Real Madrid. By the 1980s Bayern dominated in Germany, and in the post-war era English football has been dominated by Manchester United, Arsenal and Liverpool. United's 10 titles in the last 20 years may sound boring, but Liverpool won 10 in 20 between 1969 and 1988. A handful of sides have dominated for most of English football's history. Even a club as large as Newcastle have not won the title since 1927. The imbalance in England as in all European leagues was reinforced by European competition, which handed the dominant teams more money.

The old European Cup was seldom much fairer than the Champions League is now. We saw in the previous chapter that only between 1970 and 1981 did teams from modestly sized towns regularly win the trophy. Usually the cup went to the biggest provincial cities, or to Madrid. Even Platini admits: 'For 40 years it's been the biggest clubs that won the Champions League; when I played, too. With or without homegrown players, it was Real Madrid, Liverpool, Manchester, Juventus who won. English clubs won the cup 10 times in a row, I think. No? In the 1980s.'

Oh dear. Platini is not going to win any pub quizzes any time soon. In fact English clubs won six European cups from 1977 through 1982. But his point stands: inequality in the European Cup is nothing new.

He smiles, thinking again of that English dominance in the 1980s: 'It's funny. There were no great debates then, saying, "We have to change everything." Today it's the money that makes the difference.'

That is precisely the point. Today's inequality bothers people not because it is unprecedented, but because it is more driven by money than it used to be. In the old days, a middling team could suddenly enjoy years of dominance if it happened to hire an excellent manager who signed excellent players. That's what happened to Liverpool under Bill Shankly, and to Forest under Brian Clough. Today, a middling team can suddenly enjoy years of dominance if it happens to be bought by a billionaire who hires an excellent manager who signs excellent players. That is what happened to Chelsea under Roman Abramovich, and what may happen to Manchester City under Abu Dhabian rule. In short, inequality in football, as well as not being boring, is not even new. The one thing that is new is the money.

Many people tend to feel that inequality becomes unfair when it is bought with money. It disgusts them that Chelsea can sign the best players simply because they are a rich club. This is a moral argument. It's a form of idealistic egalitarianism, which says that all teams should have more or less equal resources. This stance may be morally right (we cannot judge), but it is not a practical political agenda, and it probably doesn't reflect what most football fans want. Spectators vote with their feet. It's certainly not the case that millions of them are abandoning the Premier League because the money offends them. The evidence of what they go to watch suggests that they want to see the best players competing against each other. Many people resent Manchester United. Few seem to find them boring.

THE STRANGE DEATH OF THE FA CUP

It is 'the best loved of all England's sporting institutions, a major strand of the nation's fabric and as much a part of its way of life as Sunday roast and a pint at the local', boasted *The Official History of the Football Association* in 1991. The FA Cup, like the British Christmas and so many other British traditions, was invented by the Victorians and took off from there. It will always be with us, like Brussels sprouts and the Queen's speech on Christmas Day.

True, for the very biggest clubs, the Cup is clearly no longer what it was. In 2000 the holders Manchester United didn't even bother entering, preferring the World Club Cup in Brazil instead. But for everyone else, surely, the third round in early January is still the time to dream.

You would think so. The only problem is that the data show something different: even for small clubs, the FA Cup has lost much of its magic. The Premier League is only part of the explanation, not the main culprit for the Cup's demise. This is a case-study in the decline of a British tradition.

The Cup's creator, Charles Alcock, was one of those exhausting, bewhiskered Victorians who invented much of the modern world. The son of a Sunderland shipping agent, he didn't just give us the

FA Cup (1871, with Alcock captaining Wanderers to victory) and the first unofficial sports international (England v Scotland in 1870, with Alcock captaining England), but also the first cricket Test match between England and Australia, while on the side he wrote the first history of football, started several magazines, acted as London agent for a baseball tour in 1874, played a central role in legalising professional football, and so on. Now, of course, he is virtually forgotten.

Alcock's great gift to football is the knockout format. He is said to have borrowed it from his old school Harrow, where the 'houses' played an annual knockout 'House Cup', the winner of which got to call itself 'Cock House'. The format worked so well for the FA Cup that it was later used for the first three World Cups.

Knockout competitions satisfy. Usually we separate humans into hierarchies – the seven-stone weakling does not fight the bodybuilder on the beach – but everyone loves seeing an underdog win, even if only for a day. It tells us (a) that our status can change suddenly, and therefore (b) that tomorrow could be much better than today.

The FA Cup was arguably the making of football. When Alcock launched the competition in 1871, cricket was still Britain's unchallenged national sport. England then had only 50 football clubs, many of which had been founded by cricketers looking for a way to keep socialising in winter. Even in the US, cricket was the most popular sport until another upstart, baseball, began eclipsing it at the end of the 1860s.

But in the first decade after the FA Cup began, the number of English football clubs mushroomed. New county associations everywhere (modelled on the cricket counties) created their own knockout cups. The working classes began to flock to what had once been an elite game: a great forgotten symbol of English social change was the defeat of the Old Etonians by working-class Blackburn Olympic in the Cup final of 1883.

While cricket stuck to the three- or four-day county match, convenient only for the leisured upper middle classes, football's cups found a mass market. Only after 2000 did the cricket authorities rectify their historic error, and begin to draw big crowds with the three-hour Twenty20 game.

It was football's 'cups' that gave birth to the Football League. By the mid-1880s professional, working-class clubs dominated the game. They played in several cups at once, making lots of money if they went on multiple cup runs simultaneously. But if they went out of all the cups early, they suffered. So William McGregor of Aston Villa proposed creating a competition to ensure what he called 'a fixity of fixtures'. League football began not because people wanted it, but because it made financial sense for the clubs.

The league format worked in its own way. In most countries, fans liked it even better than they did their national cups. But in England, for over a century, the FA Cup continued to dominate.

We can prove this statement through a simple test. Whenever a Cup tie involves two teams from the same division of the league, we can compare the attendance at the Cup game with that at the league fixture between the same two teams. The difference in the size of the crowds tells us something about the relative popularity of each competition.

We can see at once that there used to be a magic to the Cup. On average in the 1976–77 season, for instance, the 45 games between same-division teams in the Cup attracted 30 per cent more spectators than the equivalent league matches, even if you leave out the Cup quarter-finals, semis and final. To take one example, on 21 August 1977, Cambridge United and Colchester played each other in the fourth division of the Football League. Only 3,036 spectators turned up. But three months later, when the teams met again in Cambridge in the first round of the Cup, 5,090 watched. Those extra 2,054 people came for the magic of the Cup, even though that day there was no prospect of giant-killing.

What was true at the bottom of English football was also true at the top. On 8 January 1977, the Cup tie between Everton and Stoke City drew 32,952 people, over 10,000 more than had seen their meeting in the first division on 11 September 1976.

The Cup's magic lasted into the 1990s. Any club could guarantee that its Cup ties would produce some of its best gates of the season.

Then something changed. With hindsight we can see that the turning point was 1989–90. That season, the Cup's lead in attendances over the league dropped below 30 per cent for the first time since the 1970s. For the next few seasons the Cup's lead held fairly steady around 25 per cent, but between 1994–95 and 1997–98 it collapsed. In that last season, when Arsenal romped past Newcastle in the Cup final, Cup games for the first time drew fewer spectators than their league equivalents – only 96 per cent as many.

Never since has the Cup outdrawn the league. In this century, the competition's crowds have hovered between 80 and 90 per cent of equivalent fixtures in the league. In 2006–07, the ratio was just 84 per cent. Often the gap was even more dramatic: in 2006, when Bradford met Crewe in the first round of the Cup, 3,483 fans showed up. Their league encounter in February 2007 drew 7,778, or more than twice as many.

What is true now in the lower divisions is just as true in the Premier League. For instance, in January 2007 only 24,426 fans watched Everton v Blackburn in the third round of the Cup; the league fixture that season drew 35,593. Only for the biggest teams, the Manchester Uniteds and Liverpools, do we see anything like parity between the competitions, and then only because these clubs always sell out their games. It seems a good bet that if these clubs had unlimited seating capacity they would have bigger gates today in league fixtures than in the FA Cup, whereas the reverse was true through the Eighties. Only in Football League Two has the FA Cup maintained any kind of parity, with

Cup games drawing 2 per cent more fans than their league equivalents. In other words, only the lowest division of the professional game had less magic than the Cup.

To express the trophy's standing in absolute numbers: in 2006–07, the attendance at same-division FA Cup matches totalled 713,675. The comparable league fixtures drew 818,016. And of course average attendance in the Premier League is way above the average for the FA Cup.

Some defenders of the FA Cup have blamed the escalating cost of season tickets. They say this has forced fans to economise by cutting back on optional FA Cup games. But their argument merely demonstrates a simple economic fact: the FA Cup is an 'inferior good'. To an economist, an inferior good is something that people buy less of as they get richer. If the FA Cup were not inferior, fans would buy cheap FA Cup tickets instead of expensive season tickets. In fact people do the opposite: those who can afford season tickets for the Premier League buy them, and don't bother with the Cup, leaving tickets for everyone else. Nor is this just a story of the Premier League. As we have seen, even fans from the lower divisions treat the Cup as an inferior good.

So an article of faith of English football – the magic of the FA Cup – is simply wrong. The question is what killed the Cup.

The natural instinct is to blame the Premier League. After all, the Cup went into decline just as the FA created the Premier League in 1992. But, in fact, the strange death of the FA Cup was in the making well before that.

After the Second World War, football crowds for both the league and the Cup soared, as British men looked for entertainment in a world of austerity and rationing. In the 1948–49 season, a massive 41 million tickets to football matches were sold. However, when incomes began to rise in the 1950s, people looked for new forms of entertainment: first television, then foreign holidays, motoring and other modern pursuits.

Football came to look tired and old-fashioned. Clubs didn't invest in entertaining fans, and many fans stopped coming. The ones who stuck with the downmarket game were often young men, with their countercultures of graffiti, yobbery and hooliganism. Hooliganism sold newspapers, and so the press began to portray football as scary. In the 1985–86 season, the year after the Heysel disaster, only 16 million match tickets were sold.

In these decades Cup crowds fell along with league ones. In the 1960s well over three million people a year still watched Cup matches. By the 1980s fewer than two million did.

Then, mysteriously, league football began to recover. In every season from 1986 until 1992 – even before the Premier League began, and even as Britain went through a recession – annual attendance in the Football League grew. It's therefore wrong to say that Sky made league football a success. Rather, Sky spotted the growing demand for live football, and bet the company on the trend continuing.

Sky was right. Most club owners in the Premier League worried that more games on TV would keep fans at home. In fact, the reverse proved true: the more people could see at home, the more they wanted to go the stadium. Perhaps the mere sight of games on TV proved that football was not the bloodbath that some newspapers made it out to be. In any case, live football meant exposure, and as every contestant on *Celebrity Big Brother* knows, exposure on TV is only ever good for business.

Crucially, the Premier League had a televised twin. The Champions League was also born in 1992, and also marketed itself through TV from the start. The twins helped each other grow. One thing that made the Premier League magical was that the top few teams qualified for the Champions League. By contrast, the winner of the FA Cup suffered the ignominy of playing in the UEFA Cup. No wonder the Cup began to pale beside the Premier League.

Between 1986 and 2004 average league attendances grew at an average annual rate of 3.2 per cent, faster than the British economy. Today total league attendance hovers around 30 million, nearly twice what it was in 1986. If ticket prices had remained static this would have been a remarkable achievement, but of course they too have soared. In the mid-1980s ticket prices were still around £2.50. Today, in the Premier League, they are more like £30. That implies a growth rate of around 11.5 per cent a year for nearly a quarter of a century, way above inflation.

But unlike league football, the Cup never recovered. Since the 1981–82 season, the annual Cup crowd has fluctuated between 1.7 and 2.2 million. While the league was booming, the Cup's crowds hit an all-time low in 1999–2000. The 2006–07 season was the first time in the new millennium that they rose above two million.

FA officials occasionally say that what these static attendance figures show is not the decline of the Cup, but the rise of the league, especially the Premier League. However, they are wrong. Firstly, the five-year average attendance for the Cup over the last 20 years was trending downwards until very recently. Secondly, let's repeat that this is not just about the Premier League: if we compare matches in all divisions, the FA Cup is seen as second best measured by the number of people who bother to turn up.

It wasn't simply the Premier League and Champions League that killed the FA Cup. The real culprit is television – or in the case of the Cup, the lack of it.

Anyone over 40 who grew up in England (or indeed almost anywhere else in the Commonwealth) remembers the time when the FA Cup final was one of the few live football games on TV. Other than the Cup, only the odd European Cup tie or depressing England game was shown live on British TV. Until 1982 there were no league games at all live on television. (Yes, this is not a typo.) More than that, the Cup final was broadcast simultaneously on BBC1 and ITV. No wonder it seemed the most important game of the season, 'a major strand of the nation's fabric', as the FA's history called it. It was one of the very few games the nation could watch. Much of its magic came from television.

The financial crisis of the early 1980s finally forced the Football League to accept what most other sports (especially American ones) had already realised: live TV is good for sport. Grudgingly, the Football League agreed to broadcast first five and later 10 games a season, in exchange for a pittance from broadcasters, which was shared among all 92 league clubs.

The only identifiable change linked to league football's recovery from its 35-year decline is live broadcasting. When that recovery began, in the mid-1980s, all other conditions for football were bad: hooliganism, rising ticket prices, high unemployment among the sport's traditional audience, and the disasters at Heysel and Bradford. English teams were banned from Europe. The best players were moving to Italy. And yet spectators were starting to return to the stadiums.

Slowly, the big clubs realised that TV would make them rich. In 1992 they set up the Premier League, reinvested in stadiums after the Taylor Report, and began one of the greatest recoveries in the history of sports marketing. A decade later almost every Premier League ground was a sell-out for almost every match, despite soaring ticket prices, and even though a third of the games were being broadcast live, often at unsociable hours.

It was Sky that gave league football exposure. If Rupert Murdoch wanted to sell subscriptions, he needed fans to think the league game was sexy. Suddenly the FA Cup had a televised competitor that was marketing itself shamelessly almost every day. The FA decided to stay loyal to the BBC, and that decision made its own competition come to look old-fashioned. We kept being told we loved the tradition. The figures suggested otherwise. No wonder the biggest clubs stopped fielding their best teams in the Cup. Like everyone else, they didn't feel the magic any more.

We said at the start of this chapter that the magic of Charles Alcock's competition had a lot to do with giant-killing. But as money from TV and other sources flowed into football, and flowed particularly to the big clubs, giant-killing in the Cup died out.

Let's define giant-killing as a victory by a team that plays at least two divisions below its opponent. In the Seventies, there were on average four giant-killings a season. By the 1990s, there were only two, because the big clubs had bought up almost all the talent. Football began to bear out Damon Runyon's riff on Ecclesiastes: 'The race is not always to the swift, nor the battle to the strong, but that's the way to bet.'

We can document the growth in football's wealth gap. In the 1950s, first-division clubs spent on average just over twice as much as fourth-division clubs on players. By the 1970s they spent four times as much; by the late 1990s, more than 12 times as much.

Finally, in 2001, the FA tried to do something to resuscitate the Cup: it began offering prize money. Prizes ranged from £1,000 for winning a game in the preliminary rounds, to £2 million for winning the final. The principle was sound: attractive prizes are a proven method for luring the best competitors in sports like athletics, tennis, golf and boxing. The problem was that the prizes in the FA Cup were too small. The total prize fund of something like £20 million is less than the guaranteed TV payment to the bottom club in the Premier League.

There is a glimmer of hope for the Cup. Attendances have risen every season since 2000, if only very modestly. But this tradition isn't what it was. Like the 'Sunday roast and pint at the local', with which the FA's official history compared the Cup in 1991, the trophy has ceased to be 'a major strand of the nation's fabric'.

Perhaps the best analogy for the FA Cup is the British Christmas. Every December most British families lay on the traditional Brussels sprouts, but a cursory inspection of the Christmas washing up shows that 50 per cent goes uneaten. After Christmas lunch, the Queen speaks on television. In 1987, 28 million Britons watched her – the largest TV audience of the year. By

2007, only 7.5 million Britons still switched on. That's about the same number of viewers around the world as watched Arsenal v Manchester United in the Premier League that year. If today you had to identify 'the best loved of all England's sporting institutions, a major strand of the nation's fabric', it would be the Premier League. British traditions come and go, and Rupert Murdoch appears to have created a new one.

SECTION III

THE FANS:
Loyalty, Suicides, Happiness, and the Country
with the Best Supporters

THE COUNTRY THAT LOVES FOOTBALL MOST

Which country loves football most?

This might sound like a matter of the heart that is hard to measure, but in fact the data exist. Loving football expresses itself in three main ways: playing the game, going to the stadium, and watching football on TV. We have international figures for all three.

First, a caveat: not all the numbers are reliable. There are lies, damned lies and statistics; and statistics from outside the western world tend to be even worse. We will therefore limit our quest to Europe. Using a bit of judgement, by the end of the chapter we will be able to say with some confidence which European country cares most about the game.

PLAYERS: OH, TO BE A TINY ISLAND

In 2006 FIFA tried to count how many people in the world played football. The 'Big Count' came up with 265 million footballers, more than 90 per cent of them males. Some were registered with proper clubs. The overwhelming majority, though, were 'unregistered occasional players' who kicked around with mates on playgrounds and beaches and five-a-side courts. The only way to find out whether these people played football was by asking them – or at least a tiny representative sample of them.

None of these obstacles put off FIFA. The organisation is a bit vague about exactly how it got hold of the figures, saying it used 'the standard practice of a questionnaire as well as an online tool'. It also threw in its Big Count 2000, plus a UEFA survey and other 'internal analyses', to 'supplement missing data from associations and for plausibility purposes'. Reading between the lines of the survey, it seems that more than a fifth of national FAs didn't even bother to take part. The whole endeavour was 'scientifically observed by Lamprecht & Stamm SFB AG, a social research company based [handily] in Zurich'.

Anyway, the most ambitious survey of football participation in history came up with a list of the keenest football-playing countries. China and the US were found to have the most players (26 million and 24 million respectively), but of course the key question is which countries had the largest proportion of their inhabitants playing. Here is FIFA's list:

PERCENTAGE OF POPULATION THAT PLAYS FOOTBALL

1	Costa Rica	27	11	Anguilla	12
2	Germany	20	12	Austria	12
3	Faroe Islands	17	13	Norway	12
4	Guatemala	16	14	Slovakia	11
5	Chile	16	15	Sweden	11
6	Paraguay	16	16	Bermuda	11
7	Aruba	15	17	Iceland	11
8	Barbados	13	18	Netherlands	11
9	Vanuatu	13	19	Ireland	10
10	Mali	12	20	Cook Islands	10

It's striking how many of the keenest footballers live on little islands where there presumably isn't much else to do but play football and watch the waves roll in. The Faroe Islands, Aruba,

Barbados, Vanuatu, Anguilla, Bermuda, Iceland and the Cook Islands (combined population about a million) all make the top 20.

FIFA's list is interesting if true. Let's take the case of Mali, tenth on the list. This is a vast country with poor or non-existent roads. It stretches much of the way across the Sahara. The average inhabitant has a daily income of about $3. Who worked out that 11 per cent of the 12 million Malians play football?

Even the European figures are dubious. When the Mulier Instituut in the Netherlands set out to collate data on sports participation in the EU, it began its report with a series of caveats. Different countries use different methods to establish how many people play sport, it said. 'Even within a single year, research conducted in one and the same country can result in significant differences in the recorded figures for sport participation for up to 40 per cent.'

Still, when it comes to European countries at least, FIFA's list probably has some value. That's because Europe is an organised sort of continent where a high proportion of the people who play soccer are actually registered with a club. We have a good idea of how many registered footballers there are, because every one of them belongs to the country's FA. So the number of registered players in a European country is a fair indicator of the total of all its footballers. By way of reality check, let's see whether the European countries on FIFA's overall list of keenest players have lots of *registered* footballers too.

It turns out that Germany, Holland, Austria and Sweden – all in the top 20 of keenest football countries per capita – all also figure in FIFA's top 20 countries with the most registered footballers. Furthermore, Slovakia is in the top 20 countries with most registered *male* footballers, even though it has only 5.4 million inhabitants. In the Faroes, Norway and Ireland, also on FIFA's list of keenest countries, a mammoth 10 per cent or so of the population are registered footballers. Of the keenest European countries identified by FIFA, only Iceland lags a bit in registration: just 7 per cent of Icelanders were registered players.

So it seems that the European countries in FIFA's top 20 per capita might really play a lot of football. Without treating the Big Count as gospel, let's give those nine Europeans countries on FIFA's list a little star each, and continue our quest to find the keenest of them all.

SPECTATORS: GREAT HORDES OF PEOPLE NOT GOING TO FOOTBALL MATCHES

Playing is one way of expressing a love of football. Going to watch matches is another.

When you think of packed football stadiums, you think of England. Visually, football crowds are one of the things that the English do best. And everyone knows that the Premier League has the biggest crowds in the world.

Well, the second-biggest crowds, anyway. The average attendance in the Premier League in the 2007–08 season was 36,076. That was 3,000 fewer than went to see the average Bundesliga game that same year.

This fact comes from a weirdly addictive statistics website. The best thing about www.european-football-statistics.co.uk (run by the Dutchman Paul in 't Hout) is its collection of average attendances for almost every football league in Europe, though sadly not Albania. These stats give surprising insights into fandom, and help reveal which European country is maddest about the game.

The first thing you notice on the website is how much attendances fluctuate over time. The data on the site go back decades. Back in the 1980s, when Italian stadiums were as safe as family restaurants and Serie A was the world's best league, Italians watched far more football than the English. In the 1984–85 season the average crowd in Serie A was 38,872. Napoli, for crying out loud, drew over 77,000. Meanwhile, in the English first division in that year of Bradford and Heysel, only 21,080 braved the average league match.

How times change. By the 2007–08 season, according to the stats obtained by in 't Hout, Serie A and the Premier League had pretty much changed places: the average Italian game drew only 23,180 people, a good 13,000 fewer than the Premier League. Juventus, the Old Lady herself, averaged just 20,930. Here are a few teams in Europe that outdrew her that season: Genk in Belgium, Heerenveen in Holland, 1860 Munich (averaging over 35,000 in Germany's second division), nine clubs in the English Championship including both Sheffield sides, and Leeds United in League One.

Many other European leagues also have sharp trends in attendance over time, further evidence that fans behave much more like consumers than like addicts. French, German and Dutch attendances have soared since the 1990s. In eastern Europe, by contrast, we see what Brian Clough once called the great hordes of people not going to football matches. These empty stadiums are a post-Communist phenomenon. Back in 1989, Nicolae Ceaucescu's last year in power, the average crowd at a Romanian first-division match was officially 17,000, nearly as many as in England at the time. Now it is just 5,800.

The least popular league in Europe is Estonia's, with an average attendance in the country's top division of 184 (presumably not so hard to count). And even given that Russian men are dying at such a startling rate, it's disappointing that only 13,334 on average bother to turn up to premier league matches there. The English Championship (average: 17,483) is more popular, and in fact outdraws every league in Europe east of Germany. The English and Germans are the only Europeans who go to watch mediocre football in numbers.

However, as a friend of ours in Moscow once advised: 'Never believe any Russian statistic.' In 't Hout admits to doubting the stats for certain eastern European countries. He gets particularly suspicious when the official attendance for a game is reported as a round number – 3,000, for instance – as opposed to a precise one like 3,142. He e-mails us: 'In some leagues I found figures for one game of, for example, 2,000 and 5,000.'

The western European data tend to be more reliable. Even there, though, there are doubts. In England, is the attendance the number of people who actually went to the game, or the number who held tickets for it? After all, many season ticket holders skip some matches. At a small club at the end of a disappointing season, they might have trouble passing on their tickets. In countries such as Italy, ticket sellers have been known to wave hundreds of scary-looking away fans through without anyone paying. Some turnstile attendants might slip the odd bribe into their pockets and click somebody through, or let in friends for free. Clubs in some countries might report a lower attendance than the real figure, to reduce the tax they pay on their ticket income. Anyway, there's often nobody assiduously counting bums on seats.

Still, the figures on in 't Hout's website do tell us something. Most of them are not made up. Especially in western Europe, they probably correlate to a large degree with the number of people who actually went to games. And we can accept the general finding that eastern European crowds are low. A glance at the pictures on TV tells us that. Admittedly we can't make a precise ranking of average crowds in all European countries, but we can identify a few countries where attendances at football seem to be particularly high as a share of their population.

The way to identify these hot spots is first to count the combined average crowds for the main professional divisions in each country. Let's start with the largest European countries, which typically have three serious divisions each. England has four, but so as to compare it to France, Germany, Italy and Spain we will only analyse its top three divisions.

The 68 English league clubs in those three divisions averaged about 1.3 million spectators between them in 2007–08. (The clubs in League Two had another 104,000 in total, too few to make much difference to the national total.) That is, over two normal match days, in which every club played at home at least once, you would expect 1.3 million people to show up in England's top three divisions. That is by no means a precise figure, but it is probably a decent indication.

We then divided that spectator average by the country's population. England has 51 million inhabitants. 1.3 divided by 51 = 0.025. That means that the total combined spectator average of English clubs equals 2.5 per cent of the English population.

It turns out the English are the keenest stadium-goers of all the large European countries. Here are the (very rough) stats for the top three divisions of each big country:

TOTAL SPECTATOR AVERAGE AS PERCENTAGE OF POPULATION

1	England	2.5	4	Italy	1.2
2	Spain	1.9	5	France	0.9
3	Germany	1.5			

Spain's average only included the top two divisions – all that in 't Hout's website had. However, in the other large countries the crowds for the third division added only between 0.1 and 0.2 per cent to the national total.

So far the English have lived up to their reputation as great consumers (if not players) of football. But when we compare them to the smaller western European nations, their spectating becomes less spectacular. The Scots, for one, are much keener watchers of football. The average Scottish Premier League match drew a crowd of 15,580 in 2007–08, which is not bad for a country of 5.1 million people. If the English went in equal proportions, taking into account the fact that the English Premier League has eight more teams than Scotland's, the average top-flight English match would draw a crowd of about 90,000. You might even say that the English are somewhat lacklustre fans given that they have the best teams on earth playing in their local grounds. On the other hand, they also have to pay the highest ticket prices on earth.

The Scots are among the European spectating elite, if not at the very top. Here are the European countries whose inhabitants, according to www.european-football-statistics.co.uk, are most inclined to watch professional football:

TOTAL SPECTATOR AVERAGE AS PERCENTAGE OF POPULATION

1 Cyprus	4.8	3 Scotland	3.9
2 Iceland	4.4	4 Norway	3.7

For Scotland and Norway, we counted attendances in the top two divisions; for even smaller Cyprus and Iceland, only the top one. All the clubs in the Icelandic top division put together had a total average attendance of just 13,284, about the same as Bradford City all by itself. However, that was pretty good for a country of just over 300,000 people who were also busy buying up the world's subprime mortgages and running West Ham at the time.

It would be silly to treat these figures as exact to the decimal point. On the other hand, these are countries that tend to produce fairly reliable statistics. Norway is wealthy and hyperorganised. Iceland was wealthy until it discovered subprimes, and remains hyperorganised. Scottish football has modern stadiums and voracious marketing officials, who keep elaborate electronic databases of their supporters. They have a pretty good idea of how many come to matches. Paul in 't Hout says he considers the Norwegian, Icelandic and Scottish attendance data quite reliable, because they are reported as exact figures – 3,921 or 5,812 spectators. He is more suspicious of Cyprus, where the figures are reported as round numbers like 2,000 or 9,000. Also, he admits: 'I only have one source in Cyprus and so I cannot verify the figures.'

Still, we can say with some confidence that these top four nations love going to watch football. Their position at the top of these rankings is not a one-off. When we did this exercise in 2001, Cyprus was also in first place, and Scotland's lead over England was as large as it was in 2008. People in these countries watch in astonishing numbers given how poor their leagues are. To quote Nick Hornby, marvelling at the thousands of people who watch even the most pathetic English clubs: 'Why, really, should anyone have gone at all?'

Each of the top four gets a star in our quest to find Europe's keenest football nation. Two of the top four – Norway and Iceland – also appeared in our very cautious list of the countries that played most football. They now lead the pack with two stars each. The other keenest playing nations had unspectacular average crowds, with the Netherlands the best of the lot at 2.5 per cent of the country's population. As for the Faroes, even in 't Hout doesn't have the attendance figures.

NATIONS OF COUCH POTATOES: THE MOST POPULAR TV PROGRAMMES IN HISTORY

In our quest to establish which country cares most about football, one statistic towers over all the others: TV viewing figures. After all, relatively few people actually play football – seldom more than 10 per cent of a country's inhabitants – and even fewer watch it in stadiums. In any case, we have seen the flaws in the data for playing and spectating. But we do have good figures for the most popular way to consume football: watching World Cups and European Championships on TV. Viewing figures are the final piece of evidence to assess before we can name the most football-mad country in Europe.

TV ratings have plunged over the last 30 years. Once upon a time only the BBC broadcast in Britain, and so every programme the Corporation aired had a market share of 100 per cent of viewers. Then television expanded: first came other free channels like ITV and Channel Four, and later satellite and broadband cable.

Audiences in all rich countries splintered between the different channels. The share that any one show could command slumped. In the US for instance, 36 of the top 45 shows ever aired were shown before 1990. But here's the thing: all the top nine American programmes after 1990 were sports events. Seven were Super Bowls, and the other two were ladies' figure-skating events from the 1994 winter Olympics, which people watched because they knew that one American skater had paid someone to nobble her rival in the national team. Only sport could still unite Americans on the sofa.

It is the same in Germany, where seven out of the eight highest rated programmes of all time involve the German football team playing in a major tournament. In Britain only the 1966 World Cup final and the 1970 FA Cup final replay between Leeds and Chelsea make the top eight. Still, here too big football tournaments provide some of the communal glue once supplied by trade unions, churches and royal weddings. Possibly the best chance English people get to bond with each other nowadays, unless they are weeping over the passing of Jade Goody, is during a World Cup.

Big football matches have that sort of unifying role in most European countries. Their appeal goes beyond men. Forty per cent of the global audience for Euro 2004 was female. In fact, it is the long-term rise in female viewers that has made televised football more popular than ever before.

Before we can work out which country watches most football on TV, we need to separate the reliable viewing data from the false ones. Organisations like FIFA and the International Olympic Committee report the highest numbers they can. The more TV viewers an event attracts, the more advertising will flow to the event, and the more broadcasters will pay to screen it.

Hence the improbable tallies that organisers sometimes cite for their events. According to FIFA, a cool 715 million people watched the World Cup final in 2006. Even this claim looks modest compared to the 1.5 billion who supposedly saw the opening ceremony of the Commonwealth Games in Melbourne. What to believe?

This is where Kevin Alavy comes in. Alavy is head of analytics at Futures Sport & Entertainment. His job is to sit in London working out how many people really watch different sports events, though in fact he is far more interesting and charming than that description implies. This is how he defines his work: 'Very simply, are these sports events worth the massive investment that they typically cost, and how can my clients get even more value from their association with sport?'

Alavy can explain how the inflated numbers were invented and provide advertisers (and some of the rights-holders) with the more reliable estimates they need. He also extracts trends from the mountains of broadcasting data that exist nowadays. For this book, he gave us an insight into some of the data he has been gathering on World Cups and European Championships since 1998. Using it, we can identify the most fanatical football nation in Europe.

Around the world, TV data are extrapolated from the viewing habits of a sample of the population – in the US, about 10,000 people. Individuals used to get paid a small fee to keep a diary of their TV consumption. Then came the 'people meter': a little electronic box attached to a TV set that allows each person in a household to indicate when they are watching. Invented in Britain, the people meter is now used in most wealthy countries to measure viewing. Alavy calls it 'the gold standard of global media research'.

To see how people meter data differ from the inflated data, consider the Super Bowl. It is indisputably the most watched event in the US. The last 10 Super Bowls have been the 10 most watched American TV programmes of the last decade. But exactly how watched were they? Figures of 750 million to a billion global viewers per game get cited. Instead, using the people meter data,

Alavy puts a typical Super Bowl's average live audience at about 100 million viewers, or about one third of all Americans excluding the under-fives. (That is a mammoth figure, except when compared to the viewing figures for big soccer games. For instance, six matches at Euro 2004 drew a larger live global audience than that year's Super Bowl.)

The inflated figure of '750 million to one billion' is not an outright lie. Rather, it is a reasonable guess as to the number of people in the world who could have watched the Super Bowl on TV because they subscribe to the right channels.

Using the people meter, Alavy has collected verifiable viewing figures for sport in 54 countries. Of the countries on his list 31 are in Europe, 12 in Asia, 10 in the Americas, and only one (South Africa) in Africa, a continent where there is almost no serious measurement of viewing habits. Many poorer countries still use diaries rather than people meters. Sadly, there are no reliable viewing figures either for Cyprus, Iceland or Scotland, three of the four European countries with the highest relative attendances in stadiums. Cyprus and Iceland are too small for Futures Sport & Entertainment to bother to measure their viewing habits, and the Scottish figures are lumped together with Britain as a whole. Even so, for 33 of Alavy's 54 countries we have figures for at least four of the six major football tournaments covered since the World Cup of 1998.

The viewing figure Alavy uses for any given game or event is the 'average programme audience'. That is the average number of viewers during the entire event, rather than the peak figure, which would typically be 1.5 times higher, or the 'reach', which includes anyone who caught at least three minutes.

Alavy reports the viewing figure for any game as a percentage of all the people in each country who live in households with TV sets. In most European nations almost every household has owned a set since the 1970s. However, that is not true in less developed nations. Only about a quarter of India's population of 1.1 billion, for instance, live in households with TVs.

Alavy's collection is a treasure chest: thousands of TV ratings covering hundreds of games between national teams screened in 54 countries since 1998. However, there is an obvious problem: Germans probably watch lots of games involving Germany, and Germany has a pretty good record; how to compare the viewing figures of the successful Germans with the not-quite-so-successful English? Indeed, how to compare German viewing of Euro 2008, where their team made the final, to viewing by the English, whose team didn't even qualify? Or to cite another complication: a casual fan who only watches his own national team is surely not to be compared to the fanatic who glues herself to the sofa for every match of the tournament. Going one step further, viewers in Malaysia or Colombia who follow European Championships must surely be considered to have reached the acme of perfection in fandom.

There are other problems. The World Cup in Japan and Korea had disastrous TV ratings in Europe, because most games were played in the European late morning or at lunchtime. That is why FIFA was so keen to keep the World Cup of 2010 in South Africa despite all the problems there: Johannesburg is usually just one hour ahead of Central European Time, making it ideal for European viewers. It's less convenient for Americans. In all the agonising over the refusal of Americans to watch soccer on TV (as opposed to playing it, which American children do in great numbers) an obvious but overlooked explanation is that most of the best games are played in Europe at times when most Americans are working.

We also need to take account of the significance of each match. Obviously some matches will draw more viewers than others, but how many more?

In short, no two of our thousands of ratings are strictly comparable. Happily, there is a way to control for the differences, and so to strip down to the essence of TV fandom. We can expect viewing levels in every country to rise for the final of a tournament. We can also expect an uplift when the country's own national team plays, or when a game is shown in prime time. Once again, we need to wheel out the technique of multiple regression. A reminder: multiple regression is the mathematical formula for finding the closest statistical fit between one thing (in this case TV viewing figures) and any other collection of things (here time of match, who is playing, etc). When you have many observations – like the thousands we have here – the regression technique is extremely powerful. Not only does it give you a precise figure for the influence of one factor on another, but it can also tell you how reliable that statistical estimate is. For example, the regression can show that playing a game in prime time will add, say, 4 per cent to the size of the audience; and it can also reveal that the probability that this estimate is mistaken is less than 1 per cent.

Running a regression will allow us to isolate each contributory factor – such as kick-off time – and measure its impact on attendance. Not only will this tell us a great deal about what attracts viewers to televised football, but the final figure that we are left with after these regressions consists of two parts. One part is what is called a 'random error': that which we cannot explain because we know too little about what happened on the day. The other part, though, is a 'fixed effect': an estimate of the viewing share that a football match will achieve in a given country, stripped of all other characteristics like kick-off time, identity of teams, stage in the tournament etc.

The 'fixed effect' is what we are after. The size of the fixed effect in each country will tell us how keen that country is on watching international football on TV. The method works like this:

Our data show that the 'fixed effect' for the UK is 6.98. This means that just under 7 per cent of all British households with TV sets will watch a World Cup or European championship game, regardless of its characteristics. Seven per cent is the proportion of Brits that we can expect to have watched, say, Tunisia v Saudi Arabia at the World Cup of 2006.

However, if the game is played in the middle of prime time (meaning a kick-off between 7pm and 8.45pm) the total of British viewers rises by about 4.3 per cent. If the game is a semi-final, viewing goes up another 5.6 per cent.

So our regressions would lead us to estimate the British audience for each World Cup semi-final in 2006 at 16.9 per cent. The core audience of 7 per cent would have risen by 4.3 per cent because each game kicked off in prime time, and by another 5.6 per cent because it was a semi-final. (7 + 4.3 + 5.6 = 16.9). The actual viewing figures for each game were within two percentage points of our estimates.

This is by no means perfect, but over the hundreds of games seen in 54 countries, the errors are relatively small. The average rating figure for each game taken across all 54 countries is 8.6 per cent. Again: that is the proportion of households with TV sets that watched the game. For more than three quarters of our estimates, the error was smaller than half this number. So while we should not place too much weight on any single estimate for a particular match seen in a specific country, overall the regression summarises the data pretty well. The regression captures just over two thirds of the variation in viewing figures. The remaining third of the variation is due to unexplained random factors.

Before we ask which countries are the biggest football couch potatoes, let's pick apart the other regression effects for what they tell us about fandom. We found that only two time-of-day effects mattered: games played during 'sleep time' (midnight to 5.40am) reduced the average audience by 3.6 percentage points, while prime time added about 4 percentage points depending on the exact time.

The significance of a match was crucial. In the group stages, if one or both teams playing in the third match were already knocked out, the TV rating fell. If both teams were out, the game lost 4.7 percentage points of its rating – a giant loss, since a rating of 4.7 per cent is usually enough to keep a series on TV in the first place.

Yet when one or both teams in a third group game had nothing much to play for because they had already qualified for the next round, viewing figures barely fell. Football is soap opera. We watch it because of the story that unfolds after the game, not just because of the game itself. As long as a team is still in the tournament, its story continues.

Viewing figures rise steadily for each round of a tournament. The World Cup's round of 16 adds 1.4 per cent to the audience, while quarter-finals add 2.5 per cent, semi-finals 5.6 per cent and the final itself 10.1 per cent. Even the match for third place, often mocked as meaningless, raises audiences by 4.9 per cent – only slightly less than the semi-final effect. UEFA dropped the third place play-off from the European Championship in 1984 because the game was thought to be boring. Perhaps UEFA should reconsider.

Besides time and significance of the match, a third effect sometimes matters: who is playing. Brazil are everybody's 'second team'. Despite getting duller since 1970, they still command a viewing premium of 2.2 per cent whenever they play. Weirdly, only one other team consistently enhanced viewing figures across all 54 nations in Alavy's database: not Italy or Holland or Argentina but, yes, England. Their games boost global TV ratings by 1.4 per cent.

To sum up, imagine a World Cup final played in mid prime time between England and Brazil; this would add 10.1 (the final effect) + 4 (prime-time effect) + 1.4 (England effect) + 2.2 (Brazil effect) = 17.7 per cent to average viewership expected in any country.

There is one last factor to consider: nationalism. Its effect is enormous. For any game, for any country, broadcasting the national team added an average of 17.9 per cent to the audience. It appears that for the average person on earth, simply watching his own national team in a bog-standard group match is more attractive than watching England v Brazil in the World Cup final. People who love football are vastly outnumbered by nationalists who only tune in for 'our boys'.

If England did play Brazil in a World Cup final in prime time, how many Britons would watch? Our model would predict 7 per cent (the core audience) + 17.9 (the nationalist effect) + 16.3 (the prime-time, final and Brazil effects) = 41.2 per cent. That would equal about 25 million viewers. In fact this is almost certainly an underestimate, partly because it wouldn't count the people watching in pubs and other public places. Predictions about events that are both extremely rare and important are inevitably subject to wide margins of error. The same problem afflicts forecasting in financial markets: no statistical model can accurately predict a crash in the stock market. We have a good idea of how regular 'small' factors like the time of day will affect viewing figures. We are much less precise about the effect of big one-offs like the country's own national team playing a final.

Now we can finally open the last door: after correcting for all incidental factors, which country has the highest TV ratings for World Cups and European Championships?

THE BIGGEST FOOTBALL COUCH POTATOES

CORE TV VIEWING RATING FOR FOOTBALL AS PERCENTAGE OF HOUSEHOLDS WITH TV SETS

#	Country	Rating	#	Country	Rating
1	Croatia	12.4	11	Germany	8.6
2	Norway	11.9	12	Hungary	7.9
3	Netherlands	11.5	13	Italy	7.8
4	Uruguay	10.7	14	Argentina	7.4
5	Denmark	9.1	15	Indonesia	7.3
6	Ecuador	9.0	16	Singapore	7.1
6	Serbia	9.0	17	Romania	7.1
8	Brazil	8.8	18	UK	7.0
9	Korea	8.7	19	Lebanon	7.0
10	Sweden	8.6			

And the winner is: Croatia! Alavy notes that Croat passion goes beyond football. 'They also have very high ratings in other major sporting events,' he says. For instance, when Croatia and Spain met in the world handball final in 2005, average ratings in Croatia were nearly four times higher than in Spain. This enthusiasm may stem from having recently fought for independence in a nationalist war; or it may just be because Croatia has excellent sports teams.

The other European countries that watch most international football – the Norwegians, Dutch, Danes and Serbs – also have relatively small populations and relatively big football reputations. Quite likely, small nations score high in our rankings because they tend to be more interested in what is going on outside their borders than big nations like France or Mexico. Alavy notes: 'To have high average ratings, it's all about having a high tendency to watch when your local heroes are *not* playing.'

Britain, for all its claims to football obsession, is stuck in what Alavy calls 'a kind of mid-table mediocrity', sandwiched in 18th place between Rumania and Lebanon. Germany are the keenest couch potatoes among Europe's big countries. Eleventh in the table, they would be even higher but for their new custom of 'public viewing', as they call it in their impenetrable language. Since 2006, Germans have taken to watching games in huge crowds on big screens outside. About 12 million Germans are estimated to have chosen this method to watch their team lose to Italy in that year's World Cup semi-final. The figure was particularly impressive given that the 30 million other Germans who watched at home were by themselves the country's largest ever TV audience. At Euro 2008, the 'Fan Mile' by the Brandenburg Gate in Berlin had to be shut nearly three hours before the final of Euro 2008 because it was already packed with nearly half a million singing and dancing 'public viewers'. Yet these people do not show up in Germany's 'people meter' data.

Generally, European countries dominate at the top of Alavy's table. Partly this is because most World Cup games are played at times designed to suit them. There is a vicious (or virtuous) cycle here: because Europe has high viewing figures for football, World Cups are often held in Europe, and so European teams do well, and so European viewing figures are high. Only as Asians become richer and keener on football might this change. Chinese prime time could be a very lucrative market one day.

The Asian figures in our table need to be taken with a pinch of salt. The Korean figures are for 2002–08, so they benefited from the 'halo effect' created by South Korea's run to the semi-final in 2002. Moreover, in Korea and Indonesia the World Cup is hard to escape because it is often shown 'wall to wall' on several channels simultaneously. By contrast, Singapore scores highly partly because only the best World Cup matches are shown there – and partly because Singaporeans love betting on football the way other people love football.

And here are Alavy's least enthusiastic nations:

CORE TV VIEWING RATING FOR FOOTBALL AS PERCENTAGE OF HOUSEHOLDS WITH TV SETS

1	Australia	2.7	6	Canada	1.7
2	New Zealand	2.5	7	Latvia	1.6
3	Ukraine	2.1	8	India	1.2
4	Mexico	2.0	9	US	0.6
5	Lithuania	1.8	10	Taiwan	-0.8

The Taiwanese must really not like football. Of course even they cannot achieve a negative rating in practice, but our data combine the actual viewing figures with the specific characteristics of each game (time of day, group match, etc) to produce a final figure. In real life the Taiwanese numbers do not come out far from zero. Nor do the ratings for the US and India. An oddity of the US is that it is the only country where the nominal national team does not draw the highest ratings. At the World Cup of 2006, viewers there preferred watching Brazil, Italy and Mexico. For many people living in the US, of course, these are their true 'home' teams.

Americans, Indians and Taiwanese at least have an excuse for not watching soccer: they prefer other sports. The nations that stand out among Alavy's least enthusastic are Mexico and Ukraine, which both have respectable traditions in football. Indeed several other countries that don't care much – Spain, Portugal and France – have some of the best football teams on earth. Alavy notes that Spanish audiences for international sport tend to be relatively low, perhaps because of the country's regional divides. Basques, say, might not want to follow a Spanish 'national' team. That may now be changing: Spanish viewing figures shot up during Euro 2008 even before they reached the final.

THE KING AS SPURS FAN:
THE COUNTRY IN LOVE WITH FOOTBALL

Heia, Norge. Norway is officially Europe's kookiest nation about football. 'Why football in Norway?' ruminates Matti Goksøyr, the well-known Norwegian sports historian, when we break the happy news to him. He admits to being baffled: 'Norway, a winter nation. Impossible to play football in winter time. It's really a mystery.'

Just to recap: here is how Norway won our award. In our first category, playing football, Germany and the Faroes scored highest in Europe, at least according to FIFA. Austria, Norway, Slovakia, Sweden, Iceland, Holland and Ireland followed at some distance.

Of these keen playing countries, the only ones that were also unusually keen on spectating were Norway and Iceland. Cypriots and Scots were avid spectators, too.

So our third category, TV viewing, had to provide the decider between the front-runners, Norway and Iceland. It may be that the entire Icelandic population watches every game of every World

Cup, even the goalless draw between Bolivia and South Korea in 1994, but if so we will have to wait a couple of years to find out, because the country only introduced people meters in 2007. However, Norway did register among the continent's leading couch potatoes as compiled by Kevin Alavy, alongside Denmark, Croatia and Holland. (The Dutch and Icelanders deserve special mentions for scoring high in two of our three categories.)

Admittedly Norway got a boost from the peculiarity of its TV market. Crucially, commercial TV took a long time to get going in the country. This means that Norwegians for a long time had fewer channels than most Europeans, which in turn means that programmes on their few channels could get a larger share of the market than elsewhere. On the other hand, the Norwegian enthusiasm for watching football is remarkable because it isn't even their favourite TV sport. In surveys people claim to prefer biathlon and langlaufen, says Professor Knut Helland of the University of Bergen. So Norway win our award.

Why Norway, indeed? Early signs of dangerous obsession emerged in the late 1940s, when football pools were introduced into the country. Nowadays the whole word gambles on football, but the Norwegian oddity was that even back then, all the games on the coupon were from the English Football League. Goksøyr adds: 'And that was self-evident. It had to be like that.'

Had there been an award for most Anglophile country in Europe, Norway would probably have won that too (with Scotland and Serbia finishing joint last). Halvard Lange, Norway's foreign minister from 1946 to 1965, once said: 'We do not regard Englishmen as foreigners. We look on them only as rather mad Norwegians.' When the Germans invaded Norway in 1940, it had seemed natural that King Haakon and his Oxford-educated son Olav should flee to London, along with the Norwegian government. Later, after Olav became king, he always tried to make an autumn pilgrimage to England, where as well as dropping in on his cousin Queen Elizabeth he did his best to catch a football match. Olav supported Arsenal, which must have made for awkward dinner-time conversation with his son Harald, the current king, who is a Spurs fan.

Obsession with English football is now almost a human universal – South African cabinet meetings sometimes get interrupted by quarrels over the previous night's English games – but Norway got there first. On Saturday, 29 November 1969, decades before the Premier League formulated its secret plans for world domination, Norwegian TV broadcast its first ever live English football match: Wolves 1, Sunderland 0. Naturally, the nation was hooked. The Saturday game from England fast became an institution. 'The most important thing in Norway when it comes to affection for football is the Saturday TV games,' says Andreas Selliaas, special adviser to the Norwegian Olympic and Paralympic Committee and Confederation of Sports. 'My father supports Leyton Orient. Why?'

Orient aren't even the worst of it. There is also a Barnet Fan Club of Norway, and a Rushden and Diamonds Supporters' Club. According to the *Aftenposten* newspaper, 50,000 Norwegians belonged to supporters' clubs of British teams in 2003. King Harald was an honorary member of the Spurs fan club. That's not to mention the planeloads of Norwegians who commute to Old Trafford. And while doing all this, the Norwegians still find time to lead the world at winter sports.

When they turn to footie, in summer, the local peculiarity is that Norwegian women play it almost as keenly as men. The country's FA started hunting for women way back in the 1970s. Today about one in 23 Norwegian females is a registered footballer, the highest proportion of any country on earth. In fact, Norway has more registered female footballers than England, despite having less than a 10th of its population. Even the Norwegian FA's general secretary is a woman. It's surely no coincidence that the world's most developed country (according to the UN rankings) is also the one that gives the largest share of its inhabitants the opportunity to play and watch football.

Norwegians have always played the game, and obsessed over English teams, but for decades they barely bothered to develop an elite game of their own. Their domestic league was amateur, and the national team's matches weren't shown live on the country's sole TV channel but were squeezed into a couple of minutes on the evening news. Then, in 1992, Norwegian TV finally embraced Norwegian football. The league took off, gaining status from returning Norwegian players who had actually clumped around the holy sanctum that is English football. Many fans adopted a local side to supplement their British one.

Now one in 27 of Norway's inhabitants is a regular spectator in their domestic league, a mania untempered by the dreadfulness of the teams. Other Scandinavians, reflecting on Norway's love for almost any kind of football, like to say: 'Norwegians are not used to much.'

Norway's national team has seldom been up to much either, even if they are the only side in the world with a winning record against Brazil (played 4, won 2, drawn 2). The number of Norwegians that glue themselves to a World Cup is especially outrageous given that they usually don't have a dog anywhere in the race. Though Norway didn't qualify for Euro 2004, for instance, Norwegians watched more of the tournament than most nations that were there. If they ever get a decent team, they might really start to like football.

ARE FOOTBALL FANS POLYGAMISTS? A CRITIQUE OF THE HORNBY MODEL OF FANDOM

Just this one afternoon started the whole thing off – there was no prolonged courtship … In a desperate and percipient attempt to stop the inevitable, Dad quickly took me to Spurs to see Jimmy Greaves score four against Sunderland in a 5–1 win, but the damage had been done, and the six goals and all the great players left me cold: I'd already fallen for the team that beat Stoke 1–0 from a penalty rebound.

NICK HORNBY in *Fever Pitch* (1992)
on the origin of his lifelong love of Arsenal.

Fever Pitch is a wonderful memoir, the most influential football book ever written, and an important source for our image of the football fan. The 'Fan', as most Britons have come to think of him, is a creature tied for life to the club he first 'fell for' as a child. Hornby says his love of Arsenal has lasted 'longer than any relationship I have made of my own free will'. But is Hornby's 'Fan' found much in real life? Or are most British football supporters much less loyal than is usually presumed?

Let's start with Hornby's version, because it is the accepted story of the British Fan. As far as life allows, the Hornbyesque Fan sees all his club's home games. (It's accepted even in the rhetoric of fandom that travelling to away games is best left to unmarried men under the age of 25.) No matter how bad his team get, the Fan cannot abandon them. When Hornby watches the Arsenal of the late 1960s with his dad, their incompetence shames him but he cannot leave: 'I was chained to Arsenal and my dad was chained to me, and there was no way out for any of us.'

'Chained' is a very Hornbyesque word for a Fan's feelings for his club. Often, the Fan uses metaphors from drugs ('hooked') or romantic love ('relationship', 'fell for'). Indeed some adult Englishmen who would hardly dare tell their wives that they love them will happily appear in public singing of their love for a club, or for a player who would snub them in a nightclub if they ever managed to sneak past his entourage.

No wonder the Fan's loyalty to his club is sometimes described as a bond stronger than marriage. Rick Parry, as chief executive of the Premier League in the 1990s, recited the then dominant cliché about fandom: 'You can change your job, you can change your wife, but you can't change your football team ... you can move from one end of the country to another, but you never, ever lose your allegiance to your first team. That's what English soccer is all about. It's about fierce loyalty, about dedication.' (The Argentine variant: 'You can change your wife – but your club and your mother, never.') Recently, in more metrosexual times, football officials trying to emphasise the strength of club brands have extended the cliché by one more attachment: you can even change your gender, the officials say, but not your club.

Ideally, the Hornbyesque Fan supports his local side (even if Hornby did not). This gives the Fan roots, a sense of belonging. In a wonderful essay on fandom in the highbrow journal *Prospect,* Gideon Rachman quotes an archetypal declaration of faith from a Carlisle Fan called Charles Burgess, who wrote in the *Guardian*: 'There never was any choice. My dad ... took me down to Brunton Park to watch the derby match against Workington Town just after Christmas 41 years ago – I was hooked and have been ever since ... My support has been about who we are and where we are from.'

In real life Rachman is a commentator on international politics in the *Financial Times,* but his essay in *Prospect* is a key text in the British debate about fandom. It is the anti-*Fever Pitch.* In it, Rachman outs himself as a 'fair-weather fan, an allegiance-switcher', who at different times in his life has supported Chelsea, QPR and Spurs. So casual are his allegiances that he registered with FIFA for the World Cup of 2006 as an Ivory Coast supporter, figuring that that way he wouldn't face much competition for tickets. He got into every round including the final. For the World Cup in South Africa, Rachman is a registered Paraguay fan.

He treats the passions of Hornbyesque Fans as slightly bizarre. After all, in England a Fan's choice of team is largely random. Few clubs have particular religious or class affiliations, and few English people have an attachment dating back generations to any particular location. Some children become fans of their local team, however terrible it might be, but if you live in Cornwall or Somerset or Oxfordshire you will have no local team, while if you live in London or around Manchester you have many. As Rachman asks: 'Why devote a huge amount of emotion to favouring one part of west London over another?'

Nonetheless, the Hornbyesque Fan is a widely admired figure in Britain, at least among men. Whereas 'fanatic' is usually a pejorative word, a 'Fan' is someone who has roots somewhere. As we will argue later, this respect is connected to the quirks of British history: in this country, roots of any kind are in short supply.

However, our first question is: how true is the Hornby model of fandom? Does it really describe the way most British fans feel about their clubs?

THE CHINESE SERIAL FAN

Very little is known about sports fans who are not hooligans. The academics D.L. Wann and M.A. Hamlet estimated in 1995 that only 4 per cent of research on sport concentrated on the spectator.

So we start our quest into the nature of fandom with only one or two fairly safe premises. One is that foreign fans of English clubs, at least, are not all monogamous in their devotion. Rowan Simons explains in *Bamboo Goalposts*, his book about Chinese football, that many Chinese fans support 'a number of rival teams at the same time', and are always changing their favourite club. Simons adds: 'So dominant is the serial supporter in China that it is quite rare to find a fan with a real unflinching loyalty to one team.'

Stephanus Tekle, senior consultant at the market researchers Sport+Markt, has polling data to back up Simons's claim. Tekle says that since the late 1990s hordes of new fans around the world – particularly women – have come to football without long-standing loyalties. Many of these people appear to be 'serial supporters' who probably support Manchester United and Liverpool, or Real Madrid and Barcelona, simultaneously. No wonder that clubs like United or Real keep changing their guesses as to how many fans they have worldwide. Here are a few of United's estimates of the last few years:

Year	Estimated Fans	Source
2003	75 million	Mori
2007	About 90 million	Manchester United
2008	333 million	TNS Sport
	(including 139 million 'core fans')	

None of these estimates is necessarily wrong. There may well be 333 million people on earth who have feelings for Manchester United. However, few of these 'fans' are likely to be lifelong Horn-byesque devotees. José Angel Sanchez, now chief executive of Real Madrid, a club with its own share of foreign serial support-ers, thought many of these serial fans might eventually evolve into Hornbys. He told us in 2003: 'We used to say that the chances of changing your team is less than changing your partner or even your sex. But the way that people enter football in Asia is differ-ent: they enter through the stars. But this will not stay this way, in my opinion.' Well, perhaps.

Still, surely British fans are a lot more loyal than those fickle Chinese? Unfortunately, polling suggests otherwise. In 2008 Sport+Markt found that Chelsea had 2.4 million 'fans' in Britain. Again according to Sport+Markt, that represented a rise of 523 per cent in the five years since Roman Abramovich had bought the club. Yet even that figure of 2.4 million represented a swift decline: in 2006, when, no doubt coincidentally, Chelsea had just won the league twice running, Sport+Markt credited the club with a mammoth 3.8 million British fans.

Again, we are not saying that Sport+Markt's figures were wrong. Rather, its premise was. To serial supporters, the question 'Which is your preferred football club?' does not make sense. It presumes that everyone who likes football is a one-club Horn-byesque Fan. Instead, researchers should be asking, 'Which *are* your preferred football *clubs*?' After all, a very large proportion of people who like football are polygamous consumers. One of the authors of this book, Stefan, as a Saturday-morning coach of primary-school children, has seen the colour of the shirts switch from red to blue and back again depending upon who last won the league. Newly rising clubs like Chelsea are particularly prone to attracting short-term fans, says Tekle of Sport+Markt. Clubs like Liverpool or Manchester United with stronger brands tend to have more loyal long-term supporters, he adds. In fact the likes of

Manchester United are likely to have both far more Hornbys *and* far more casual fans than other clubs. But detractors of United tend to seize upon the hordes of casual fans, and don't mention the Hornbys.

Hornby himself recognised the prevalence of casual fans in football. Many of the people who pop up briefly in the pages of *Fever Pitch* enjoy the game but are not wedded to a particular club. Hornby calls this type the 'sod-that-for-a-lark floating punter', and speaks of it with admiration: 'I would like to be one of those people who treat their local team like their local restaurant, and thus withdraw their patronage if they are being served up noxious rubbish.'

SPECTATORS: THE HARD CORE

We know there are broadly speaking two types of football fan: the Hornbys and the sod-that-for-a-lark floating punters. We know that the sod-that-for-a-lark people are heavily represented among foreign fans of clubs like United, and even seem to be pretty common in Britain. By 2006, if we can believe Sport+Markt's figures, about 90 per cent of Chelsea's fans were people who had not supported them in 2003. No doubt a club like Hartlepool has a higher percentage of devoted Hornbys among their fans, but then clubs like Hartlepool don't have many fans full stop.

One might carp that the sod-that-for-a-lark lot are mostly just armchair fans, and that 'real' fans tend to be Hornbys. However, it would be wrong to dismiss armchair fans as an irrelevance. The overwhelming majority of football fans in Britain are armchair fans, in the sense that they hardly ever go to games. In a Mori poll in 2003, 45 per cent of British adults expressed an interest in football. But we've seen that the total average weekly attendances of all professional clubs in England and Scotland equal only about 3 per cent of the population. In other words, most of the country's football fans rarely or never enter football stadiums.

Fletcher Research, in one of the first serious market analyses of English football in 1997, found that only about 5 per cent of supporters of Premier League clubs attend even one match in an average season. If only a small minority of football fans get to the stadium at all, even fewer see every single home game for years on end as Hornby did.

Most football fans are armchair supporters. If we want to unearth the Hornbys, we need to concentrate on the elite of fans that actually go to games: the spectators.

We know that, in the Premier League at least, most spectators now watch every home game their club plays. Often they have to: at the most successful clubs, only season-ticket-holders can get seats. Many of these regular spectators may be sod-that-for-a-lark punters at heart, who have been enticed by ticketing policies to show up every week. However, it's among this group of week-in-week-out spectators that we must look for the small hardcore of lifelong Hornbys in English football. At moments of high emotion, the TV cameras like to zoom in on spectators in the stands – heads in hands, or hugging their mates – as if these people incarnated the feelings of the club's millions of supporters. They don't. Rather, they are the exceptions, the fanatical few who bother to go to games. Some of these spectators presumably support their club 'through thick and thin', watching them unto eternity as Hornby does.

At least, that is the theory. But we studied attendances in English football over the last 60 years, and found that even among the actual spectators, a startlingly high proportion appeared to be sod-that-for-a-lark types.

Nobody seems to have tried before to calculate how many British fans are Hornbys. Yet the figures required to make some sort of estimate do exist. Paul in 't Hout's marvellous website www.european-football-statistics.co.uk has statistics on attendances and league performance for all clubs in the top four divisions of

English football from 1947 through 2008. Using this data, we can find out (a) the annual mortality rate of football spectators – how many of the people who watched last season don't come back the next? – and (b) the sensitivity of new spectators to the success of teams – do most newcomers flock to Chelsea when Chelsea win the league?

Our model itself reveals some of the logic of football fandom. Generally speaking, teams cannot both have very loyal Horn-byesque fans (i.e. a low mortality rate) and at the same time be capable of attracting large numbers of new spectators when they are successful. If most of the crowd consisted of Hornbys who never gave up their seats, then when a team did well, there would be no room in the stadium for all the new fans who wanted to watch them. So floating supporters can only get tickets if the mortality rate of the existing spectators is high enough.

Previous studies have shown that a club's attendance tends to rise and fall with its league position. (The rare exceptions include Newcastle, Sunderland and the Manchester City of the late 1990s.) In our data for the 61-year period, there were 4,454 changes in clubs' league position. In 64 per cent of the cases where the club rose in the league, its home crowd increased too. In 74 per cent of the 'down' years, home attendance fell. This means that 69 per cent of all cases confirmed the simple hypothesis that fans respond to performance. Simply put: there is a market in football spectators. The few academics who study fandom – most of them in the US – explain the fans' motives through the psychological phenomenon of 'BIRGing', or 'Basking in reflected glory'.

To account for the ebb and flow of English football fans, we have constructed a very simple model. It consists of two elements. First, there are the 'new fans' coming into the game. New fans are estimated as the difference between the total atten-dance for the season and the number of loyal fans left over from the previous season. We divide new fans into two groups: the

BIRGers, who come to watch the team depending on its success; and those who come for reasons we can't explain. We will treat these reasons as random factors, although each person probably had a good reason to come to the game at the time – a friend invited them, a girlfriend left them, etc.

The second element of our model are the 'loyal fans': those who came back from the previous season. Loyal fans are estimated as the difference between the total attendance for the season and the new fans entering the game. Of course, the difference between the loyal fans plus the new fans and last season's attendance is the 'lost fans'. We can think of these lost fans as falling into two groups as well: the BIRGers who were lost to the club because its performance declined, and those who were lost for other reasons that we cannot measure (got back together with girlfriend, took up DIY, etc).

Now, we are not claiming that we can identify new fans, loyal fans and lost fans *individually*. However, we can identify these categories *in a statistical sense*, as groups. We know how many people are in each group, even if we do not know their names.

Our model produces two results. Firstly, it gives us an estimate of the BIRGers: the fraction of new fans that a team can expect to attract as a result of the position it achieves in the league. Looking at the annual changes in attendances, we found that spectators are only mildly sensitive to a team's performance. Our estimates implied that the club that won the Premier League would attract 2.5 per cent of all new spectators entering the league the next season. However, a team that finished at the bottom of the Premier League, or the top of the Championship, does almost as well: it attracts 2 per cent of all the league's new spectators. Teams in the middle of the four divisions (i.e. those ranked around 46th in England) would attract 1 per cent of all new spectators, while teams at the very bottom of the fourth tier would attract almost nobody. In short, while new spectators do like success, the vast majority of them are not simple BIRGers, glory-hunters. Judging by the ebb and flow of crowds over the 61 years, most people seem to go to a plausible club playing near their home.

That is the profile of the newcomers. But how many of last year's crowd do they replace? What is the mortality rate of the existing spectators?

We know how many spectators each club lost or gained, season by season, for 61 years. We also know how many spectators the league as a whole lost or gained. That means that for every club we can calculate the average percentage of last season's fans who did not come back for the new season. And the percentage that fits the data best? 50. Yes: on average in the post-war era, half of all spectators in English football did not take their seats again the next season.

Here's an example of how the model works:

Bristol City finished the 2006–07 season in second place in League One. Their total attendance that season was 295,000. The total attendance for all four divisions was 29.5 million.

The next season,

(a) The total attendance for all four divisions rose by 400,000, to 29.9 million.
(b) Bristol City came fourth in the Championship – a rise of 22 places.

So to calculate Bristol City's expected attendance in 2007–08, we estimate their numbers of loyal 'returning' fans and of new fans:

(c) Loyal fans are 50 per cent of the previous season's total: 148,000.
(d) New fans are calculated by estimating Bristol City's share (based on league performance) of new fans of the entire league:

(e) We predict 15.1 million new spectators for English football as a whole. That equals this year's total attendance (29.9 million) minus loyal fans from last year (50 per cent of 29.5 million = 14.8 million) = 15.1 million (29.9 – 14.8).

(f) Given that Bristol City finished 24th out of 92 clubs, we estimate their share of all new fans in the country at 1.7 per cent. Their number of new fans should therefore equal .017 x 15.1 million = 257,000.

(g) So City's loyal + new spectators = 148,000 + 257,000 = 405,000.

(h) Bristol City's actual number for 2007–08 was 374,000, so our model overestimated their support by 31,000, or 8 per cent.

(i) For the sake of simplicity, we have rounded up all numbers.

Obviously the model does not work perfectly for every club. However, taking all 92 clubs together, the estimate that fits the data best is that 50 per cent of last season's fans do not return. To quote one analysis of the English game:

> One Third Division club in the London area, for example, has an estimated 'hard core' support of about 10,000; this rises to 20,000 according to the team's success and the standing of the visiting team.

These words were written in 1951, in an economic study of football published by the Political and Economic Planning think tank. They remain a good summary of English fandom as a whole since the war.

The discovery that half of all spectators – supposedly the hardest of hardcore fans – do not bother to return the next season conflicts with the Hornby version of loyal one-club fandom. Yet it has to be true, to explain the churn we see in attendances. Even a club like Leeds, noted for its devoted fans – while stuck in

League One draws significantly larger crowds than Juventus – it has seen attendance fall from a peak of 755,000 in the 2001–02 season to only 479,000 in 2006–07.

Nor is this high mortality rate a new phenomenon. The 61 years of attendance data suggest that habits of English spectators have changed little over the years. While there has always been a hard core of Hornbys, it seems it has also always been the case that the majority of people who go to English football matches go only once in a while, and are often quite fluid about who they choose to watch. And given that spectators are the fans who commit most time and money to the game, their devotion is in most cases really rather limited. The long-term devoted spectator of the kind that Hornby described in *Fever Pitch,* far from being typical, is a rare species. Committed one-club lifelong fandom is a beautiful theory – or, as Gandhi supposedly said when asked what he thought of modern civilisation, 'That would be a good idea.' The reality is that in English football, the loyal Hornbys are a small shoal in an ocean of casual Rachmans. England may be a nation of fans, but it's scarcely a nation of Hornbys.

CALL YOURSELVES 'LOYAL SUPPORTERS'

In 1996 Alan Tapp, a professor of marketing at Bristol Business School, started to develop a relationship with a struggling club in the Premier League. Over the next four years he met the club's executives, got to see the data they had on their supporters, and assembled a team of researchers who conducted hundreds of interviews with the club's fans. Tapp eventually published two papers about his work in academic marketing journals. Together they add up to a rare, marvellous study of how the spectators of one club actually behave. Tapp titled his second paper, published in 2004, 'The loyalty of football fans – we'll support you ever-more?' – with a very pregnant question-mark. What he found was that fans talk loyal, but don't always act it.

The club Tapp and his colleague Jeff Clowes studied – based in a Midlands town that is quite easy to identify – was not very good. It wasn't the sort of outfit to attract many BIRGing glory-hunters. Most of the club's spectators lived locally. In a survey in 1998, a massive 87 per cent of them agreed slightly or strongly with the phrase, 'I would describe myself as a loyal supporter.'

Well, they would say that, wouldn't they? Tapp cautions that many of those 87 per cent might have been engaging in 'socially desirable responding'. After all, almost nobody in English football calls himself a 'sod-that-for-a-lark floating punter'. That would be socially taboo. Most fans told Tapp and Clowes that they regarded sod-that-for-a-lark types as 'pariahs'. As Rick Parry said, English fans pride themselves on their loyalty.

Yet when Tapp studied how these spectators behaved, he found a peculiar lack of loyalty. To start with the most basic fact: the club's average crowd during the four-year period of study slipped from about 24,000 to just 16,000.

The average across the period was about 21,000, which broke down as follows:

- About 8,000 season ticket holders.
- Another 8,000 places typically filled from a group of 15,000 or so regular attenders.
- 5,000 spectators who came from a 'revolving door' of perhaps 20,000 'casual fans'.

Tapp came up with three labels for the different groups: 'fanatics', 'committed casuals', and 'carefree casuals'.

The 'fanatics', or Hornbys, were mostly season-ticket-holders. Tapp said some of these people were veritable '"football extremists" who had commitment to the sport and the club that is arguably unparalleled in other business or leisure sectors'. There was the man who, when asked by Tapp's team what he would save if there were a fire in his house, replied: 'Oh, my [match] programmes and tapes. No question. And my wife and kids of course.' Many of the fanatics came from the local area, and had supported the club since childhood.

But even some of the fanatics were less fanatical than they claimed to be. Tapp found that each season, on average, 1,000 of the 8,000 season ticket holders did not renew their seats and were replaced by new people. 'Even at the fanatic end, the loyalty bucket had significant leaks,' he remarked.

The team was playing badly. In one season, a mere 2 per cent of fans proclaimed themselves 'very satisfied' with performances. However, it was not the bad football that was driving them away. When Tapp's team asked people why they were letting their season tickets lapse, the lapsers usually talked about their lives away from the stadium. Fans were much more likely to give up their season tickets if they had children aged under five, or if they described their lives as 'complicated'.

So it wasn't that the lapsers felt less loyal to the team than the people who kept going year in, year out. They were simply at different stages in life. Some regular fans admitted that at one point in life 'they had simply lost interest, often in their late teens and early twenties'. Others had been 'triggered' by a son or daughter to return to the stadium. Older people, whose lives were presumably more stable, were the most likely to renew their season tickets. Tapp surmises that they 'have simply settled into some form of auto-repurchase'. In other words, showing up to the stadium year in, year out is not a good marker of loyalty. Rather, it is a good marker of age.

At the far end of the scale from the 'fanatics' were the 'carefree casuals'. Few of the carefree casuals claimed to be 'loyal supporters'. They were 'football fans' rather than 'club fans', they preferred to see a good game than a victory for their team, and they treated football as just one of several possible activities on a Saturday. Tapp noted: 'Being club supporters is not part of their self-image.'

Many of the 'carefree casuals' sometimes went to watch other teams. Tapp reckons that it is probable that some regulars at Derby County, for instance, also occasionally show up at Nottingham Forest, even if this flies in the face of everything we are always told about English football fans.

Tapp adds that these people are mostly not 'brand-switchers', who switch from supporting one club to supporting another. Very few people love Derby one year, Forest the next, and Carlisle the year after. Rather, these adulterous spectators are engaging in what marketing experts call 'repertoire buying': they purchase different brands at different times. In normal consumer markets in almost every country, 'repertoire buyers' are thought to outnumber both 'brand-loyal' and 'price buyers'. In football too, repertoire buyers seem to be fairly common. Tapp says: 'Repertoire fans took a lot of pleasure from a multiplicity of aspects of the game itself, while single club fanatics were less interested in football, more devoted to the club as an entity.'

Tapp's middle group of spectators at the Midlands club were 'committed casuals'. These people didn't go to every match, but they did tend to describe themselves as 'loyal supporters'. They rarely watched other clubs, and were more interested than the 'carefree casuals' in seeing their team win. However, they too treated football as just one option for their Saturday. Tapp said they 'perhaps have their football support in perspective with the rest of their lives'.

In short, through close-up study very rare in English football, Tapp has got past the cliché of 'We'll support you evermore'. Instead he found the same thing that we did: there are some Hornbys in British football, but even among the self-proclaimed 'loyal supporters' of an inglorious club they are outnumbered by casual fans who can take it or leave it. Tapp ends by cautioning sports marketers that for all the rhetoric of undying love pervading English football, fans' loyalty 'cannot be relied upon'. He urges marketers to 'look under the surface of supporter loyalty', where they will find 'loyalty patterns quite similar to, say, supermarket goods sectors'.

HORNBYS, CLIENTS, SPECTATORS AND OTHERS

It turns out that few British football fans are either Hornbys or BIRGing glory-hunters. Rather, most have a shifting relationship with the club or clubs that they support. Of the 50 per cent of spectators who do not show up at their club the next season, the largest group may well continue to be monogamous fans of that club. They just can't afford to go any more, or are busy raising children, or have moved to another part of the country, or simply care less than they used to. The object of their love might not have changed, but the intensity has. Many of them may once have been Hornbys who fell for a team as an eight-year-old when their father took them to their first game. However, by the time they are 28 or 88 they are no longer the same fan. For many people, fandom is not a static condition but a process.

Other lapsed fans will have lost interest altogether. Others still might be shifting their allegiances to another club or clubs, either because they have moved to a new town, or have started to follow the team their kids support, or have simply fallen for better football elsewhere. Rachman, for example, explains in his *Prospect* essay that he stopped supporting Chelsea 'because they were a terrible team, followed by violent cretins'.

Instead, he made a 4-kilometre (2½-mile) journey within west London and became a QPR fan. In the rhetoric of English football, the choice facing the supporter is often presented as stark: either he sticks with his local team or he becomes a BIRGing glory-hunter. However, reality is more nuanced. England is so densely stuffed with professional football clubs – 43 within 150 kilometres (90 miles) of Manchester, as we saw – that many people can find a new local side without going to the trouble of moving house.

Then there is a dirty secret of English football: many fans support more than one team. If you live in Plymouth, say, you might support Plymouth Argyle, Chelsea and Barcelona, and have a fondness for half a dozen other clubs, even though if Plymouth ever make the FA Cup final you will travel to Wembley decked out as a 'lifelong Plymouth fan'. Hornby himself, in *Fever Pitch,* supports Cambridge United as well as Arsenal. In fact, whereas the usual analogy for football fandom is idealised monogamous marriage, a better one might be music fandom. People are fans of The Beatles, or The Cure, or The Pixies, but they generally like more than one band at the same time, and are capable of moving on when their heroes fade.

As usual, it was Arsène Wenger who put this best. In January 2009 he gave Arsenal's website an untraditional account of how he thought fandom worked:

> Football has different types of people coming to the game. You have the client, who is the guy who pays one time to go to a big game and wants to be entertained. Then you have the spectator, who is the guy who comes to watch football. These two categories are between 40 and 60 [years old].
>
> Then you have two other categories. The first is the supporter of the club. He supports his club and goes to as many games as he can. Then you have the fan. The fan is a guy between 15 and 25 years old who gives all his money to his club.

Obviously, Wenger's four categories are not exact. Here and there they even conflict with those of Tapp and Clowes, who found that many fans *lose* interest between 15 and 25. But Wenger agrees with them that there are several different categories of spectator, of varying emotional intensity, and that people move between these categories depending largely on their time in life.

Ties in football fandom are much looser than the rhetoric of 'We'll support you evermore' suggests. In that regard, they resemble ties of real existing marriage in Britain today. People still get married promising 'till death do us part', but in 2000 there were 141,000 divorces in England and Wales, six times as many as in 1960. About half of all adults in England and Wales are not presently married. A lifelong monogamous marriage has become almost as rare as a lifelong monogamous love of a football club.

THE INAUTHENTIC NATION

Against all evidence, the stereotype persists that the typical British football fan is a full-on Hornby. No wonder it does, because the tiny percentage of fans who are Hornbys dominate the national conversation about fandom. Of course they do: they are the people who are most motivated to join the conversation. For them, following football is not just a hobby but an identity. Also, they make up a disproportionately large share of the football economy – 'the most valuable customers', Tapp calls them – and so clubs and media listen to them more than to the sod-that-for-a-lark punters. And the Hornbys have a compelling story to tell. Most of the best stories are about love, and these are people who proclaim their love in public every week.

Yet there is a deeper reason why the Hornby account of fandom has been so easily accepted in Britain. That is because it tells a story of roots, of belonging – a lifelong love of the club your father or grandfather supported before you – in a country that is unusually rootless. In transient Britain, the story of the rooted Fan is especially seductive.

Britain was the first country on earth where peasants left their native villages to go and work in rootless industrial cities. It was among the first countries where the churches began to empty; a tie that helps root people all over the world has long been extraordinarily weak among native Britons.

Even after the Industrial Revolution, the British never settled down much. The average Briton now changes his residence about once every seven years, more often than all other Europeans except the Nordics and the Dutch, according to a Eurobarometer survey for the European Commission in 2005. Many Britons emigrate. About six million of them now live outside Britain, as do another 50 million-odd people with British ancestry. Probably only India and China have produced diasporas that are as large and as widely spread, says the British government.

It is hard for people this transitory to build up deep ties of any kind, even to football clubs. Admittedly Tapp and Clowes found that many of the 'fanatical' supporters of the club they studied had spent their lives in the local town. But it was the club's 'casual' fans, who 'had often moved to the area as adults', who were more typical of British migratory patterns. For instance, Tapp and Clowes identified one group whom they called 'professional wanderers': 'people (mainly managers/professionals) who have held jobs in a number of different places who tended to strike up (weakly held) allegiances with local teams, which they retain when they next move.' Like most Britons, the professional wanderers were too rootless to become Hornbyesque Fans. *None* of the casual fans interviewed by Tapp and Clowes 'felt a close part of the local community, in contrast to the fanatics'.

And Britons have suffered yet another uprooting: as well as leaving their place of birth, many of them have left their class of birth too. This upheaval began on a large scale in the 1960s. As the economy grew, and more Britons stayed on at school and went to university, a mostly working-class nation turned into a mostly middle-class one. For many people this was a traumatic change. Their fathers had been factory workers, and now they were managers/professionals, with the different set of experiences and attitudes that that entails. They lost touch with their roots. Naturally, many of them began to worry about their authenticity deficits. In the 1990s, when football went upmarket and the proverbial prawn sandwiches replaced the proverbial pies, there were endless laments for a lost cloth-capped proletarian culture from people who themselves somewhere along the way had ceased to be cloth-capped proletarians. They yearned to be authentic.

All this makes the true Fan a particularly appealing character to Britons. He is our version of a blood-and-soil myth. The Fan has roots. Generations may pass, and blue collars turn to white, but he still supports his 'local' team in what is supposed to be the 'working man's game'. Many Britons who aren't Hornbyesque Fans would like to be. The Fan is more than just a compelling character. He is a British national fantasy.

A FAN'S SUICIDE NOTES: DO PEOPLE JUMP OFF BUILDINGS WHEN THEIR TEAMS LOSE?

It is one of the eternal stories that are told about football: when Brazil get knocked out of a World Cup, Brazilians jump off blocks of flats. It can even happen when Brazil wins. One writer at the World Cup in Sweden in 1958 claims to have seen a Brazilian fan kill himself out of 'sheer joy' after his team's victory in the final. Janet Lever tells that story in *Soccer Madness*, her eye-opening study of Brazilian football culture published way back in 1983, when nobody (and certainly not female American social scientists) wrote books about football. Lever continues:

> Of course, Brazilians are not the only fans to kill themselves for their teams. In the 1966 World Cup a West German fatally shot himself when his television set broke down during the final game between his country and England. Nor have Americans escaped some bizarre ends. An often cited case is the Denver man who wrote a suicide note – 'I have been a Bron-

cos fan since the Broncos were first organized and I can't stand their fumbling anymore' – then shot himself.

Even worse was the suicide of Amelia Bolaños. In June 1969 she was an 18-year-old El Salvadorean watching the Honduras v El Salvador game at home on TV. When Honduras scored the winner in the last minute, wrote the great Polish reporter Ryszard Kapuscinski, Bolaños 'got up and ran to the desk which contained her father's pistol in a drawer. She then shot herself in the heart.' Her funeral was televised. El Salvador's president, ministers and the country's soccer team walked behind the flag-draped coffin. Within a month, Bolaños's death would help prompt the 'Soccer War' between El Salvador and Honduras.

Then there was the Bangladeshi woman who reportedly hanged herself after Cameroon lost to England in the World Cup of 1990. 'The elimination of Cameroon also means the end of my life,' said her suicide note. In fact, if *The Hindu* newspaper in India is right, Bangladeshis have a terrible proclivity for football suicides. After Diego Maradona was thrown out of the World Cup of 1994 for using ephedrine, 'about a hundred fans in Bangladesh committed suicide', said an article in the newspaper in 2006. (It would be fascinating to know *The Hindu*'s source.)

By now the notion that football prompts suicide has become a truism. It is often cited to show the grip of the game over its devotees, and as one reason (along with heart attacks on sofas during televised matches) why the average World Cup causes more deaths than goals.

We found that there is indeed an intimate connection between suicide and football. However, the connection is the opposite of what is commonly believed. It's not the case that fans jump off buildings when their teams lose. Working with a crack team of Greek epidemiologists, we have found evidence that rather than prompting suicide, football stops thousands of people from killing themselves. The game seems to be a life-saver.

* * *

Each year about a million people worldwide commit suicide, esti-mates the World Health Organisation. That is nearly twice the number that die of breast cancer, and five times as many as died in war in 2002. To use Germany as an example: in 2005, a total of 10,260 Germans officially died by suicide, more than died in traffic accidents, illegal drugs, HIV, and murder and other violence put together. For Germans aged under 40, suicide was the second most common cause of death. And the reported figures for suicides are understatements, says the University of Hamburg-Eppendorf, which runs a therapy centre for people at risk of suicide: 'There may be a significant share of unrecognised suicides among the death types labelled "traffic accidents", "drugs" and "causes of death unknown".'

The suicide risk varies depending on who in the world you are. If you are an elderly, alcoholic, clinically depressed, divorced Lithuanian man, be very afraid; but suicide rates are relatively low in Latin America, leaving aside for the moment the issue of World Cups. Globally, women attempt suicide more often than men do, but most 'successful' suicides are males. In the US, for instance, 80 per cent of the 30,000 people who manage to kill themselves each year are male. For reasons that nobody quite understands, suicide peaks in spring, when daylight hours are longest. In the northern hemisphere, that means May and June.

The question of why people commit suicide has preoccupied sociologists since sociology began. In 1897 Emile Durkheim, descendant of a long line of French rabbis, published his study *Suicide*. It wasn't just the first serious sociological study of suicide; it was one of the first serious sociological studies of almost anything. Drawing on copious statistics, Durkheim showed that when people lost their connection to wider society because of a sudden change – divorce, the death of a partner, a financial crisis – they sometimes killed themselves. He concluded that this particular form of suicide 'results from man's activities lacking regulation and his consequent sufferings'.

A few decades later, sociologists began to wonder whether man's sufferings might possibly include the results of sports matches. The numbers of suicides this caused might be significant: after all, most suicides are men, and sports give meaning to many men's lives. Frank Trovato, a sociology professor at the University of Alberta in Canada, was among the first to investigate the suicide–sport nexus. He found that when the Montréal Canadiens ice hockey team – once described as the national team of French Canada – got knocked out of the play-offs early between 1951 and 1992, Québecois males aged 15 to 34 became more likely to kill themselves. Robert Fernquist, a sociologist at Central Missouri State University, went further. He studied 30 American metropolitan areas with professional sports teams from 1971 to 1990, and showed that fewer suicides occurred in cities whose teams made the play-offs more often. Routinely reaching the play-offs could reduce suicides by about 20 each year in a metropolitan area the size of Boston or Atlanta, said Fernquist. These saved lives were the converse of the mythical Brazilians throwing themselves off apartment blocks.

Later, Fernquist investigated another link between sport and suicide: he looked at the suicide rate in American cities after a local sports team moved to another town. It turned out that some of the fans abandoned by their team killed themselves. This happened in New York in 1957 when the Brooklyn Dodgers and New York Giants baseball teams left, in Cleveland in 1995–96 when the Browns American football team moved to Baltimore, and in Houston in 1997–98 when the Oilers American football team departed. In each case the suicide rate was 10 to 14 per cent higher in the two months around the team's departure than in the same months of the previous year. Each move probably helped prompt a handful of suicides. Fernquist wrote: 'The sudden change brought about due to the geographic relocations of pro sports teams does appear to, at least for a short time, make highly identified fans drastically change the way they view the normative order in society.' Clearly none of these people killed themselves just because they lost their team. Rather, they were very troubled individuals for whom this sporting disappointment was too much to bear.

Perhaps the most famous recent case of a man who found he could not live without sport was the Gonzo author Hunter S. Thompson. He shot himself in February 2005, four days after writing the following note in black marker entitled 'Football Season Is Over':

> No More Games. No More Bombs. No More Walking. No More Fun. No More Swimming. 67. That is 17 years past 50. 17 more than I needed or wanted. Boring ...

Thompson, an occasional sportswriter, loved American football. One night during the presidential campaign of 1968, he took a limousine journey through New Hampshire with his least favourite person, the Republican candidate Richard Nixon, and they talked football non-stop on the back seat. 'It was a very weird trip,' Thompson wrote later, 'probably one of the weirdest things I've ever done, and especially weird because both Nixon and I enjoyed it.' The reminiscence, in *Fear and Loathing on the Campaign Trail '72,* segues into an ominous musing on suicide, as a Nixon aide snatches away the cigarette Thompson is smoking over the fuel tank of the candidate's plane. Thompson tells the aide: 'You people are lucky I'm a sane, responsible journalist; otherwise I might have hurled my flaming Zippo into the fuel tank.'

'Not you,' the aide replies. 'Egomaniacs don't do that kind of thing. You wouldn't do anything you couldn't live to write about, would you?'

'You're probably right,' says Thompson. As it later turned out, he was wrong. His ashes were fired from a cannon in Aspen, Colorado.

So much for suicides and North American sports. We know much less about the connection between suicides and European football. In one of the very few European studies done so far, Mark Steels, a psychiatrist at the University Hospital in Nottingham, asked whether Nottingham Forest's worst defeats prompted local suicides. He looked at admissions for deliberate self-poisoning to his hospital's accident and emergency department on two bad days for Forest: after the team's defeats in the FA Cup final of 1991, and the FA Cup quarter-final of 1992. He found that both games were followed by an increase in self-poisonings. After the Cup final, the rise was statistically significant, meaning that it was unlikely to have happened by chance. Steels concluded 'that a sudden disappointment experienced through an entire community may prove one stress too many for some vulnerable members of this community'.

All this is fascinating but inconclusive. For a start, the sample sizes of all these studies are pretty small. How many people are admitted to a Nottingham hospital for self-poisoning after a football match? (Answer: 10 in the 12 hours after the 1991 Cup final; nine after the 1992 quarter-final.) How many people kill themselves in Cleveland in any given month? The other problem is that almost all these researchers pursued what you might call the Brazilian apartment-building hypothesis: that when people suffer a sporting disappointment, they kill themselves. Mostly, these are studies of the dogs that barked: people who did commit suicide.

But what if the relationship between suicide and sport is deeper than that? If sport gives meaning to fans' lives, if it makes them feel part of a larger family of fans of their team, if fans really do eat and sleep football as in a Coca-Cola ad, then perhaps sport might stop some of these fans from killing themselves. We wanted to find out if there were dogs that didn't bark: people who didn't commit suicide because sport kept them going.

It so happens that we have a case-study. Frederick Exley was a fan of the New York Giants American football team, whose life alternated between incarcerations in mental hospitals and equally unhappy periods spent in the bosom of his family. In 1968 Exley published what he called 'a fictional memoir', *A Fan's Notes,* one of the best books ever written about sport. Nick Hornby gave *Fever Pitch* the subtitle 'A Fan's Life' in part as a tribute to Exley.

The Exley depicted in *A Fan's Notes* is a classic suicide risk. He is an alcoholic loner separated from his wife. He has disastrous relationships with women, alienates his friends, and spends months at a time lying in bed or on a sofa at his mother's or aunt's house. For a while his only friend is his dog, Christie III, whom he dresses in a mini blue sweatshirt like his own, and teaches to stand up like a man. 'Like most Americans,' Exley writes, 'I had led a numbingly chaste and uncommitted existence in which one forms neither sympathies nor antipathies of any enduring consequence.'

Only one thing in life provides him with any community: the New York Giants. While living in New York City he stands on the terraces every home game with a group of Brooklyn men: 'An Italian bread-truck driver, an Irish patrolman, a fat garage mechanic, two or three burly longshoremen, and some others whose occupations I forget … And they liked me.'

When the Giants are not playing, Exley spends much of his time drinking alone. But when a game is on, he watches – depending on the stage of his life – with his Brooklyn group, or with other people in bars, or with his stepfather at home. Exley is the stepfather's eternal house guest from hell, but 'things were never better between us than on autumn Sunday afternoons':

> … after a time, hardly noticeable at first, he caught something of my enthusiasm for the beauty and permanent character of staying with someone through victory and defeat and came round to the Giants.

Fittingly, the stepfather dies just before a Giants game: 'Seated on the edge of the davenport watching the starting line-ups being introduced, he closed his eyes, slid silently to the floor, and died painlessly of a coronary occlusion.'

Inevitably, at one point in the memoir, Exley contemplates suicide. He has convinced himself he has lung cancer. Determined to avoid the suffering his father went through, he decides to kill himself instead. Drinking with strangers in bars, he gets into the habit of working 'the conversation round to suicide', and soliciting their views on how best to do it. The strangers are happy to oblige:

> Such was the clinical and speculative enthusiasm for the subject – 'Now, if I was gonna knock myself off ...' – that I came to see suicide occupying a greater piece of the American consciousness than I had theretofore imagined.

Only one thing keeps Exley going. The Giants are 'a life-giving, an exalting force'. He is 'unable to conceive what my life would have been without football to cushion the knocks'. The real-life Frederick Exley lived to the age of 63, dying in 1992 after suffering a stroke alone in his apartment. He might never have got that old without the Giants.

There may be a great many Exleys around. The viewing figures we saw earlier in the book suggest that sport is the most important communal activity in many people's lives. Nearly a third of Americans watch the Super Bowl. However, European soccer is even more popular. In the Netherlands, possibly the European country that follows its national team most keenly, three quarters of the population watch Holland's biggest football games. In many European countries, World Cups may now be the greatest shared events of any kind. To cap it all, World Cups mostly take place in June, the peak month for suicides in the northern hemisphere. How many Exleys have been saved from jumping off apartment buildings by international football tournaments, the world's biggest sporting events?

This is not just a rhetorical question. A study of football tournaments and suicide would bring together both an incomparably compelling communal event and a sample the size of several countries. So we set about finding the data.

We needed suicide statistics per month over several years for as many European countries as possible. These figures do not seem to be published anywhere. Luckily we found out that the Greek epidemiologists Eleni Petridou and Fotis Papadapoulos had laboriously got hold of these data years earlier by writing to the statistical offices of several countries. A statistician who works with Petridou and Papadapoulos, Nick Dessypris, went through the numbers for us. He found that in almost every country we know about, fewer people kill themselves while the national team is playing in a World Cup or a European Championship. Dessypris said the declines were 'statistically significant' – unlikely to be due to chance.

Let's take Germany, the biggest country in our study and one that always qualifies for big tournaments. Petridou and Papadapoulos had obtained monthly suicide data for Germany from 1991 through 1997. A horrifying total of 90,000 people in Germany officially killed themselves in this period. The peak months for suicides were March through June.

But when Germany were playing in a football tournament – as they did in the Junes of 1992, 1994 and 1996 – fewer people died. In the average June with football, there were 787 male and 329 female suicides in Germany. A lot more people killed themselves in the Junes of 1991, 1993, 1995 and 1997 when Germany were not playing football. In those football-free Junes, there were an average of 817 male and 343 female suicides; or 30 more dead men and 14 more dead women than in the average June with a big tournament. For German men and women alike, the June with the fewest suicides in our seven-year sample was 1996, the month that Germany won Euro 96.

We found the same trend for 10 of the 12 countries we studied. In Junes when the country was playing in a football tournament, there were fewer suicides. These declines are particularly remarkable given how much alcohol gets consumed during football tournaments, because drinking would normally be expected to help prompt suicides. Only in the Netherlands and Switzerland did football tournaments not seem to save lives; these two countries saw very slight increases in the suicide rate during tournaments. In the other countries, the life-saving effect of football was sometimes spectacular. Our data for Norway, for instance, run from 1988 through 1995. The most football-mad country in Europe played in only one tournament in that period, the World Cup of 1994. The average for the seven Junes when Norway were not playing football was 55 suicides. But in June 1994 there were only 36 Norwegian suicides, by far the lowest figure for all eight Junes in our dataset. Or take Denmark, for which we have suicide tallies from 1973 through 1996, the longest period for any country. In June 1992 the Danes won the European Championship. That month there were 54 male suicides, the fewest for any June since 1978, and 28 female suicides, the joint lowest (with 1991) since the dataset began.

We have tried to make some very rough estimates of how many lives these tournaments saved in each country. 'Lives saved' represents the decline in deaths during the average June when a country's national team is playing in a World Cup or European Championship compared to the average June when the team isn't playing. Here is the tally:

	Male lives saved	Female lives saved
Austria	9	–3
Czech Republic	14	6
Denmark	4	4
France	59	8
Germany	30	14
Greece	0	5
Ireland	2	1
Netherlands	–5	0
Norway*	[19 lives saved spread across both genders]	
Spain	4	1
Sweden	4	15
Switzerland	–1	–2

* The data for Norway was not broken down by gender.

The figures are negative for the Netherlands and Switzerland because more people killed themselves when their teams were playing than when there was no football.

The next question is what happens after a team is knocked out. Do all the people who had been saved from suicide by football then fall into a void and jump off apartment buildings? If so, you would expect a rise in suicides in the period after the tournament.

However, we found that in 10 of our 12 countries, suicides *declined* for the entire year when the national team played in a big tournament. Only in the Netherlands did suicides rise in the year when the team played; in Spain the difference was negligible. But in the other 10 countries, even after the team got knocked out and the euphoria ended, there was no compensating rise in suicide. To the contrary: it seems that the uniting effect of the tournament lasted for a while afterwards, continuing to depress the suicide rate. For each of these 10 countries, more lives were saved on average over the entire year than in June alone. Here are our very rough estimates for lives saved over the entire year when the national team plays in a tournament ('lives saved' represents the decline in deaths during a 'football' year compared to the average year):

	Male lives saved	Female lives saved
Austria	46	15
Czech Republic	55	12
Denmark	37	47
France	95	82
Germany	61	39
Greece	9	13
Ireland	19	−10
Netherlands	−10	−1
Norway	[92 lives saved spread across both genders]	
Spain	2	−3
Sweden	44	16
Switzerland	20	2

Very roughly, football tournaments in these periods appear to have helped save several hundred Europeans from suicide.

We couldn't find any monthly suicide data for any of the British nations. However, the only two previous studies on this topic that we know of in Britain suggest that the life-saving effect works there too.

'Parasuicide' is a suicidal gesture in which the aim is not death, but rather self-harm, or a cry for help. One example of parasuicide is taking an insufficient overdose. George Masterton, a psychiatrist in Edinburgh, and his co-author J.A. Strachan studied Scottish parasuicides during and immediately after the World Cups of 1974, 1978, 1982 and 1986. Each time, Scotland had qualified for the tournament. Each time, Masterton and Strachan found a fall in parasuicide for both genders during the tournament 'which has been sustained for at least eight weeks after the last game'. The Scottish case is a pretty strong piece of evidence against the apartment-building theory of football suicides, because if there was ever an excuse for football fans to try to kill themselves, it was Scotland's performance at the World Cup of 1978. (Their fantasist manager, Ally McLeod, had boasted beforehand that they would leave with a 'medal of some sort'.)

Later Masterton and Anthony J. Mander studied the numbers of people who came to the Royal Edinburgh Hospital with psychiatric emergencies during and after the World Cups of 1978, 1982 and 1986. The researchers found 'reductions in all illness categories during and afterwards (with the exception of alcoholism during)'. The decline in emergencies applied to both genders, and was more marked after each World Cup than during it. For instance, there was a 56 per cent fall in admissions of male neurotics in the weeks after a tournament.

The authors then tried to explain what was going on here:

> There are few outlets which permit a wide and acceptable expression of Scottish nationhood – sport is perhaps the most powerful, and football is the national game … We would speculate that such a common interest and endeavour, fused with a surge of nationalism, might enhance social cohesion in the manner proposed by Durkheim to explain the decreased suicide rates that accompany times of war.

'Social cohesion' is the key phrase here. This is the benefit that almost all fans – potential suicides and the rest of us – get from fandom. Winning or losing is not the point. It is not the case that losing matches makes significant numbers of people so unhappy they jump off apartment buildings. In the US, fans of longtime losers like the Chicago Cubs and the Boston Red Sox baseball teams have not killed themselves more than other people, says Thomas Joiner, author of *Why People Die by Suicide*, whose own father died by suicide.

Joiner's article 'On Buckeyes, Gators, Super Bowl Sunday, and the Miracle on Ice' makes a strong case that it's not the winning that counts but the taking part – the shared experience. It is true that he found fewer suicides in Columbus, Ohio, and Gainesville, Florida, in the years when the local college American football teams did well. But Joiner argues that this is because fans of winning teams 'pull together' more: they wear the team shirt more often, watch games together in bars, talk about the team and so on, much as happens in a European country while the national team is playing in a World Cup. The 'pulling together' saves people from suicide, not the winning. Proof of this is that Joiner found fewer suicides in the US on Super Bowl Sundays than on other Sundays at that time of year, even though few of the Americans who watch the Super Bowl are passionate supporters of either team. What they get from the day's parties is a sense of belonging.

That is the life-saver. In Europe today, there may be nothing that brings a society together like a World Cup with your team in it. For once, almost everyone in the country is watching the same TV programmes and talking about them at work the next day, just as people used to do 30 years ago before cable TV arrived. Part of the point of watching a World Cup is that almost everyone else is watching too. Isolated people – the types at most risk of suicide – are suddenly welcomed into the national conversation. They are given social cohesion. All this helps explain why big football tournaments seem to save so many female lives in Europe, even though relatively few women either commit suicide or (before about 2000 at least) watch football. The 'pulling together' during a big football tournament is so universal that it drags many women along in a way that club football does not. It may also be that, during tournaments, some troubled women benefit from a brief holiday from male partners who are distracted by football.

Other than sport, only war and catastrophe can create this sort of national unity. Most strikingly, in the week after John F.

Kennedy's murder in 1963 – a time of American sadness but also of 'pulling together' – *not one* suicide was reported in 29 cities studied. Likewise, in the US in the days after the September 11 attacks, another phase of national 'pulling together', the number of calls to the 1-800-SUICIDE hotline halved to about 300 a day, 'an all-time low', writes Joiner. And in Britain in 1997, suicides declined after Princess Diana died.

Joiner speculates that 'pulling together' through sport may particularly suit 'individuals who have poor interpersonal skills (often characteristic of severely depressed or suicidal persons)'. You don't have to be charming to be a fan among fans.

In 1956 Frederick Exley was drunk, unemployed and loveless in Chicago. He writes: 'Though I had completely disregarded football my first year in that happy city, during the autumn of 1956, after losing my job, I once again found that it was the only thing that gave me comfort.' At some point or other in life, we have all known how that feels.

HAPPINESS: WHY HOSTING WORLD CUPS IS GOOD FOR YOU

In the 1920s, the belief arose in the poor black Transkei region of South Africa that black Americans were going to arrive in aeroplanes to destroy the white men and save the chosen. This was supposed to happen in 1927.

Today in South Africa you can find a similar belief: that in 2010 the rich people of the world will arrive in aeroplanes and save the whole nation. On the day in May 2004 that South Africa was awarded the World Cup, people celebrating in Soweto shouted, 'The money is coming!'

Half the people you meet in Johannesburg have a scheme for 2010: buying apartments just to rent them out during the tournament; selling sausage and maize pudding outside stadiums; corralling peasant women to weave bead flags in the colours of all the participating teams. Much of South African conversation now is about such schemes, and in newspaper profiles, when a celebrity describes what he is working on, he generally adds, 'The key thing is to be ready for 2010.' The year has become a magic number, like the Year of the Beast, or 1927.

South Africans may sound as if they are on a collective space trip organised by the government and scheduled to end with a bump on 12 July 2010, the day after the final. However, they are merely expressing in extreme form a conventional belief: that hosting a big sports event can make a place rich. Whenever a country bids to host the World Cup or the Olympics, its politicians prophesy an 'economic bonanza'. They invoke hordes of shopaholic visitors, the free advertising of host cities to the world's TV viewers, the long-term benefits of all the roads and stadiums that will get built. No wonder that nowadays almost every country seems to want to host these events. The bidding to stage the World Cup of 2018 is the most competitive ever.

In fact, staging sports tournaments doesn't make you rich at all. The reason why countries are so eager to host is an altogether different one: hosting makes you happy. Strangely, though, the wannabe hosts don't seem to understand their own motives.

The 1989 movie *Field of Dreams* is a sentimental redemption story starring Kevin Costner as an Iowa farmer. Growing up the son of a baseball nut, the farmer had dreamt of being a baseball star. As an adult, he hears a voice telling him to build a baseball diamond on his cornfield. 'If you build it, he will come,' is the film's catchphrase. The moral: building stadiums where they do not currently exist is uplifting and good for you. This originally American idea has since spread to soccer in Europe.

There is in the US a small industry of 'consultants' who exist to provide an economic rationale for 'If you build it, he will come.' In almost any city in the US at almost any time, someone is scheming to build a spanking new sports stadium. The big prize for most American cities is to host a major-league team; ideally an American football one, but if that can't be had then baseball, basketball or, if nothing else is going, ice hockey or, at worst, soccer. Hosting an American sports 'franchise' has a lot in common with hosting a World Cup. Both the franchise and the

World Cup are mobile beasts. Their owners are generally willing to move to whichever city or country offers them the best deal. In the US, owners of sports teams usually demand that the host city's taxpayers stump up for a stadium, with lucrative car parks thrown in. All this is then handed over to the franchise owner, who also gets to keep the money he makes from selling tickets. About 70 new major-league stadiums and arenas have been built in the US in the last 20 years. The total cost: $20 billion, about half of which came from the public. In New Orleans, for instance, the taxpayer paid for the Superdome but not for better levees.

In 1989 there was a typical case in which 70 investors, including the son of the then American president George H.W. Bush, paid $83 million for the Texas Rangers baseball club. The Bush group wanted a bigger stadium. Strangely for a phalanx of right-wing millionaires, it decided that local taxpayers should finance it. If that didn't happen, the new owners threatened to move the Rangers elsewhere. The people of the local town of Arlington duly voted to increase the local sales tax by half a per cent, raising the $191 million needed for the ballpark.

The president's son, George W., became the Rangers' managing director. Mostly, this just meant being the official face of the club. He would sit in the stands during games handing out baseball cards with pictures of himself. When he ran for governor of Texas in 1994, he constantly cited his experience in baseball. There wasn't much else on his CV at the time. He was duly elected, and decorated his Austin office with 250 signed baseballs.

In 1998 the Bush group sold the Rangers to Tom Hicks for $250 million. Most of the value was in the stadium that the taxpayers had built. Bush personally netted $14.9 million. He admitted: 'When it is all said and done, I will have made more money than I ever dreamed I would make.' Meanwhile he was already beginning to parlay his governorship into a bigger political prize.

So the trick for American club owners is to persuade the taxpayer to cough up for stadiums. This is where economists come in handy. Economists like to say that people respond to incentives. Well, economists certainly respond to incentives. Anyone hoping to persuade taxpayers to stump up for a stadium in the US commissioned an economist to write an 'economic impact' study. By a strange coincidence, these studies always showed that the stadium would make taxpayers rich. (One book describing this racket is aptly called *Field of Schemes*.)

The argument typically went as follows: building the stadium would create jobs first for construction workers, and later for people who worked in it. Fans would flock in from all around ('If you build it, he will come'), and they would spend money. New businesses would spring up to serve them. As the area around the stadium became populated, more people would want to live there, and even more businesses (and jobs) would spring up. 'The building of publicly funded stadiums has become a substitute for anything resembling an urban policy,' notes Dave Zirin in his *People's History of Sports in the United States*.

The 'economic impact' study then typically clothes this model with some big numbers. If you put your mind to it, you can think up a total in benefits that runs into the billions, whatever currency you happen to be working in. Best of all, no one will ever be able to prove that number wrong. Suppose you promise that a stadium will bring a city economic benefits of $2 billion over ten years. If the city's income (hard to measure in the first place) rises by only $1 billion over the decade, then, of course, it was something completely different (the world economy, say) that restricted the income. You could only prove the original estimates wrong if you could estimate how much economic growth there would have been had the stadium never been built – but this 'counterfactual' figure is unknowable, precisely because it is a counterfactual. The same economists soon branched out into writing studies that justified ever more extravagant spending on the Olympics.

It would have seemed rude to derail this industry with anything so inconvenient as the truth. But then along came Rob Baade.

The quiet, courteous academic seemed an unlikely figure to be taking on the stadium lobby. After all, he is a former top-class athlete himself: at college, Baade captained the Wisconsin basketball team. When the white coach seemed antagonistic to the majority of black players, Baade found himself championing players against coach in what he describes as one of the most difficult years of his life.

Afterwards he wanted to do graduate work in public finance, a branch of economics that usually involves many equations and few words. But he also wanted to coach basketball, and to apply something of what he had learnt while in the Wisconsin team. A colleague told him about a job at Lake Forest College, an idyllic little place just outside Chicago. To the dismay of some of his purist professors, he went to Lake Forest on a temporary appointment and ended up coaching there for 18 years, while also rising to full professor of economics. He was a good coach, too: the year before he arrived the team had not won a single game, but within four years they were winning 85 per cent of their games.

When you start out as an academic you try to write papers that will grab your colleagues' attention. Baade used his own background to enter the economics of sports, then still almost virgin terrain. At a seminar in New York he presented a paper entitled 'The Sports Tax'. Journalists from the *New York Times* and the *Wall Street Journal* happened to be in the audience, and they zeroed in on what had been almost a throwaway line in his talk: public investment in stadiums does not provide a good return for taxpayers. As a coach himself, Baade might have been expected to join the stadium boosters. Had he done so, he could have earned himself good money in 'consulting'. Instead he went into opposition.

The Heartland Institute, a conservative think tank, asked him to write up his thoughts. There are few issues in American political life where the right joins with an intellectual liberal like Baade, but the paper he published in 1987 laid out the problem clearly: 'Contrary to the claims of city officials, this study has found that sports and stadiums frequently had no significant positive impact on a city's economy and, in a regional context, may actually contribute to a reduction in a sports-minded city's share of regional income.'

Baade had asked the awkward questions that stadium boosters always ignored. For instance, where would all the construction workers for the new stadium come from? Wouldn't they have jobs already, and therefore wouldn't a shortage arise somewhere else? Worse still, as competition for their skills intensified, wouldn't costs rise?

Once you start thinking of people as having alternatives, rather than just standing around waiting for the stadium to arrive, the economics begin to look less appealing. For every dollar going in, there is probably a dollar going out somewhere else. In particular, if a city has to balance its budget, then spending more on stadiums must mean spending less on hospitals and schools. These lost jobs have to be counted against the stadium's benefits. And if the city doesn't balance its budget, isn't it storing up future burdens for taxpayers, who will have to forego something, some day?

That is bad enough, but what if the stadium doesn't produce the promised benefits? After all, most stadiums are only used for a few hours a week, and barely at all in the off-season. Even allowing for the occasional rock concert (and there is a limit to how many times Elton John can play in your town), most of the time the neighbourhood around the stadium will be deserted. Nobody wants to live in a place like that. The neighbourhoods around the new Wembley or Old Trafford have hardly become des res, for instance.

Nor did Baade believe that a stadium would draw in much spending from outside the city. Most out-of-town fans would buy a hot dog and beer, watch the game, and leave – hardly an economic bonanza. A mall, or a Cineplex, or even a hospital, would generate more local spending.

Around the end of the 1980s other economists, too, began asking these awkward questions. However, Baade went one better. In order to show that the boosters' numbers didn't add up, he generated some numbers of his own. Perhaps he couldn't measure the counterfactual, but he could get close by comparing economic growth in cities that had major-league teams with those that didn't. After all, he reasoned, if the boosters were right, then over time cities with stadiums must do better than cities without stadiums.

Baade examined data such as income per head, and the numbers of new businesses and jobs created in various cities. The more he looked, the less difference he found between the economic profiles of cities with and without stadiums. All this spending was evidently producing no benefit.

Gradually people took notice. Other economists started to replicate Baade's findings, and to find new ways to test the proposition that stadiums create wealth. 'Anti-stadium movements' began in many American cities.

In the mid-1990s Baade was asked to testify before Congress. On the day of his testimony, Congress was also holding hearings on the Clinton Whitewater affair and on military intervention in Bosnia, but when the stadium hearings started, the other chambers emptied. One of the people in the room was Paul Tagliabue, commissioner of the NFL and someone all the Congressmen wanted to be seen with. Powerful people like Tagliabue were getting quite irritated with Baade's awkward facts.

Academic freedom is a cherished value of American universities, but, as Baade was starting to realise, so is making money. He recalls an old guy coming up to him after one meeting, and saying: 'You might be right, Professor, but if I were you I would watch my back. You're getting in the way of a whole lotta commercial projects.' A university seldom likes seeing its employees upset local politicians and business people. Lake Forest College always supported Baade, but at times it would have been convenient had he thought differently.

He kept on telling the truth regardless. Among economists, often not the sportiest of types, he developed a special credibility as a former athlete. This sometimes came in handy, for example when a questioner in a public debate asked, 'No disrespect, Professor, but what does an economist like you know about athletics?'

Eventually Baade descended on soccer. He and Victor Matheson conducted a study of the impact of hosting the World Cup of 1994 in the US. They looked for evidence of faster economic growth in the host cities, and as usual they found nothing. Meanwhile, the old bogus American arguments for hosting sports had spread to other countries.

The raising and dashing of hopes of an 'economic bonanza' has since become as integral a part of a modern football tournament as the raising and dashing of hopes that England will win it. A few months after England hosted Euro 96, for instance, a report by a body called Tourism Research & Marketing said that fewer than 100,000 overseas fans had visited England for the tournament, against a forecast – admittedly plucked out of thin air by the FA – of 250,000. Nor had the visitors spent much. Euro 96 generated about £100 million in direct income for Britain. This was peanut dust beside the £12.7 billion spent by all overseas visitors to the country in 1996. Meanwhile, a study by Liverpool University and the city council found that the 30,000 visitors to Liverpool during Euro 96 spent only £1.03 million between them. How many jobs did that create? Thirty, all of them temporary.

A few years later Japanese and Korean government officials were predicting that the World Cup of 2002 could boost their economies by a staggering $26 billion and $9 billion respectively. Of course, after the event there was little sign of any such boost, and indeed some evidence that tourists had stayed away for fear of football hooligans.

Finally the weight of this research was starting to stack up. It was becoming obvious that even if you build it, he doesn't necessarily come. The boosters' claims of economic benefits were growing muted. The estimates produced for the World Cup in Germany in 2006 were altogether more sober. Even a study sponsored by the German football federation suggested a mere $2 billion in new benefits. (Similarly in London now, estimates of the likely economic benefits from the 2012 Olympics are kept studiously vague.)

Perhaps the best estimate we have of how much visitors to football tournaments actually spend was done at the German World Cup. This was the biggest media event in history, a month-long party (except for the boring football), and yet even here the hosts didn't make much money.

A team of economists, led by Holger Preuss from the University of Mainz, decided to work out how much 'new' money visitors to the World Cup actually spent. In the old days, when boosters estimated economic bonanzas, they simply multiplied the number of seats in stadiums by some imaginary spending number (counting meals, hotels, and transport as well as tickets) to produce an enormous hypothetical sum.

The problem with this method, as serious economists pointed out, is that not every visitor to an event really injects extra spending into the economy. Preuss's team surveyed a large sample of visitors to the World Cup, and found that only about a fifth of them were foreigners who had travelled to Germany specifically for the football. Over half the 'visitors' were in fact Germans. For the most part these Germans would have been in Germany anyway, and had there been no World Cup they would presumably have spent their money on other forms of entertainment (such as going to cinemas or restaurants). If they spent money on the World Cup, they spent less elsewhere in the German economy, which largely offset any economic benefit from the football. Of course, some Germans who might otherwise have been spending their money in Spanish bars stayed home for the football. However, their spending was probably offset by other Germans who went abroad precisely in order to avoid the madness of the World Cup.

The remaining foreign visitors to the World Cup – about a quarter of all visitors – were either 'time-switchers', who would have come to Germany anyway at some point, and simply timed their visit to coincide with the World Cup, or foreigners who would have been in Germany during the World Cup anyway, and just decided to go along and see what all the fuss was about. Preuss's team called this last category 'casuals'.

'Time-switchers' and 'casuals' would have added little to spending, because even without the World Cup they would have spent their money in Germany. Preuss's team asked their respondents detailed questions about their spending plans. They concluded that the World Cup generated spending by visitors of €2.8 billion. That was negligible besides the Paris Hiltonesque €1,000 billion-plus spent annually by consumers in Germany. It was also much less than the German state spent preparing for the tournament. Remarkably, more than a third of that visitor income came from people who never got inside a stadium but merely watched the games on big screens in public places. In short, even the World Cup was barely a hiccup in the German economy.

Almost all research shows the same thing: hosting sports tournaments doesn't increase the number of tourists, or of full-time jobs, or total economic growth. The next World Cup will not be an aeroplane dropping dollars on South Africa. When the country's finance minister flew three eminent sports economists to Pretoria for a workshop, the trio argued that the best South Africa could hope for was that the World Cup would *not reduce* economic growth. Even the 500,000 or so expected foreign visitors would not be a bonanza. In 2007, South Africa attracted an average of more than 750,000 foreign visitors a month.

None of this is to mention the host's costs. If the economic benefits of putting on these tournaments are muted, the expenses seldom are. The economists Brad Humphreys and Szymon Prokopowicz made some rough estimates of the costs to Poland of hosting just half of Euro 2012. Poland will need to lay on a lot more than just new stadiums, airports, and hotels for fans. UEFA requires, for its own officials and guests, the use of one entire five-star hotel within 45 minutes' drive of every stadium. The teams need another 16 hotels, most of them five-star. The referees have to be in five-star hotels near the stadiums. The doctors who perform the doping controls need five-stars 'in the countryside'. Much of the cost of these hotels will come courtesy of the Polish government. It will also have to put up surveillance cameras all over its stadiums and towns.

In all, Humphreys and Prokopowicz estimated that Poland would have to spend about $10 billion on Euro 2012. True, some of the infrastructure the country is buying will have its uses after the tournament. However, much of it won't, because the things you need for a football tournament are never quite the same as the things you need for daily life, which is why the Japanese stadiums for the World Cup of 2002 are now mostly empty. All those Polish cameras, roads to stadiums and luxury hotels in provincial towns may never quite pay for themselves.

Ah, say the boosters, but the biggest economic benefits are intangible. Michael Katz is a millionaire Johannesburg lawyer who sits on the organising committee for the South African World Cup. In his air-conditioned office in the business district of Sandton, he says the World Cup will show 'that foreigners can invest here, trade here with confidence'. The tournament will boost South Africa's brand.

However, that is true only if things go well. What if three days into the tournament an English fan is carjacked, and later an American sponsor who has come to Johannesburg to watch games and schmooze is raped? The news will be repeated non-stop on CNN for a month. Statistically, this is quite likely to happen. The armed robbers of Johannesburg have undoubtedly already cancelled all leave for June and July of 2010.

Katz responds: 'On that basis you must never host a World Cup, you must never do anything in business, because something may go wrong.' But we know that hosting a sports tournament can seriously damage your brand. It happened to the Olympic hosts Munich in 1972, Montreal in 1976, and Atlanta in 1996. The 2010 World Cup might persuade people that South Africa is not a poor, corrupt, diseased, crime-ridden country; alternatively, it might persuade them that South Africa is precisely that.

Most economists now agree with Rob Baade: hosting a sports tournament doesn't make a place rich. The question then is why countries still bother. Why do the US, Russia, Australia, England, Indonesia, Mexico, Japan, Spain and Portugal, Holland and Belgium all want to stage the World Cup of 2018? The answer has nothing to do with money. Rather, it reveals something about the new politics of happiness now emerging in the rich world.

In recent years, social scientists have learnt a lot about happiness. Their best source in Europe is the Eurobarometer research programme, which is funded by the European Commission. Each year it asks about 1,000 citizens from each European country how happy they are. To quote the exact question: 'On the whole, are you very satisfied, fairly satisfied, not very satisfied, or not at all satisfied with the life you lead?'

The survey has been conducted for about 40 years. By now, some insights have accumulated. Perhaps the most interesting is that having money in itself doesn't make you happy. 'There is a paradox at the heart of our lives,' is how Richard Layard opens his book *Happiness: Lessons from a New Science,* one of a flood of recent works on the subject. 'Most people want more income and strive for it. Yet as Western societies have got richer, their people have become no happier.' Layard (sometimes described as the British government's 'happiness czar') says that in the US, Britain and Japan, people have got no happier in the last 50 years even as average incomes have more than doubled.

It seems that we humans adapt quickly to our environment. The things we once thought of as luxuries soon become necessities (although, by the same token, our sense of well-being would quickly adapt to losing half our income). What we care about is not our absolute wealth but our rung on the ladder. Ruut Veenhoven, a leading researcher of happiness, says: 'When we have overtaken the Joneses, our reference drifts upward to the Smiths, and we feel unhappy again.'

Only in countries where income per capita is below about £11,000 – countries such as Mexico, the Philippines or India – has increased wealth brought some happiness. Layard writes: 'The reason is clear – extra income is really valuable when it lifts people away from sheer physical poverty.' But that very rarely happens in Europe any more.

Some other truths emerge from the European data. Scandinavians are very happy; eastern Europeans are not. The Irish both north and south of the border are surprisingly happy. Age, sex and social status matter too. In western Europe at least, the average person's happiness tends to decline with age until he is 26 years old, and then starts to rise again. Women seem to be happier than men, which might help account for their much lower rates of suicide. The more educated people are, the happier they tend to be. Married people are generally happier than unmarried ones. What happens around you in society also matters: when unemployment or inflation rises, people tend to grow unhappier. Spending time with friends and family makes people happy.

And, we discovered, so does hosting football tournaments. Staging a World Cup won't make you rich, but it does tend to cheer you up.

The day before the World Cup final of 2006, one of the authors, Simon, visited the street where he used to live in Berlin. Fifteen years before, the Hohenfriedbergstrasse had been a dull-brown place with toilets on the stairwells where nobody ever spoke to anyone else. This time, he had to check the street sign to make sure it was the same place. Flags were flying from every house – German flags made in China, but also flags of many other nations – and everywhere there were children playing, even though they had supposedly gone extinct in Germany. The World Cup seemed to have made a usually gloomy nation happy.

This is typical. Georgios Kavetsos and Stefan Szymanski (with a lot of help from Robert McCulloch, guru of happiness research) took the European Commission's happiness data for 12 western European countries from 1974 to 2004, and checked whether it correlated at all with sports tournaments. The obvious first question was whether people became happier when their national team did well. It turned out that they didn't: there was no visible correlation. Then Kavetsos and Stefan looked at hosting and happiness, and here they found a link. After a country hosts a football tournament, its inhabitants report increased happiness.

What Kavetsos and Stefan did was to replicate existing studies of happiness using all the measures researchers usually consider (income, age, marital status, etc), and then to see whether living in a host country made a difference as well. Their data on happiness covered eight separate hosts of tournaments: Italy and France for the World Cups of 1990 and 1998; and for the European Championships, Italy (1980), France (1984), West Germany (1988), England (1996) and Belgium and the Netherlands (2000). In all but one of these eight host countries, there was a significant up-tick in self-reported happiness just after the tournament. The only exception was the UK, where happiness fell slightly just after Euro 96, but then we all know that the UK is not England.

This evidence is persuasive. However, given that so many other factors influence happiness, we wanted to test whether this effect could be measured even after allowing for the other factors. To do this, several large databases have to be welded together, and in the process the data from some years was lost. For instance, it turns out that the income of respondents was not surveyed in every single year. That left us with data for five hosts: Italia 90, and the Euros of 1984, 1988 and 2000, the last of which had two hosts. Admittedly this is a small sample, but in all five host countries, happiness rose after the tournament, even allowing for all the other effects that influence happiness. The inhabitants reported a higher level of happiness the year after the tournament than they had the year before; and they reported more happiness in the autumn surveys (i.e. after the tournament) than in the spring surveys (held before the tournament).

The jump in happiness was quite large. Citizens of wealthy countries like the Netherlands or France would need to make hundreds of euros more a month to experience a similar leap. One way to express this is that the average person gains twice as much happiness from hosting a football tournament as from having higher education. The effect can also be likened to an unexpected increase in income that takes someone from the bottom half of the income distribution to the middle of the top half. It's not quite winning the lottery, but very satisfying nonetheless. If you calculate this for an entire nation, then the leap in happiness from hosting can easily be worth a few billion euros.

In general in the host countries, older men gained the most extra happiness, presumably because many of them were sitting in front of their television sets with little else to do. Lesser-educated people gained more happiness than better-educated ones. Of all the subgroups we studied, only one (a significant one) did not get any happier: women.

The gain in happiness lasts at least a couple of months, given that the tournaments are played in midsummer and the survey is carried out in the autumn. For World Cups, the gain was quite persistent: even two and four years after the tournament, every subgroup we looked at was still happier than before the tournament. European Championships, though, lifted happiness only briefly. We found no impact on happiness in the host country a year after the Euro.

But if people gain a lot of happiness after hosting a tournament, they lose a little happiness before it. The ritual fuss over whether the stadiums will be ready, whether English thugs will invade their country, whether their team will be made to look ridiculous etc, appears to cause stress. Six years and four years before hosting a tournament, many of the subgroups we studied showed a decline in happiness.

It turns out that hosting doesn't make you rich, but it does make you happy. This begs a question. If countries want to host football tournaments (and American cities want to host major-league teams) as part of their pursuit of happiness, why don't they just say so? Why bother clothing their arguments in bogus economics?

The answer is that it took politicians a long time to discover the language of happiness. Until very recently, European politicians talked mostly about money. Anything that served only to make people happy was derided with the contemptuous phrase 'feel-good factor', as if politics should be above such trivialities. Only on the political fringes did happiness get any play, such as in the Liberal Party Report of 1974: 'Once the basic needs of food and shelter are met, the individual's greatest satisfactions are to be found in love, trust and friendship, in beauty, art and music, and in learning, none of which are served by the mythology of growth for its own sake.'

However, nobody listened to the Liberals. Other politicians simply assumed that the real business of government was to make people richer. For one thing, measuring income was easier than measuring happiness. And so, when politicians argued for hosting tournaments, they typically used the language of money. It was almost the only vocabulary they had.

But it gradually became clear that in rich countries, more money didn't make people happier. Robert Kennedy was one of the first to see this, remarking in March 1968, three months before he was murdered, that gross domestic product 'measures everything ... except that which makes life worthwhile'.

Only in the last few years have many European politicians begun talking less about money and more about happiness. In Britain, the change is clear: Gordon Brown is an old-fashioned 'money' politician, whereas David Cameron is more of a new-fangled 'happiness' one. In a speech in 2006, Cameron tried to introduce the acronym 'GWB' – 'general well-being' – to counter the decades-old 'GDP' for gross domestic product.

He said, 'Improving our society's sense of well-being is, I believe, the central political challenge of our times ... Politics in Britain has too often sounded as though it was just about economic growth.' Instead, Cameron wanted politics 'to recognise the value of relationships with family, friends and the world around us'.

It seems that football tournaments create those relationships: people gathered together in pubs and living-rooms, a whole country suddenly caring about the same event. A World Cup is the sort of common project that otherwise barely exists in modern societies. We've seen that the mere fact of following a team in the World Cup deters some very isolated people from committing suicide. If playing in a tournament creates social cohesion, hosting one creates even more. The inhabitants of the host country – and certainly the men – come to feel more connected to everyone else around them. Moreover, hosting probably boosts the nation's self-esteem, and so makes people feel better about themselves.

Even politicians are made happy by hosting. Most of their work is frustrating. You try to get money to build, say, roads, but other politicians stop you. Even when you get the money, it's hard to build the roads because people pop up to object. It's the same with housing or foreign policy or recycling: being a politician is an endless tedious struggle with your enemies.

But it isn't when you want to host a sports tournament. Suddenly, everyone gets on board. While London was bidding for the Olympics, the rower Steve Redgrave pulled an Olympic gold medal out of his pocket during a meeting at the House of Commons, and MPs of all parties began drooling over him. Even going to war doesn't create that sort of unanimous sentiment any more.

The end of ideology – the disappearance of nationalism, socialism, religion, communism and Fascism from western Europe – has left many politicians with little better to do than to plug sports events using specious arguments. Ken Livingstone wrote when he was mayor of London: 'Crucially, the Olympics will also bring much-needed new facilities: an Olympic-size swimming pool in a city that has just two Olympic pools to Berlin's 19, and a warm-up track that would be turned over to community use.'

Plainly, arguments like these are just excuses. If you want to regenerate a poor neighbourhood, regenerate it. Build nice houses and a train line. If you want an Olympic pool and a warm-up track, build them. You could build pools and tracks all across London and it would still be cheaper than hosting the Olympics. The only good reason to host an Olympics is that it makes people happy. The politicians behind London's bid did not say so, because when the city was bidding in the early 2000s they hadn't yet discovered the politics of happiness. But they did sense that the voters would reward them for winning the Games.

The London Games may pay for themselves in terms of happiness. After all, in 2008 the monthly income of the third quartile of British earners was £1,033, while the top quartile earned £2,608. Based on past data, the increase in happiness from hosting could be as much as £1,575 per employee, or a staggering national total of £31 billion worth of happiness. The eight million Londoners, in particular, have the highest incomes in the European Union, and so would need to receive a fortune in tax rebates to buy the happiness that the Games could bring them.

Puritans might rightly argue that even a rich country like Britain has better things on which to spend money. However, the likely gain in happiness from the Olympics does mean the politicians are canny to give the people bread and circuses. In post-materialist countries like Britain, the maths of hosting and happiness probably stack up.

But it's much less likely that South Africa will get its money's worth in happiness from hosting the World Cup. This is still very much a sub-£11,000 country, where putting more money in people's pockets would make them happier. About a third of all South Africans live on less than $2 a day. These people need houses, electricity, holidays, doctors.

We already know that the World Cup won't make Sowetans richer. It's also questionable whether it's an efficient way to make them happier. At the last count, the ever-rising bill for the stadiums alone for the World Cup stood at nine billion rand (up from an initial estimate of two billion rand). Lungile Madywabe, who is writing a book about South African soccer, notes that for R9 billion you could build a quarter of a million houses for poor people. That is more than the South African government builds each year.

Driving out of Soweto, you see the pain in the advertisements painted on the roadside hoardings: 'Motaung Funeral Directors – We Salute the Spirit of Ubuntu!' There are also the '21st Century Funeral Brokers', or you can buy a 'rasta funeral'. Just outside town, you pass a flowerbed beside the roadside where the flowers form the shape of a number: '2010'. It's the year the Americans will land in aeroplanes and save everybody.

SECTION IV

THE COUNTRIES:
Rich and Poor, Tom Thumb, Ghiddink, Saddam,
and The Champions of the Future

THE CURSE
OF POVERTY:
WHY POOR
COUNTRIES ARE
POOR AT SPORT

When Didier Drogba was five, his parents put him on a plane in the Ivory Coast and sent him to live with an uncle in France. The six-hour flight, alone with his favourite toy, passed in a blur of tears and tissues.

About a decade later Drogba's father lost his job at a bank in the Ivory Coast, and the family moved to a suburb of Paris, where they were reunited with their exiled son. Eight Drogbas ended up living in a flat about 10 metres (33 feet) square. 'A very large wardrobe, really,' Drogba recalled in his autobiography. 'Hard. Very hard. Even enough to drive you crazy.' The flat was cold, and his little brothers were so noisy that he couldn't concentrate on his schoolwork. 'Luckily, my father had allowed me to start playing football again.'

There is a myth that poor people are somehow best equipped to make it as sportsmen. A cliché often used about them is that sport is their 'only escape route from poverty'. The poor, supposedly, are figuratively 'hungrier' than the rich. If they are black, like Drogba, they are sometimes thought to have greater genetic gifts than white people. And the evidence that poor people excel at sport seems to be in front of our eyes. England is not the only national football team dominated by players from lowly backgrounds. France since the 1990s have generally fielded a majority of non-white players, and few Brazilian internationals are sons of corporate lawyers either. Most of the world's best footballers started life poor: South Americans like Diego Maradona, who as a toddler almost drowned in a local cesspit, Africans like Samuel Eto'o, who appear to support hundreds of people back home, or European immigrants like Zlatan Ibrahimovic or Zinedine Zidane, who grew up in some of the toughest neighbourhoods on the continent. Drogba's childhood was only slightly more Dickensian than most. The origins of American basketball players and football players are mostly lowly too. The best preparation for sporting greatness seems to be a poor childhood.

And yet it is not. The facts show that the world's poor people and poor countries are worse at sport than rich ones. It is true that poorer immigrants in rich countries often excel at sport, but the reasons for that have nothing to do with skin colour or 'hunger'.

Let's look at poor countries first. The vast majority of countries on earth are firmly excluded from sporting success, simply because they are poor. This becomes apparent in a simple exercise to discover which country is the world's best at sport, and which country is best for its size.

To find the best countries, we combined the historical results from many major international sporting events: the summer and winter Olympics, World Cups in several sports, and the most popular individual sports. For some sports the data go back more than a century; for others, only a couple of decades. For all sports, we took 2006 as the end-point.

Our methodology is not perfect. We started with the men's World Cups in biggish sports that have seldom or never featured at the Olympics. We ranked the top five countries in these sports, based first on the number of world titles they won, and in case of ties, on finishes in the final four. We gave the best country in each sport five points, the second four, the third three, the fourth two, and the fifth one. There is no need to read the rankings for every sport, but here are the detailed points tallies for those who are interested:

RUGBY UNION: TOP 5 COUNTRIES

1	Australia	5	4	South Africa	2
2	New Zealand	4	5	France	1
3	England	3			

KARATE (ONLY COUNTING TEAM EVENTS): TOP 5 COUNTRIES

1	Japan	5	4	Spain	2
2	France	4	5	Italy and Turkey	1 each
3	England	3			

CRICKET: TOP 5 COUNTRIES

1	Australia	5	4	Pakistan	2
2	West Indies	4	5	Sri Lanka	1
3	India	3			

Baseball was trickier. Historically the US dominates the sport. However, it traditionally sends amateurs or minor-leaguers to the World Cup. The US ranks only third all-time in the tournament. But we used our judgement to rank it as the world's best country in baseball, producing this ranking:

BASEBALL: TOP 5 COUNTRIES

1	US	5	4	Colombia	2
2	Cuba	4	5	South Korea	1
3	Venezuela	3			

Basketball is an Olympic event. However, as the world's second-most popular team game it deserves additional input in this quest. We therefore added the results of the basketball World Cup. Again the US rarely fielded its best players, and historically ranks second behind Yugoslavia. But using common sense we placed the US first here too, producing this ranking:

BASKETBALL: TOP 5 COUNTRIES

1	US	5		4	Brazil	2
2	Yugoslavia	4		5	Argentina	1
3	USSR	3				

Favouring the US in baseball and basketball did not affect the outcome of our quest.

The only women's World Cup we counted was soccer. Women's soccer is an Olympic event too, but far more popular than most other women's team games, and therefore it seemed to merit more input. The rankings for women's football:

WOMEN'S FOOTBALL: TOP 5 COUNTRIES

1	US	5		4	Sweden	2
2	Norway and Germany 4 each			5	China	1

We also assessed popular individual sports that are seldom or never represented in the Olympics. We rewarded countries for triumphs by their citizens. In tennis we counted men's and women's Grand Slam tournaments – tennis being a rare sport in that it is played widely by women. We only used results from the 'open era' starting in 1968, when tennis became very competitive.

MEN'S TENNIS: TOP 5 COUNTRIES

1	US	5		4	Czechoslovakia	2
2	Sweden	4		5	Spain and Switzerland 1 each	
3	Australia	3				

WOMEN'S TENNIS: TOP 5 COUNTRIES

1	US	5	4	Yugoslavia	2
2	Germany	4	5	France	1
3	Australia	3			

In golf we used the results of the men's majors:

GOLF: TOP 5 COUNTRIES

1	US	5	3	South Africa	3
2	Britain (including all four home countries)	4	4	Australia	2
			5	Spain	1

In chess we ranked countries by the number of years that they provided the world champion:

CHESS: TOP 5 COUNTRIES

1	USSR/Russia	5	4	US	2
2	Germany	4	5	Cuba	1
3	France	3			

In cycling we counted victories by citizens of each country in the Tour de France, a more prestigious event than the world championship:

CYCLING: TOP 5 COUNTRIES

1	France	5	4	Italy	2
2	Belgium	4	5	Spain	1
3	US	3			

In motor racing we chose the most prestigious competition, Formula I, thus discriminating against the US, which prefers its own races. Again, we counted world championships by citizenship. The rankings:

MOTOR RACING: TOP 5 COUNTRIES

1	Britain	5	4	Argentina	2
2	Brazil	4	5	France, Australia and Austria	1 each
3	Germany	3			

We did not include the World Cups of popular sports like volleyball and ice-hockey, because these are Olympic sports, and so we will assess them through their role in the Olympics' all-time medals table. Boxing was too hard to assess as there are various rival 'world championships'. We also excluded the athletics World Cup. Athletics is copiously represented at the Olympics, and for most of the history of its World Cup, the entrants have been entire continents rather than single countries.

Clearly the summer and winter Games deserve to carry more weight in our quest than any single World Cup. In the summer Olympics of 2004, medals were awarded in 28 sports. Many of these, such as archery or kayaking, are played by very few people. Still, because of the event's profusion of sports and its prestige, we gave the summer Games 10 times the weighting of World Cups in individual sports. So we gave the top country in the all-time medals table 50 points, rather than five points for a single World Cup. Because the whole planet competes in the Olympics – unlike say in baseball or cricket – we rewarded the top 10 rather than five countries in the all-time medals table. The ranking:

SUMMER OLYMPICS: TOP 10 COUNTRIES

1	US	50	6	Hungary	8
2	USSR/Russia	40	7	East Germany	6
3	Britain	30	8	Germany	4
4	France	20	9	Sweden	2
5	Italy	10	10	Australia	1

We gave the winter Olympics three times the weighting of a World Cup. Because few countries play winter sports, we rewarded only the top five in the all-time medals table:

WINTER OLYMPICS: TOP 5 COUNTRIES

1	Norway	15	4	Germany	6
2	US	12	5	Austria	3
3	USSR/Russia	9			

Finally, the football World Cup. Football is an Olympic sport, but it is also the planet's most popular game. We gave its World Cup six times the weighting of World Cups in other sports, and rewarded the top 10 countries in the all-time points table. The ranking:

FOOTBALL WORLD CUP: TOP 10 COUNTRIES

1	Brazil	30	6	France	5
2	Germany	24	7	Spain	4
3	Italy	18	8	Sweden	3
4	Argentina	12	9	Netherlands	2
5	England	6	10	Russia/USSR	1

We then totted up all the points. Here is our top 20 of best sporting countries on earth:

TOTAL POINTS ACROSS ALL SPORTS AND OVERALL RANKING

1	US	92	10	Argentina	15
2	USSR/Russia	58	11	Sweden	11
3	Britain	51	12	Spain	9
4	Germany	45	13	Hungary	8
5	France	40	14	East Germany and Yugoslavia	6
6	Brazil	36			
7	Italy	31	16	South Africa, Japan and Cuba	5
8	Australia	20			
9	Norway	19	19	New Zealand, Austria and Belgium	4

The winner, the US, deserves particular praise given that we omitted two of its favourite sports, American football and NASCAR racing, because nobody else plays them. The USSR/Russia in second place can be slightly less pleased with itself, because it won most of its points when it was still a multinational empire. Third place for Britain/England shows that the country has punched above its weight, though more so in the distant past than recently. Germany, in fourth place, is a dangerous sleeper. If we credit the united country with East Germany's Olympic medals (and forget all the male growth hormones that went into winning them), then Germany jumps to second place overall with 77 points.

Australia in eighth place did brilliantly given that we ignored its prowess at Australian rules football and rugby league. Brazil was the best developing country, and would have been even if it didn't play football, thanks to its successful diversification into basketball and Formula One. India (1.1 billion inhabitants, 3 points for cricket) and China (1.3 billion, 1 point for women's football) were the biggest flops per capita.

But which country is world champion per capita? To find out, we worked out how many points each country scored per million inhabitants. That produced this top 10 of overperformers:

TOTALS

#	Country	Points
1	Norway	4
2	Sweden	1.22
3	Australia	0.98
4	New Zealand	0.97
5	United Germany (including the GDR's Olympic medals)	0.94
6	Britain/England	0.85
7	Hungary	0.8
8	West Indies*	0.77
9	France	0.67
10	Italy	0.54

* Or the nations that together supply almost all West Indian cricketers, namely Jamaica, Trinidad and Tobago, Guyana, Barbados and Antigua.

Heia Norge, again. The country that we have already crowned as the most football-mad in Europe now turns out to be the best per capita at sport. Norway's lead is so large that it would most probably have won our sporting Tom Thumb trophy even with a different scoring system; even, say, if we had valued the winter Olympics only as much as a cricket or baseball World Cup. This is a country where at a state kindergarten in suburban Oslo in mid-afternoon, among the throng of mothers picking up their toddlers, someone pointed out to us an anonymous mum who happened to be an Olympic gold medallist in cross-country skiing. Norway won more points in our competition than all of Africa and Asia (excluding Oceania) put together. We could even have omitted the winter Olympics – almost a Norwegian fiefdom – and the country would still have made the top five of our efficiency table thanks to its prowess at women's football.

But the main thing the top of our rankings demonstrates is the importance of wealth. Our efficiency table for sport bears a curious resemblance to another global ranking: the United Nations' human development index. This measures life expectancy, literacy, education and living standards to rank the countries of the world according to their well-being. We found that a nation's well-being is closely correlated with its success in sport. Which country is top of the UN's human development index for 2008 (based on data for 2006)? *Heia Norge,* again.

Joint first in the index with Norway was Iceland, though the country that turned itself into a hedge fund and then blew itself up may have slipped a little since. Iceland, with only 300,000 inhabitants, was never going to win any of our sporting points. But Sweden was second in the world for sports and seventh for human development. And the fourth country in the UN's human development index, Australia, was our sporting number three. In all, eight of the countries in our sporting top ten were also among the UN's twenty-three most developed countries on earth. The only poorer nations that snuck into our sporting top 10 were Hungary (with its vast Olympic programme under communism) and the West Indian nations. However, even these poor cousins were all classified by the UN as 'highly developed' countries except for Jamaica and Guyana, whose development was 'medium'. Generally, the most developed countries also tend to be best at sport.

The case of Norway shows why. It's Norwegian government policy that every farmer, every fisherman, no matter where he lives in the country, has the right to play sport. And Norway will spend what it takes to achieve that. Just as supermarkets have sprouted all over Britain, there are all-weather sports grounds everywhere in Norway. Even in the unlikeliest corners of the country there's generally one around the corner from your house. Usually the changing-rooms are warm and the coaches have acquired some sort of diploma. A kid can play and train in a proper team for well under £100 a year, really not much for most Norwegians. Almost everyone in the country plays something. Professor Knut Helland of Bergen University, who has written a book on Norwegian sport and media, notes that Norway has the biggest ski race in the world with about 13,000 participants. 'I'm taking part in it myself,' he adds. When the European Commission studied time use in European countries in 2004, it found that the Norwegians spent the most time playing sport: on average, a whopping 13 minutes a day. People all over the world might want to play sport, but to make that possible requires money and organisation that poor countries don't have.

In short, poor countries are generally poorer at sport. It's no coincidence that China won nothing at sport before its economy took off, and that it topped the medals table at the Beijing Olympics afterwards. Most African countries barely even try to compete in any sports other than football and a few track events. And the best place to find out why the world's poor do worse than the world's rich is South Africa, where some very poor and very rich neighbourhoods are almost side by side, separated only by a highway or a golf course.

South Africa is the one African country to score any points at all in our sporting table. Yet it owes almost all those points to an ethnic group that makes up less than 10 per cent of the country's inhabitants: white people.

Only about 4.3 million of the 48 million South Africans are white. Nonetheless, whites accounted for 14 of the 15 players in the Springbok rugby team that won the World Cup in 1995, and 13 of the 15 that won it in 2007, as well as all five South African golfers who have won majors and all the country's best cricketers. If we treated white South Africa as a separate country, then their five sporting points would have put them in third place in the world in our sporting efficiency table. That is entirely predictable. South African whites were nurtured under apartheid on almost all the resources of the country.

The national teams of South African whites now dominate their respective sports. At the time of writing, the country's mostly white cricket team is ranked second in the world, while the mostly white Springbok rugby team are world champions. Non-white South Africa's national team does less well. As we write the 'Bafana Bafana' football team, sometimes known at home as the 'Banana Banana', are 77th in FIFA's rankings, several spots behind Wales and Cyprus.

Here are five vignettes to explain why black South Africa and other poor nations fail at sport:

YOU ARE WHAT YOU EAT

JOHANNESBURG

Steven Pienaar, Everton's South African midfielder, has the frame of a prepubescent boy. There's hardly a European footballer as reedy as he is. But in South African football his body type is common. Frank Eulberg, a German who spent about five minutes as assistant coach of the Kaizer Chiefs, South Africa's best team, says that when he arrived at the club, 16 of the players were shorter than 1.75 metres (5ft 9in). 'I sometimes thought, "Frank, you're in the land of the dwarves."'

Most likely, Pienaar is reedy because he grew up malnourished and without much access to doctors. He was born in a poor Coloured township in 1982, at the height of apartheid, when almost all money and healthcare went to whites. Growing tall is not just a matter of what you eat; when children become ill, their growth is interrupted, and because poor children tend to get ill more often than rich ones, they usually end up shorter.

Most of the players who will represent South Africa in 2010 were born in non-white townships in the 1980s. And so the ghost of apartheid will bug the Bafana at the World Cup. One reason South Africans are so bad at football is that most of them didn't get enough good food.

Apartheid, based on the bogus ideology that races are different, ended up creating white, black, 'Coloured' and Indian South Africans who really were like separate peoples. The whites on average tower over the blacks. No wonder the cricket and rugby teams are so much better than the Bafana. 'Well, they have their moments,' laughs Demitri Constantinou.

This descendant of Greek immigrants, an exercise scientist at Wits University in Johannesburg, directs FIFA's first medical centre of excellence in Africa. When we met, he was running a project with the South African Football Association to help develop young footballers. Constantinou's team tested the health of all the players selected for SAFA's programme. In a Woolworths tearoom in one of Johannesburg's posh northern suburbs, among white ladies having afternoon tea, he says, 'The biggest issue was nutrition.' Is malnutrition one reason why African teams perform poorly at World Cups? 'I think yes. And I think it has been overlooked as a possible cause.'

Hardly any players in the latter stages of the World Cup of 2006 were shorter than about 1.73 metres (5ft 8in), Constantinou notes. 'There is a minimum height.' If a large proportion of your male population was below that height, you were picking your team from a reduced pool. Conversely, though he didn't say it, one reason that Norway and Sweden (two of the three tallest countries in the world) excel at sport is that almost all their male inhabitants are tall enough. They are picking their teams from a full pool.

A BEAST INTO A TOOTHPICK

CAPE TOWN

George Dearnaley is a big ruddy white man who looks like a rugby player, but in fact he was once the Bafana's promising young centre-forward. Dearnaley never got beyond promising, because when he was in his early twenties his knee went. He didn't mind much. He spoke a bit of Zulu, and had studied literature and journalism at college in Toledo, Ohio, and so he joined the football magazine *Kick Off*. Now he is its publisher as well as the author of an excellent column.

Over an English breakfast in a Cape Town greasy-spoon near the *Kick Off* offices, Dearnaley reflected on the Amazulu team in Durban where his career peaked. Seven of his teammates from the Amazulu side of 1992 were now dead, out of a squad of about 24. Dearnaley said: 'One guy died when his house exploded, so that was probably a taxi war or something. But the rest must have been AIDS. One player, a Durban newspaper said he was bewitched. A six foot four [1.93m] beast of a man, who was suddenly whittled down to a toothpick.'

Constantinou says it's quite possible that a fifth of the Bafana's potential pool of players for 2010 carries the HIV virus. How many South Africans who could have played in 2010 will be dead instead?

THE DARK SIDE OF THE MOON
SANDTON, JUST OUTSIDE JOHANNESBURG

It is quite a step for Danny Jordaan to be organising a World Cup, because until he was 38 he had never even seen one.

The chief executive officer of the FIFA World Cup 2010 grew up a million miles from the world's best football. Being in South Africa under apartheid was not quite like being on the moon, or being in North Korea, but it was almost as isolated. South Africa was the last industrialised country to get television, in 1976, because the white government was afraid of the device. Even after that hardly any blacks had TV sets, and FIFA did not allow its World Cup to be broadcast in the apartheid state. So the first time Jordaan saw a World Cup on television was in 1990.

The country's isolation continued even after that. As far as most South Africans were concerned, international football still might as well have been happening on Mars. Jordaan says, 'South Africans played on their own. We thought we were so smart. That's why when we played our first competitive match against Zimbabwe [in 1992], every South African knew we were going to hammer Zimbabwe. But Zimbabwe had this little player called Peter Ndlovu. Nobody knew Peter Ndlovu. By half-time it was 3–0 for them. That was the first entry into international football. That really shook this country.'

As late as 1998, when South Africa entered its first World Cup, large swathes of the population assumed that the Bafana would win it. After all, everyone knew that their native style of 'tsamayas and shoeshine' – essentially, doing tricks on the ball while standing around – was just like Brazilian football but better. The Bafana did not win the World Cup.

Black South Africa was isolated twice over: first by sanctions, then by poverty. However, isolation – a distance from the networks of the world's best football – is the fate of most poor countries. Their citizens can't easily travel to Italy or Germany and see how football is played there, let alone talk to the best coaches. Some can't even see foreign football on television, because they don't have a television. And only a couple of the very best players in these countries ever make it to the best leagues in the world.

One reason why poor countries do badly at sport – and one reason why they are poor – is that they tend to be less 'networked', less connected to other countries, than rich ones. It is hard for them just to find out the latest best practice on how to play a sport.

Playing for national teams in Africa hardly lifts the isolation much. Most poor, isolated African countries compete only against other poor, isolated African countries. At best, they might encounter the world's best once every four years at a World Cup. No wonder they have little idea of what top-class football is like.

'THE ORGANISERS. IT'S THE BIGGEST PROBLEM'

LONDON

For mysterious reasons, someone decided that the Bafana should play their annual charity match, the Nelson Mandela Challenge, not in the magnificent 78,000-seat FNB Stadium just outside Johannesburg, but more than 8,000 kilometres (5,000 miles) away at Brentford's Griffin Park.

On a grey November London afternoon the day before the game, the Bafana were in their grey-coloured three-star hotel on the outskirts of Heathrow Airport. In the lobby were flight crews, travelling salesmen and cheery men in green-and-yellow tracksuits hanging with their entourage: the Bafana Bafana. Their opponents, the Egyptians, who were also staying in the hotel, had congregated in the bar. Apparently Egypt were furious. They had been promised a five-star hotel, and a match fee that had yet to materialise.

Pitso Mosimane, the Bafana's caretaker manager – a big, bald, bullet-headed man – was also hanging around the lobby. Mosimane complained that African coaches never got jobs in Europe.

He gestured towards the bar: 'The coach of Egypt, who won the African Cup of Nations. Don't you think he could at least coach a team in the English first division?' Then Mosimane went off for pre-match training at Griffin Park.

Minutes later he was back at table. 'That was quick,' someone remarked. 'No, we didn't train!' Mosimane said. Nobody had bothered telling Brentford the Bafana were coming, and so the field wasn't ready for them. Now they would have to play the African champions without having trained on the pitch. 'And I'm carrying players who play for Blackburn Rovers and Borussia Dortmund, and you know? We're laughing about it.' Mosimane jerked a thumb towards four men in suits drinking at the next table: 'The organisers. It's the biggest problem. This wouldn't happen with any other national team.'

He was wrong. Organisational mishaps are always happening to national teams from poor countries. Senegal, for instance, clean forgot to enter the World Cup of 1994. In most sub-Sahara African national teams that do make it to a World Cup, players and officials have a ritual dispute over pay about a week before the tournament. In 2002 Cameroon's dispute got out of hand, whereupon the squad made a brief aeroplane odyssey through Ethiopia, India and Thailand before finally landing in Japan four days late. Jetlagged and confused, they were knocked out in the first round. In 2006 Togo's players spent much of their brief stay at the country's first ever World Cup threatening to go on strike because of their pay dispute. They worried that after the tournament was over, Togo's federation might never get around to paying them. Eventually FIFA sidestepped the federation, paid the players' bonuses directly, and told them to play or else, but it is little wonder that the team lost three matches out of three.

To win at sport, you need to find, develop and nurture talent. Doing that requires money, know-how and some kind of administrative infrastructure. Few African countries have enough of any of them.

'COLOURED' BEATS 'BLACK'

THE CAPE FLATS

If you stand on Table Mountain at night and look down at Cape Town, you will see a city of lights. Next to the lights are the railway tracks. And on the far side of the tracks are 'black spots': Coloured townships without lights. These are the rainy, murderous Cape Flats, where most of South Africa's best footballers grew up.

Benni McCarthy of Blackburn comes from the Cape Flats. So does his old mate Quinton Fortune, for years a loyal reserve at Manchester United. So does Shaun Bartlett, formerly of Charlton, the most capped player in South African history.

The key point is that according to the racial classifications of apartheid, still tacitly used by South Africans today, none of these players is 'black'. They are 'Coloured': a group of generally lighter-skinned people, mostly derived from the lighter African tribes of the Cape, though some descend from Asian slaves and mixed white–black liaisons. Less than 10 per cent of South Africans are Coloured, while about three quarters are black. However, Coloureds often make up as much as half the Bafana side. Pienaar and the striker Delron Buckley, for instance, are from Coloured townships in other parts of South Africa. This density of Coloured talent is a legacy of apartheid.

Under apartheid, the Coloureds were slightly better off than the blacks. They had more to eat, and more opportunities to organise themselves. In the Coloured Cape Flats, for instance, there were amateur football clubs with proper coaches such as you might find in Europe. Not so in black townships, where a boys' team would typically be run by a local gangster or the shebeen owner, who seldom bothered much with training.

At the World Cup of 2010, to the irritation of many South African blacks, the Bafana will still be a largely 'Coloured' team. The blacks are simply too poor to compete within their own country, let alone with Europeans. Even in the simplest game, the poor are excluded by malnutrition, disease and disorganisation.

That leaves one thing unexplained. Why is it that so many of the best European footballers – Zidane, Drogba (officially an Ivorian but raised in France), Ibrahimovic, Wayne Rooney, Cristiano Ronaldo – come from the poorest neighbourhoods in Europe?

It cannot be that boys from the ghetto have an unquenchable hunger to succeed. If that were so, they would do better at school and in jobs outside football. There must something about their childhood that makes them particularly well suited to football. That reason is practice.

Malcolm Gladwell, in his book *Outliers: The Story of Success*, advanced the '10,000-hour rule'. This is a notion from psychology, which says that to achieve expertise in any field you need at least 10,000 hours of practice. 'In study after study, of composers, basketball players, fiction writers, ice-skaters, concert pianists, chess players, master criminals,' says the neurologist Daniel Levitin in *Outliers,* 'this number comes up again and again … No one has yet found a case in which true world-class expertise was accomplished in less time.'

In football, it is the poorest European boys who are most likely to reach the 10,000-hour mark. They tend to live in small apartments, which forces them to spend time outdoors. There they meet a ready supply of local boys equally keen to get out of their apartments and play football. Their parents are less likely than middle-class parents to force them to waste precious time doing homework. And they have less money for other leisure pursuits. A constant in footballers' ghosted autobiographies is the monomaniac childhood spent playing non-stop football and, in a classic story, sleeping with a ball. Here for instance is Nourdin Boukhari, a Dutch-Moroccan footballer who grew up in an immigrant neighbourhood of Rotterdam, recalling his childhood for a Dutch magazine:

I grew up in a family of eight children … There was no chance of pocket money … I lived more on the street than at home … And look at Robin van Persie, Mounir El Hamdaoui and Said Boutahar. And I'm forgetting Youssef El-Akchaoui. [Like the other players Boukhari mentions, El-Akchaoui is a current professional footballer.] Those boys and I played on the street in Rotterdam together. We never forget where we came from and that we used to have nothing except for one thing: the ball.

… What we have in common is that we were on the street every minute playing football, day and night. We were always busy, games, juggling, shooting at the crossbar. The ball was everything for me, for us. We'd meet on squares …'

By the time these boys were 15, they were much better players than suburban kids. The 10,000-hour rule also explains why blacks raised in American ghettoes are over-represented in basketball and American football.

But it would be misleading to say these European footballers grew up 'poor'. By global standards, they were rich. Even in Cristiano Ronaldo's Madeira, Rooney's Croxteth or Zidane's La Castellane, children generally got enough to eat and decent medical care. It is true that Cristiano Ronaldo grew up in a house so small that they kept the washing machine on the roof; but in black South Africa, that washing machine would have marked the family out as rich. Beside the 10,000-hour rule, there is another rule that explains sporting success: the 15,000-dollar rule. That's the minimum average income per person that a country needs to win anything. There is only one way around this: be Brazil.

TOM THUMB: THE BEST LITTLE FOOTBALL COUNTRY ON EARTH

In 1970, when Brazil won their third World Cup, they got to keep the Jules Rimet trophy. The little statuette of Nike, then still known as the Greek goddess of victory, ended up in a glass case in the Brazilian federation's offices in Rio de Janeiro. One night in 1983 the trophy was stolen, and was never seen again.

However, the point is that everyone agrees that Brazil deserves the Jules Rimet trophy. The five-fold world champions are undoubtedly the best country in football history. Our question here is a different one: which country is best taking into account its population, experience and income per capita? If Brazil are the absolute world champions, who are the relative ones, the biggest overperformers? That overachieving country deserves its own version of the Jules Rimet trophy – call it the Tom Thumb. And which countries are the worst underachievers relative to their resources? Along the way we will have to consider several impressive candidates and make some judgement calls before coming up with our winner and loser.

* * *

First of all, if we are dealing with statistics, we have to construct our arguments on the basis of large numbers of games played. There have only been 18 World Cups, and most of these involved hardly any countries from outside Europe and Latin America. So crunching the numbers from World Cups might at best tell us something about the pecking-order among the long-established large football nations. But when the difference between, say, Argentina's two victories and England's one comes down to as little as the hand of God, or the difference between Italy's four and France's one to a pre-match pep talk given by Benito Mussolini to the referee in 1934 and a comment by Marco Materazzi about Zidane's parentage in 2006, then the statistician needs to look elsewhere.

Happily, since national teams play a lot of games, we have plenty of data. As in chapter 2, we will rely on the remarkable database of 22,130 matches accumulated by the maths professor Russell Gerrard.

The number of international matches has soared over time. Between the foundation of FIFA in 1904 and the First World War the number rose quickly to 50 per year. After 1918, growth resumed. By the eve of the Second World War, there were more than 100 international matches a year. But this was still a world dominated by colonial powers, and only with the independence movement after the war did international competition mushroom. In 1947 there were 107 international matches; by 1957 there were 203; by 1967, 308. Few new countries were founded in the next two decades, but the number of international matches continued to rise thanks to the jet plane, which made travel less of a pain and more financially worthwhile. In 1977 there were 368 international matches; in 1987 there were 393. At that point the world seemed to have reached some sort of stable equilibrium.

But then the Soviet Union broke up into 15 separate states, and Yugoslavia collapsed. The new countries flocked into FIFA. At the same time the commercial development of football meant that cash-hungry national associations were keen to play lucrative friendlies. In 1997 there were 850 international games, more than double the figure of a decade before.

If we concentrate on just the last 20 years or so of Russell's database, from 1980 to 2001, a list of the most successful teams features the usual suspects. Let's rank the top 10 countries by the percentage of games won, or, given that around one third of matches are draws, by the 'win percentage' statistic calculated by valuing a draw as worth half a win.

TOP 10 NATIONAL TEAMS BY WIN PERCENTAGE, ALL GAMES 1980–2001

	Team	Played	Won	Draws	Win %	Goal diff
1	Brazil	285	0.625	0.235	0.742	1.29
2	Germany (united)	128	0.609	0.219	0.719	0.97
3	France	188	0.590	0.239	0.710	0.98
4	Italy	203	0.557	0.276	0.695	0.78
5	Iraq	146	0.548	0.288	0.692	1.13
6	Czech Republic	83	0.554	0.217	0.663	0.88
7	Yugoslavia (Serbia & Montenegro)	65	0.523	0.277	0.662	0.78
8	Spain	198	0.520	0.273	0.657	0.88
9	West Germany	102	0.520	0.265	0.652	0.76
10	England	228	0.491	0.320	0.651	0.84

The top four is exactly as you would expect. Even in a 22-year period when Brazil won just one World Cup and tried to reinvent their national style of football, their 'win percentage' was almost 75 per cent. That equates to bookmakers' odds of 3–1 on, or about as close as you can get to a sure thing in a two-horse race.

Strangely, the old West Germany appears only near the bottom of the top 10, alongside England with a 'win percentage' of around 65 per cent. Moreover, England's average goal difference was actually slightly higher than West Germany's. It's just that West Germany had a knack of winning the matches that counted.

Only when we get down to fifth place do we find our first big surprise: Saddam Hussein's Iraq. This was the sole country other than Brazil in this period to win its matches by an average of more than a goal a game. Of course, the Iraqis' presence illustrates the problem of ranking national teams in the absence of a league format. It is hard to imagine that they would have done all that well against the other teams in the top 10. In fact they did not meet any of them in full internationals during this period (Saddam's boys didn't get many invitations to friendlies at Wembley). Mostly, Iraq beat Middle Eastern and other Asian countries.

Yet whatever their route to the top 10, getting there was some achievement. The years from 1980 to 2001 – wars, massacres, sanctions, Saddam – were not happy ones for Iraq. Nonetheless, the country produced a 'golden generation' of footballers.

It did so under the thumb of the ruling family, which loved sports. Each April Baghdad celebrated Saddam's birthday by hosting the 'Saddam Olympics'. You may not have caught these on Sky, but as late as 2002, with Baghdad's Russian–Iraqi Friendship Society as sponsor, they attracted athletes from 72 countries. And not many people know that Baghdad was also bidding to host the real Olympics in 2012 before events intervened.

Saddam left control of the football team to his bestial son Uday. A playboy and pervert, paralysed from the waist down in an assassination attempt, Uday motivated his players by threatening to amputate their legs if they lost. One former international reported being beaten on the soles of his feet, dragged on his bare back through gravel, and then dipped in raw sewage so that his wounds would be infected. Some players spent time in Abu Ghraib prison. After Kuwait came to Baghdad in 1981 and won, one of the ruling family's helpers beat up the referee, who was then 'driven hurriedly to the airport and put bleeding on a plane out of the country,' writes Declan Hill in his book on global match-fixing, *The Fix*.

Stories like these from Iraqi defectors prompted FIFA to send a committee to Iraq to investigate. The Iraqis produced players and coaches who swore blind that it was all lies. FIFA believed them, and so the Lions of Mesopotamia were allowed to keep on collecting prizes.

Only when American troops entered Baghdad in 2003 did they find the prison Uday maintained in the basement of Iraq's Olympic headquarters. It featured 'a rack and a medieval torture device used to rip open a man's anus,' writes James Montague in his *When Friday Comes: Football in the War Zone.*

But despite everything, under Saddam the Lions of Mesopotamia were the strongest team in the world's largest continent. Though they had to play on neutral ground for much of Saddam's reign due to the war with Iran, they qualified for the World Cup of 1986 and for three Olympics. They won the 1982 Asian Games, four Arab Nations Cups, three Gulf Cups of Nations, and the 1985 Pan Arab Games despite fielding a B team. As their fans used to chant (often while firing bullets into the air): 'Here we are Sunni – yah! Here we are Shiite – yah! Bring us happiness, sons of Iraq!' Even Kurds supported the Lions. Montague calls the team 'arguably the last symbol of national unity left in Iraq'. Only in the 1990s, as Saddam's regime became even more isolated and brutal, did Iraqi football decline.

All this may be a case of people immersing themselves in football because it was their only form of public expression. Huthyfa Zahra, an Iraqi artist who now produces football-themed 'pop art' from the safety of nearby Abu Dhabi, says, 'Even during the wars, in the Nineties, there were bombs above us, and we were playing in the streets. Because we didn't have anything to do.'

Why were the Lions so good under Saddam? Zahra is surprised to hear that they were. 'We are much better now,' he replies. 'Because the players play without fear now. If you don't feel comfortable, you can't play.' He points out that since the fall of Saddam and Uday, Iraq's Lions have finished fourth in the Athens

Olympics and won the Asian Cup of 2007. If Iraq ever becomes a halfway normal country, then watch out Brazil.

Also in our top 10 of most successful football countries, the new Czech and Serbian Republics inherited proud footballing traditions. Even so, their performances are remarkable: each country has only about 10 million inhabitants, compared to the 40–80 million of the large European nations and Brazil's 178 million.

Some readers may be surprised to see Spain and England complete the top 10, given that both countries are often described as 'notorious underachievers' – meaning that they don't win as many championships as the very best teams.

Pace Brazil and Iraq, one thing the table tells us is that Europeans dominate world football. The continent has eight countries in the top 10. The most obvious explanation for that is tradition: European nations are generally older, and have played international football for longer, than the rest of the world. It may also help that control of global football has largely remained in Europe. FIFA makes the rules of the game from a posh suburb of Zurich, and although western Europe has only 6 per cent of the world's population, it has hosted ten out of 18 World Cups.

But tradition does not in itself secure dominance. If it did, then British companies would still dominate industries like textiles, shipbuilding and car making. Dominance is transitory unless producers have the resources to stay ahead of the competition. The key resource in football is talent. Generally speaking the more populous countries are more likely to have the largest supply of talented people. We have also seen that rich countries are best at finding, training and developing talent. In short, it takes experience, population and wealth to make a successful football nation.

The easy bit is recognising this. The hard work is assembling the data to answer our question: which countries do best relative to their resources of experience, population and wealth?

Thankfully, Russell's data can help us with the issue of experience. He has a complete list of every single international game in history. With it, we can measure the cumulative number of games a country had played up to any given date. Sweden is the most experienced nation in football, with 802 internationals played up to 2001, while England had played 790, Argentina 770, Hungary 752, Brazil 715 and Germany (including West but not East Germany) 713. Pedants might dispute some of these numbers – identifying international games is often a judgement call if we go back more than 50 years, when arrangements could be quite informal – but even if these figures were off by 5 per cent, it wouldn't significantly affect the statistical analysis.

We also have data on each country's income. The measure typically used is gross domestic product. GDP is the total value of all goods and services bought and sold within an economy. (It includes imports and exports, but excludes income from assets owned overseas and profits repatriated to foreign countries.) The best source for GDP figures is the Penn World Tables, produced by the Center for International Comparisons at the University of Pennsylvania. The Center has estimates of GDP for 188 countries between 1950 and 2004. To measure the economic resources available to each person, it divides GDP by population. Admittedly there are all sorts of finicky issues involved in making comparisons across countries and across time, not to mention worries about measurement error and statistical reliability. Nonetheless, these data are the best we've got.

Now we run the multiple regressions we described in chapter 2. Our aim is to find the connection between goal difference per game and our three key inputs – population, wealth and experience – while also allowing for home advantage.

After all these pyrotechnics, we can make another ranking. But this time, we can compensate all the world's national teams for that trio of factors beyond their control: experience, population and income per head.

Oddly, if we rank every team no matter how few international matches they have played, it is the 'Stans' of central Asia that emerge as the world's leading overperformers relative to their experience, income and populations. Uzbekistan, Tajikistan, Turkmenistan and Kazakhstan all feature in our first draft of a top 10 of overachieving countries. All the Stans are poor in experience and income, while Tajikistan and Turkmenistan are short of inhabitants too. Most of the Stans have a negative goal difference, but they do not lose as badly as they had reason to fear. Even so, their high rankings feel counterintuitive: name five great Uzbek footballers. The fact is that these countries do well not because they are particularly good at football but because they have exploited a geographical loophole.

When the 'Stans' were still Soviet republics, they were a part – albeit a distant part – of European football. Their clubs played in Soviet leagues, and their best players dreamt of playing in all-Soviet 'national' teams for their age groups. That means their benchmark was Europe, where the world's best football was played. They were learning football in the top school. They became pretty decent at it.

Then, after the Soviet Union broke up, the 'Stans' joined the Asian Football Confederation. (Kazakhstan switched to UEFA only in 2002, after the period covered by our database.) Suddenly they could flaunt their European know-how against much weaker Asian countries. Of course they did well. But the 'Stans' have played too few matches to accumulate much of a sample size. Here we will concentrate on the teams that play more often. Below is our 'efficiency table' of the 10 best countries in the world relative to their resources, including only those that played over 100 games in the period:

TOP 10 NATIONAL TEAMS IN THE WORLD ALLOWING FOR POPULATION, WEALTH AND EXPERIENCE, ALL GAMES 1980–2001 (TEAMS PLAYING MORE THAN 100 GAMES)

	Team	Played	Won	Goal Draws	Over-Win %	diff	performance
1	Honduras	167	0.491	0.275	0.629	0.84	0.978
2	Iraq	146	0.548	0.288	0.692	1.13	0.882
3	Syria	104	0.375	0.269	0.510	0.54	0.852
4	Iran	163	0.515	0.264	0.647	1.10	0.730
5	New Zealand	124	0.379	0.210	0.484	0.37	0.691
6	South Africa	111	0.450	0.261	0.581	0.23	0.673
7	Brazil	285	0.625	0.235	0.742	1.29	0.665
8	Spain	198	0.520	0.273	0.657	0.88	0.585
9	Australia	162	0.475	0.235	0.593	0.90	0.569
10	Irish Republic	172	0.395	0.308	0.549	0.34	0.547

The final column of the table is the one to notice. It shows what you might call each country's 'outperformance', the gap between the goal difference they 'should' have achieved against opponents given their national resources and experience and what they actually did achieve (listed in the penultimate column). Honduras, the most overachieving country in football according to this table, score 0.978 goals per game more than you would have expected judging by their resources. All our top 10 scored on average between half and one goal per game more than their resources would predict. Of our original 'absolute' top 10, only Iraq, Brazil and Spain survive in this 'relative' top 10. It turns out that 'notorious underachievers' Spain have in fact long been over-achievers. Everyone instinctively benchmarks the Spanish team against Germany, Italy and France, but that is unfair. Spain is a much smaller country, and though its economy has been catching up fast, it's still significantly poorer. Consider for instance Spain's record against Italy in these 22 years. Over the period Spain's population, income per head and international experience was on average about 30 per cent inferior to Italy's. Given that, we would have expected Spain's goal difference to be about minus two over its four games against Italy. Instead Spain over-achieved, notching a win, two draws and a defeat with a goal difference of zero.

The only other European side in the top 10 of overachievers is the Irish Republic. Ireland performed brilliantly between 1980 and 2001 despite having only four million inhabitants and, for most of this period, relatively low income per capita. Not until 1994 did an economist from the Morgan Stanley bank coin the phrase 'Celtic Tiger'.

However, once again we have the difficulty that many of the teams in our top 10 compete almost exclusively against weak opponents. Syria and Iran played much the same easy schedule as Iraq did. Honduras is a titan of central America. Australia and New Zealand spent much of their time tonking tiny Pacific Islands. South Africa make the top 10 largely because they have so little experience: they only rejoined FIFA in 1992. Furthermore, GDP statistics for poorer countries outside Europe tend to be notori-ously unreliable. In general, there is more 'noise' in all the data for countries outside Europe, meaning that we struggle to pick up the influence of the factors we are interested in. It's like listening to a radio with poor reception: the meaning of the words becomes hard to make out.

It therefore makes more sense to focus on Europe alone. Europe is a more homogeneous place than the world as a whole, meaning that differences, especially in incomes and experience, tend to be smaller. Secondly, the data is better: Europeans have been collecting it for longer, and they have a relatively long history of transparent recordkeeping (though there are some very dodgy European statistics). Lastly, most of the world's dominant teams are grouped together in Europe, playing against pretty much the same set of opponents. It all adds up to a fairly accurate picture of how well each European team performs.

Let's first rank the best European teams on their absolute performance, without taking into account their population, experience or GDP. Taking only those games played between European teams (i.e. eliminating games where at least one team comes from outside Europe), here is the 'absolute' top 10 ranked by win percentage.

TOP 10 EUROPEAN TEAMS BY WIN PERCENTAGE, GAMES BETWEEN EUROPEAN COUNTRIES 1980–2001

	Team	Played	Won	Draws	Win %	Goal diff
1	Germany	97	0.608	0.227	0.722	0.98
2	West Germany	81	0.580	0.259	0.710	0.98
3	France	160	0.581	0.238	0.700	0.94
4	Italy	170	0.565	0.253	0.691	0.78
5	Czech Republic	70	0.557	0.200	0.657	0.91
6	Spain	172	0.529	0.256	0.657	0.91
7	Croatia	69	0.493	0.319	0.652	0.65
8	England	172	0.483	0.320	0.642	0.87
9	Netherlands	156	0.494	0.282	0.635	0.92
10	Russia	75	0.493	0.280	0.633	0.69

Crowded at the top, with almost indistinguishable records, are Germany (West and united), France and Italy. This trio is a clear notch ahead of the Czech Republic, Spain, Croatia, England, Holland and Russia. None of this is very surprising.

However, things become more interesting after we correct for population, experience and GDP. Now a new picture emerges. We find that in Europe, home advantage boosts the home team by a little under half a goal per game, compared with two thirds of a goal in global football. Experience also counts for less in Europe than in the world in general, though it remains the most important of our key variables in winning football matches. Having twice the experience of your opponent gives you an advantage of about 30 per cent of a goal per game. By contrast, population and GDP count for more in European football than they do in global football. Having twice the population of the opposing country is worth a quarter of a goal per game in Europe. Having twice the opponent's income per capita is worth about one goal every six games. So the factors in order of importance are – 1: Playing at home. 2: Experience. 3: Population. 4: GDP.

The European efficiency table (the first of its kind, as far as we know) may be the most telling we have, so let's rank every team for which we have data:

OVERACHIEVERS: RANKING OF EUROPEAN NATIONAL TEAMS CORRECTING FOR POPULATION, WEALTH AND EXPERIENCE, ALL GAMES BETWEEN TWO EUROPEAN OPPONENTS 1980–2001

	Team	Played	Won	Drawn	Win %	Average goal difference per game	Overachievement: Actual minus expected goal difference
1	Georgia	61	0.361	0.164	0.443	-0.11	1.167
2	Yugoslavia (S&M)	42	0.452	0.333	0.619	0.74	1.099
3	Croatia	69	0.493	0.319	0.652	0.65	0.901
4	Iceland	113	0.274	0.195	0.372	-0.50	0.837
5	Irish Republic	144	0.410	0.306	0.563	0.42	0.702
6	Armenia	42	0.119	0.310	0.274	-1.10	0.629
7	Czech Republic	70	0.557	0.200	0.657	0.91	0.598
8	Portugal	151	0.483	0.285	0.626	0.51	0.550
9	Netherlands	156	0.494	0.282	0.635	0.92	0.486
10	Bulgaria	78	0.449	0.218	0.558	0.37	0.406
11	Denmark	181	0.508	0.188	0.602	0.44	0.400
12	Moldova	51	0.157	0.216	0.265	-1.25	0.359
13	Northern Ireland	128	0.305	0.266	0.438	-0.32	0.334
14	Belarus	47	0.170	0.298	0.319	-0.77	0.284
15	Spain	172	0.529	0.256	0.657	0.91	0.241
16	Sweden	178	0.506	0.236	0.624	0.63	0.238

17	Romania	179	0.441	0.302	0.592	0.44	0.225
18	Norway	162	0.383	0.340	0.552	0.33	0.211
19	West Germany	81	0.580	0.259	0.710	0.98	0.168
20	East Germany	57	0.491	0.193	0.588	0.46	0.096
21	Scotland	140	0.400	0.271	0.536	0.10	0.086
22	Albania	70	0.214	0.171	0.300	-0.83	0.063
23	England	172	0.483	0.320	0.642	0.87	0.051
24	France	160	0.581	0.238	0.700	0.94	0.029
25	Belgium	136	0.375	0.309	0.529	0.23	-0.004
26	Wales	114	0.325	0.211	0.430	-0.33	-0.023
27	Israel	126	0.294	0.254	0.421	-0.25	-0.073
28	Bosnia-Herzegovina	29	0.276	0.207	0.379	-0.48	-0.077
29	Lithuania	79	0.291	0.165	0.373	-0.68	-0.087
30	Italy	170	0.565	0.253	0.691	0.78	-0.119
31	Slovakia	67	0.388	0.254	0.515	-0.03	-0.136
32	Slovenia	64	0.297	0.281	0.438	-0.30	-0.157
33	Switzerland	149	0.329	0.302	0.480	-0.01	-0.171
34	Greece	169	0.349	0.266	0.482	-0.13	-0.198
35	Latvia	73	0.233	0.151	0.308	-0.64	-0.200
36	FYR Macedonia	51	0.275	0.275	0.412	-0.31	-0.212
37	Cyprus	121	0.174	0.182	0.264	-1.36	-0.217
38	Germany	97	0.608	0.227	0.722	0.98	-0.224
39	Poland	174	0.391	0.282	0.532	0.13	-0.304
40	Hungary	168	0.339	0.292	0.485	-0.04	-0.374
41	Austria	125	0.344	0.248	0.468	-0.16	-0.384
42	Russia	75	0.493	0.280	0.633	0.69	-0.390
43	Azerbaijan	52	0.115	0.154	0.192	-1.75	-0.423
44	Finland	146	0.212	0.281	0.353	-0.73	-0.651
45	Ukraine	57	0.368	0.333	0.535	0.05	-0.748
46	Malta	139	0.072	0.144	0.144	-2.04	-0.807
47	Estonia	91	0.099	0.220	0.209	-1.57	-0.984
48	Turkey	130	0.300	0.223	0.412	-0.66	-1.044
49	Luxembourg	100	0.030	0.090	0.075	-2.27	-1.050

Again, the most important number is in the last column: each country's 'relative goal difference'. It turns out that the top 10 of overachievers with the best relative goal difference is monopolised by small nations. Holland with its 15 million inhabitants is the giant of the 10. The Portuguese, Serbs (and Montenegrins) and Czechs all have populations around the 10-million mark, while the Croats are at just 5 million.

This European top 10 looks more credible than our global one featuring Honduras et al, because a number of the teams on the European list – chiefly the Dutch, Czechs, Croats and Portuguese – have achieved genuine success despite being small. However, one cannot but notice that at the very top of our table is a team whose winning percentage is a mere 44 per cent: Georgia.

Georgia comes top largely because its official footballing history is so short. Only on 27 May 1990 did the country play its first official international. In truth the match was a 2–2 draw between the Georgian club Dinamo Tblisi and the Lithuanian club Zalgiris Vilnius. Georgia and Lithuania did not exist as independent states at the time, and so couldn't very well play an international. But in 1991 both nations gained their independence from the USSR, and soon afterwards they agreed to redefine the club friendly as their maiden international. By 2001 Georgia had still played only 71 internationals in its history, fewer than a tenth as many as England. Armenia, another surprise entrant in our top 10, had played just 57.

Of course the notion that these nations only started gaining experience in international football in 1990 is a fiction. Georgia and Armenia, like the 'Stans', had been learning the game for decades in the USSR. Yet for the purposes of our table, we have treated them almost as football virgins, and thanks to this statistical quirk they rocket to the top. If we credited these states with the experience of the hundreds of international matches played by the USSR, they would tumble down our rankings.

Nonetheless, Georgia clearly has potential. The country is small (5 million people), and horribly poor (even today, average income is below £2,500 per year). If the Georgians could just become as rich as Croatia, they too could start beating England at Wembley.

Perhaps the most surprising thing about our top 10 is the countries that don't make it. Germany, France and Italy – the dominant European nations – turn out to perform not much better or even a little worse against other Europeans than you would expect. We saw at the start of the book that these countries benefited from their location at the heart of western Europe, smack in the middle of the world's best knowledge network. Those networks correlate pretty well with high income and long experience in football. These are wealthy, large nations that have been playing the game for over a century. They *should* win prizes, and they do. In the decade from 1980 to 1990, West Germany reached three straight World Cup finals, winning one, and won a European Championship. Yet their performance against European teams was only 0.15 goals per game better than you would have expected based on the country's vast population, experience and income per capita. In fact, once you allow for these advantages, West Germany performed worse than Rumania and only fractionally better than the improbable trio of East Germany, Scotland and Albania.

France won two European Championships and one World Cup between 1980 and 2001. Yet against fellow Europeans they scored just one goal every 34 games more than they 'should' have done. England – which won nothing in the period – 'outperformed' their population, experience and income by more than France did.

Italy were world champions in 1982. Nonetheless, against fellow Europeans they were a goal every nine games *worse* than they should have been given their resources.

At the bottom of our rankings of relative performance, Turkey and Luxembourg are the shockers. The Turks clearly suffered from being so far adrift from the western European network of football know-how. As we will explain in the final chapter, they have recently rectified this defect and are now one of our countries of the future.

If you judge by the map, Luxembourg were smack in the middle of said western European network. But networks are never simply geographical. Nobody in football wanted to network with Luxembourg, because the country of a little over half a million inhabitants was too small to support a decent league or to produce many good players. Top-class foreign coaches and players were never spotted at the Jeunesse Esch ground passing on their know-how. And so Luxembourg never gained any. They are so bad at football that they are even worse than they should be. Admittedly their dry spell of 15 years without a win ended with Paul Koch's legendary last-minute penalty save against Malta in 1995, but even after that they hardly hit the heights. In 2001 Joel Wolff, secretary general of the country's FA, confessed to us in a world exclusive interview: 'Let's say that we have arrived at a relative nadir.' Whenever football managers invoked the verity, 'There are no more minnows in international football,' they were forgetting Luxembourg.

We award the country both our relative and absolute prizes for worst football team in Europe. In our global efficiency table of national teams (after correcting for experience, population and income) Luxembourg is 174th, the lowest of any country in the world that played at least 100 matches in the period.

Yet Luxembourg probably do not deserve the title of relatively worst football team on earth. Using a little bit of judgement, we reserve that honour for India. With a win percentage of just 46 per cent, and a goal difference of −0.26 per game, they really should be doing better. And it's a myth that Indians are not interested in football. The sports pages of their newspapers are almost as full of the carryings-on in the English Premier League as they are of cricket matches. It's true that India's poverty makes it hard to convert all those budding Rooneys and Ronaldos in Rajasthan and Orissa into stars (though that hasn't stopped their cricket team). Still, from our model we estimated that India should be outscoring their opponents by more than a goal a game.

Admittedly the country of 1.1 billion inhabitants is one spot above Luxembourg in our global efficiency table, but once you take into account that India plays most of its matches in weak Asia, whereas Luxembourg plays its in strong Europe, the Indians have it by a nose. A good indication is India's FIFA ranking (at the time of writing) of 146th in the world, six whole spots behind the Pacific island of Vanuatu.

But who gets the Tom Thumb trophy – the poor, small, inexperienced man's Jules Rimet – for the relatively best team on earth? Which country does best allowing for experience, population and income? Well, one day we'd like to see this played out on grass. Let's have a World Cup in which teams start with a handicap, settled by a panel of econometricians chaired by Professor Gerrard. But until that great day comes, all we have is our model. The best little country on earth might be Honduras or Georgia, but not even the authors believe that. A safer conclusion is that the Yugoslavs, Croats and Czechs do wonders with their modest resources. However, the country that stands out most given what it has to work with is Iraq, even taking into account its easy Asian schedule. If the country ever sorts itself out, then watch out, world.

CORE TO PERIPHERY: THE FUTURE MAP OF GLOBAL FOOTBALL

On a snowy night in Amsterdam, a dozen or so Dutch football writers and ex-players have gathered in a flat in the dinky city centre. Guus Hiddink walks in, and grabs someone's shoulders from behind by way of greeting. Growing up with five brothers gave him a knack for the right matey gesture. (Hiddink appears to be equally relaxed with women, and his cohabitation with his then mistress in Seoul shocked Koreans.)

The evening starts with a football quiz, at which the future manager of Chelsea and Russia performs indifferently. Then there is food and football talk until the early morning. Though Hiddink is the senior figure at table, he never tries to dominate. He likes telling stories – about his former player Romario, or his old team-mate at the San José Earthquakes, George Best – but when others interrupt he is just as happy to lean back in his chair and listen. He is a solid, soothing, jowly presence. 'You can feel he's at ease,' Boudewijn Zenden, one of his former players, told us, 'so if he's at ease, the others are at ease. He creates this environment where you feel safe.'

Hiddink has a special place in the latest stage of football's history. In the twenty-first century, he has been the world's leading exporter of football know-how from western Europe to the margins of the earth. We saw in chapter 1 that from about 1970 to 2000, the six founding members of the European Economic Community dominated football thinking and won almost all the game's prizes. These countries perfected what you might call the EEC style: a fast, physical, collectivist football.

But then these countries began exporting their expertise. Hiddink and other Dutch, German, French and Italian expat managers established themselves in Hiltons and westerners' compounds around the planet. In the last few years they have helped several new football countries – Russia, Australia, South Korea, Turkey and Greece to name a few – overtake the managers' own native countries. It's because of men like these that England will not be the best football country of the future. Hiddink's native Holland appear even more thoroughly doomed. On the new map of football, which Hiddink is helping to draw, his own country will shrink to a dot.

FROM THE BACK CORNER TO THE WORLD

Born in 1946, Hiddink grew up close to what was then just becoming the epicentre of global football knowledge. He is the son of a village schoolteacher and Resistance hero from a small town in the Achterhoek, or 'Back Corner', about 8 kilometres (5 miles) from the German border. The Back Corner is wooded and quiet, one of the few empty bits of the Netherlands, and on visits home from stints in Seoul or Moscow, Hiddink enjoys tootling along its back roads on his Harley Davidson Fatboy. 'Pom-pom-pom-pom-pom,' he goes, puffing out his cheeks to mimic the motor's roar.

He grew up milking cows, ploughing behind two horses, and dreaming of becoming a farmer. But Dutch farms were already dying, and he became a football coach instead. At 19 he took an assistant's job at the Back Corner's semi-professional club, De Graafschap, where his father had played before him. He then made an unusual career move: from coach to player. The head coach, seeing that his young assistant could kick a ball, stuck him in the team, and thus began a 16-year playing career.

The handsome, round-faced, wavy-haired playmaker was too lazy and slow for the top, yet he was present at a golden age. The Dutch sides of the 1970s shaped Hiddink. Holland, playing what foreigners called 'total football', a new kind of game in which play-ers constantly swapped positions and thought for themselves, reached two World Cup finals. Dutch clubs won four European Cups. Off the pitch, Dutch players of Hiddink's generation would answer foreign journalists' questions with sophisticated discourses in several languages. For a keen observer like Hiddink, the players' constant squabbles provided object lessons in how to keep stars just about functioning within a collective.

Dutch football's renown at the time helped even a second-rate player like Hiddink find work abroad, with the Washington Diplo-mats and the San José Earthquakes. 'I was Best's roommate,' says Hiddink, enjoying the quirky American word, and he mimics himself fielding the phone calls from Best's groupies: 'George is not here. George is sleeping.'

It was the start of a world tour that culminated in a suite in a five-star hotel in Moscow where, according to the president of the Russian FA, he spends a fortune ordering cappuccinos from room service. At Euro 2008 Hiddink got Russia playing the best foot-ball in their history, just as he had previously got South Korea and Australia playing their best football in history. Hiddink has helped to draw the new map of footballing power.

1889–2002: OFF THE PLANE WITH A LEATHER FOOTBALL

Football seems to have a quality that enables it eventually to conquer every known society. The first wave of exporters of the game were Victorian British sailors, businessmen, missionaries and colonial officers. In 1889, to cite a typical story, the 21-year-old Englishman Frederick Rea disembarked on the island of South Uist off the west coast of Scotland to work as a headmaster. A couple of years later two of his brothers visited, carrying with them a leather football. Within two decades the game had conquered South Uist. Shinty, a stick sport that had been played there for 1,400 years, 'was wiped like chalk from the face of the island', wrote Roger Hutchinson in the British football journal *Perfect Pitch* in 1998, 'supplanted, like a thousand of its distant relatives from Buenos Aires to Smolensk, by a game almost as young and innocent as Frederick Rea himself'. Today football is the dominant sport on South Uist. It conquered because of its magic.

Victorian Britons spread the game to continental Europe, Latin America and bits of Africa. However, for a century Asia and North America remained almost immune. Contrary to myth, soccer took a long time to become a global game. What people called the 'World Cup' should until the 1980s have been called 'the Euro–Latin American Duopoly'. Though most people on the planet lived in Asia, the continent's only representative at the World Cup of 1978 was Iran. Even in 1990 the British Isles had more teams at the World Cup (three) than all of Asia combined (two). Many Asian countries still barely knew about football. When that year's World Cup final was shown on Japanese television, there was a surprising studio guest: the baseball player Sadaharu Oh. 'Mr Oh,' he was asked during the match, 'what is the difference between sliding in baseball and in soccer?' In Australia, too, soccer was then still marginal. Johnny Warren, an Australian international and later TV commentator on the game, called his memoirs *Sheilas, Wogs and Poofters,* because, according to Australian myth in the years before Hiddink landed there, those were the three core elements of the national soccer public.

But by 1990 the so-called 'third wave of globalisation' was under way. Increased world trade, cable television, and finally the internet brought soccer to new territories. Roberto Fonta-narrosa, the late Argentine cartoonist, novelist and soccer nut, said: 'If TV were only an invention to broadcast football, it would be justified.'

Suddenly the Chinese, Japanese, Americans and even some Indians could see soccer's magic. They saw it even more clearly than the people of Uist had a century before. Soccer by now had the prestige of being the world's biggest sport, and everyone wanted a piece of its fans' passion. Football is often mocked for its low scores, but precisely because goals are so scarce, the release of joy is greater than in other sports. When the former goalkeeper Osama bin Laden visited London in 1994, he watched four Arsenal matches, bought souvenirs for his sons in the club shop, and remarked that he had never seen as much passion as among football supporters.

Just then football was capturing the last holdouts. On 15 May 1993, Japan's J-League kicked off. The next year China acquired a national professional league, and in 1996 the US and India followed. The new marginal countries began to hire European coaches who could quickly teach them the latest in football.

By the turn of the millennium, Hiddink was an obvious candidate for export. He had won the European Cup with PSV Eindhoven, had managed clubs in Turkey and Spain, and had taken Holland to the World Cup semi-final in 1998. After he passed 50, he felt his ambition begin to wane. Never a workaholic to start with, the boy from the Back Corner had by now proved himself. He had met with triumph and disaster and treated those two imposters just the same. He had gone from villager to cosmopolitan. He had fallen in love with golf. Football was becoming just a hobby.

He took a break, and in 2001 popped up in his first missionary posting, as manager of South Korea. As part of the globalisation of football, the country was due to co-host the 2002 World Cup with Japan. South Korea had played in several World Cups before, but had never won a single match, and in 1998 had lost 5–0 to Hiddink's Holland.

When Hiddink landed in Seoul, history was beginning to work in his favour. Like many emerging nations, the South Koreans were getting bigger. Thanks to increased wealth, the average height of a South Korean man had risen from 1.63 metres (5ft 4in) in the 1930s to about 1.73 metres (5ft 8in) by 2002. That meant a bigger pool of men with the physique required to play international football. In an interview during a Korean training camp in the Back Corner, a year before the World Cup, Hiddink told us he'd caught Koreans using their smallness as an excuse in football. 'But I won't allow that,' he added. 'I won't let them say beforehand, "They're a bit bigger and broader, we're small and sad." And gradually, I notice that some of our players are big too, and know how to look after themselves.' The 'height effect' was also quietly lifting many other emerging football countries, from China to Turkey.

But the Koreans had other problems. The Dutch psychological quirk had been squabbling. The Korean disease, as Hiddink soon discovered, was hierarchy. In Korean football, the older the player, the higher his status. A 31-year-old veteran international was so respected that he could coast. At meals, the group of older players would sit down at table first, and the youngest last.

Whereas Dutch players talked too much, Koreans were practically mute. 'Slavishness is a big word,' Hiddink said that day in the Back Corner, 'but they do have something like: "If the commander says it, we'll follow it blindly." They are used to thinking, "I'm a soldier, I'll do what's asked of me." And you have to go a step further if you want to make a team really mature. You need people who can and will take the team in their hands.' Hiddink wanted autonomous, thinking, 'Dutch' players: a centre-half who at a certain point in the game sees he should push into midfield, a striker who drops back a few yards. He was teaching the Koreans the Dutch variant of the EEC style.

Hiddink said of his players: 'Commitment is not their problem. Almost too much. But if your commitment is too high, you often lose the strategic overview.'

Hiddink had started out in Korea by kicking a couple of the older players out of his squad. He made a young man captain. He asked his players to make their own decisions on the field. 'That makes them a bit freer, easier,' he said. Shortly before the World Cup, he brought back the jilted older players, who by then were pretty motivated.

However, the educational process in Korea was always a two-way one. During his 18 months in the country, Hiddink learnt a few things himself. Already during his stints in Turkey and Spain, he had begun freeing himself from the national superiority complex that pervades Dutch football: the belief that the Dutch way is the only way. In Holland, football is a thinking man's game. When the Dutch talk about it, the concepts to which they always return are '*techniek*' and '*tactiek*'. '*Passie*', or passion, was a quality they associated with unsophisticated footballers from other countries. In Korea, Hiddink learnt that it was actually pretty important. Even when speaking Dutch he tends to describe this quality with the English word 'commitment', perhaps because there is no obvious Dutch equivalent.

He had also learnt what every successful missionary knows: respect the native way of life, or at least pretend to, because otherwise the natives won't listen to you. That afternoon in the Back Corner he said, 'I don't go to work on the culture of the country. I just leave it, I respect it. I only do something about the conditions that they need to perform on the pitch. And of course there are a couple of things off the field that do influence that.'

At the 2002 World Cup the Koreans played with a fervour rarely seen in football. Helped by bizarre refereeing decisions, the country from football's periphery reached the semi-final.

Korea had craved global recognition, and Hiddink achieved it. Korean cities planned statues in his honour, and a caricature of his face appeared on Korean stamps. Hiddink's autobiography appeared in a Korean print run of half a million, despite having to compete with an estimated 16 Hiddink biographies. In the Back Corner, Korean tour buses made pilgrimages to the Hiddink ancestral home. Soon after the World Cup, the man himself dropped by to visit his octogenarian parents. 'Well, it wasn't bad,' admitted his father. 'Coffee?'

2002–2004: THE PERIPHERY TAKES OVER INTERNATIONAL FOOTBALL

During that World Cup of 2002, other peripheral football countries were emerging too. Japan reached the second round, the US got to the quarters, and Korea's conquerors in the match for third place were Turkey, which hadn't even played in a World Cup since 1954.

We said at the start of this book that a country's success in football correlates strongly with three variables: its population, its income per capita, and its experience in football. For Turkey, as for many other emerging countries, all three variables were improving fast.

We have seen that from 1980 to 2001, Turkey were the second worst underperformers in European football. They scored a full goal per game fewer than they should have done given their vast population, their decent experience in international football, and their admittedly low incomes.

But just as the period we measured was ending, the Turks were beginning their rise. It is no coincidence that the country went from being a pathetic football team to one of the best in Europe at the same time as it grew from a mid-sized European state into the continent's third most populous nation. Turkey had 19 million inhabitants in 1945, double that by 1973 and about 72 million by 2008. In Europe, only Russia and Germany have more. While Turkey's population grows, most European countries are losing people. Add several million Turks in the diaspora, and the youth of most Turks, and the country starts to rival even Germany in its football potential. And Turkey is just one of many developing countries whose population is fast outstripping those of rich countries.

At the same time Turkey's economy was booming, and it was using some of the new money to import football knowledge. In that early chapter, we had measured a country's football experience by how many matches its national team had played. However, there is a shortcut to gaining experience: import it. This process began for Turkey in June 1984, when West Germany got knocked out of the European Championship. The Germans sacked their coach, Jupp Derwall. That year he joined Galatasaray, and began to import the EEC style of football into Turkey.

Derwall and other German coaches (as well as the Englishman Gordon Milne at Besiktas) got Turkish players actually working. They also introduced the novel idea of training on grass. Turkish television began showing foreign matches, which introduced some Turkish viewers to the concept of the pass.

Before Derwall's arrival, the average Turkish footballer had been a selfish midget dribbler. Derwall shipped German-born Turks into Galatasaray. The German Turks were bigger than Turkish Turks, thanks to a better diet, and they trained like Germans. Admittedly, soon after arrival in Istanbul they were exposed to the sultanesque harem lifestyle of many Turkish footballers, and their game deteriorated, but it was a start. Diaspora Turks – from Germany, France, but also the Londoner Colin Kazim-Richards at Euro 2008 – have continued to give Turkey a fast track to European football know-how. No other national team in Europe includes as many players who grew up in other European countries.

In 1996 Turkey qualified for their first major tournament since 1954. Though they didn't score a goal or register a point at Euro 96, they were judged to have done quite well. They have since reached two semis and a quarter-final at major tournaments.

In short, globalisation saved Turkish football. Turks came to the realisation – as every marginal country needs to – that there is only one way to play good football: you combine Italian defending with German work ethic and Dutch passing into the EEC style. ('Industrial football,' some Turks sulkily call it.) In football, national styles don't work. You have to have all the different elements. You cannot win international matches playing traditional Turkish football. You need to play EEC football.

Both Hiddink's experiences and Turkey's point to an important truth: in football, 'culture' doesn't matter much. Turkey may well have had 'a different culture, a different approach, a different way of life', as the French grandee Giscard d'Estaing said when he drafted the European Union's failed constitution, but it didn't stop the Turks in football. Cultures are not eternal and unalterable. When they have an incentive to change – like the prospect of winning more football matches, or perhaps the prospect of getting richer – they can change.

Turkey was one of the first countries brave enough to jettison its traditional football culture. Most countries on the fringes of Europe had dysfunctional indigenous playing styles. The ones on the southern fringe – Greece, Turkey, Portugal – favoured pointless dribbling, while the British and Scandinavians played kick-and-rush. Gradually they came to accept that these styles didn't work.

Nobody did better out of abandoning their roots and adopting EEC football than Turkey's friends across the water, the Greeks. The Greek national team had traditionally played terrible football in front of a couple of thousand spectators. During foreign trips, their camp followers – friends, journalists and miscellaneous – would hang around the team hotel drinking espressos with players until the early morning. When Greece somehow made it to the World Cup of 1994, they ended up regretting it. At their training sessions outside Boston, an outfield player would stand in goal while the others blasted shots into the bushes. They spent most of the tournament travelling the East Coast of the US to receptions with Greek–Americans, though they did find time to be thrashed in three matches. In 2002 Greece gave up on the Greek style and imported a vast chunk of experience in the person of an ageing German manager, Otto Rehhagel.

The Rhinelander was the prototype post-war West German collectivist. He had grown up a healthy drive across the border from Hiddink, amid the ruins of post-war western Germany. An apprentice housepainter and bone-hard defender, Rehhagel was brought up on the 'German virtues' of hard work and discipline. As a coach in Germany for decades, he aimed to sign only collectivist, EEC-type players whose personality had been vetted by his wife over dinner in the Rehhagel home. Everywhere he tried to build an organisation. Sacked as manager of Arminia Bielefeld, he sighed: 'At least thanks to me there is now a toilet at the training ground.' On later visits to Bielefeld with other clubs, he always enquired after his toilet.

Rehhagel quickly rooted out Greece's cult of the soloist, introduced EEC football, and took the team to Euro 2004 in Portugal. There he went around saying things like, 'Now that I am coaching Greece, I want to make one philosophical statement. Please write it down: Man needs nothing more than other people.' Banal as this sounded, it must have resonated in post-war West Germany. Certainly the Greek players, who pre-Rehhagel never seemed to have heard of collective spirit, had begun preaching the notion in many languages. 'We was very good organised,' said Zisis Vryzas after Greece beat France in the quarter-finals. Andreas Charisteas, the reserve at Werder Bremen who would become the highest scorer of Euro 2004, eulogised: 'We have a German coach, he has a German mentality, and we play like a German team.' In fact, Greece had made the same journey as Turkey: from midget dribblers to boring EEC football thanks to German coaching.

Rehhagel himself called it 'learning from European football'. Becoming 'European' – code for becoming organised – is the aspiration of many marginal European countries, in football and outside. Just as these countries were joining the European Union, they were absorbing EEC football. The final of Euro 2004 pitted Greece against another recently marginal country. The Greeks beat the Portuguese 1–0 thanks to another header from Charisteas, who soon afterwards would be a reserve again at Ajax. It turned out that with merely half-decent players, a good EEC coach and time to prepare, almost any marginal country could do well.

2005–2006: EVEN AUSTRALIA

In this new climate, the best EEC coaches could pick their posts. Hiddink received many offers to take teams to the World Cup of 2006, but he chose the most marginal country of all: Australia.

In 1974, while Hiddink was still absorbing total football in the Back Corner, Australia had qualified for its first World Cup as Asia's sole representatives. The Socceroos of the day were part-timers, and some had to give up their jobs to go to Germany. The German press was particularly interested in the milkman-cum-defender Manfred Schaefer, who had been born in Hitler's Reich in 1943 and emigrated to Australia as a child refugee after the war. At one point in the tournament West Germany's striker Gerd Müller asked him if he really was an amateur. Well, Schaefer proudly replied, he had earned $4,600 by qualifying for the World Cup. 'That's what I earn a week,' said Müller.

The Australians achieved one draw in three matches at the World Cup. 'However,' writes Matthew Hall in his excellent book about Australian soccer, *The Away Game*, 'their thongs, super-tight Aussie Rules-style shorts and marsupial mascots endeared them to the German public.'

In the next 30 years, soccer sank so low in Australia that the country's soccer federation was sometimes reduced to filming its own matches and giving them to TV channels for free. Australian club football was punctuated by weird vendettas between Balkan ethnic groups. Only in 1997, during the new wave of globalisation, were the Socceroos of 1974 publicly honoured in their own country.

Then, in 2005, Hiddink landed with a mission to teach EEC football. First he gathered the Australian team in a training camp in his native Back Corner. His first impression: 'What a bunch of vagabonds. Everyone came in wearing a cap, or flip-flops. One had on long trousers, another shorts, and another Bermuda shorts. I said, "What is this?" "Well, that's how we live." "Hello, but you probably play like that too."'

Hiddink spent Australia's first training session in the Back Corner watching his new charges fly into each other like kamikaze pilots. 'You don't have to chase these guys up,' he remarked. After half an hour he stopped the game. When the players' cries of 'Come on, Emmo!', 'Hold the ball, Johnno!', 'Let's go!' and the streams of 'Fucking' had finally faded, Hiddink asked them to shout only when a teammate was in trouble and needed coaching. That would improve everyone's vision of play, he said. The game resumed in near silence. It was Australia's first baby step towards EEC football.

Just as he had with the Koreans, Hiddink was turning the Australians into Dutch footballers. That meant giving them the intellectual discipline needed for the World Cup. The Australian way was to train hard, play hard, but then relax with late-night beers in the hotel bar. Hiddink wanted the players thinking on their own about their jobs. Working hard wasn't enough. Since the Australians already had 'commitment' and *passie*, Hiddink was teaching them to think like Dutchmen. The Socceroos tended to run to wherever the ball was. Hiddink forbade them from entering certain zones. In EEC football, doing the right things is always better than doing lots of things.

He had noticed at the Confederations Cup of 2005, shortly before he took over, where the Socceroos had lost all their three games and conceded ten goals, that all four Australian defenders would often stay back to mark a single forward. That left them short elsewhere on the pitch. No semi-professional Dutch team would be so naïve.

Hiddink was surprised that the Australians were so willing to listen to him. They understood that they had a chance to learn the EEC style from the man himself. Hiddink had always excelled in dealing with difficult characters: Romario, Edgar Davids, or the Korean Ahn Jung-Hwan. He knew just how to touch them. But the Australians, he admitted, were 'zero difficult'.

Except perhaps Mark Viduka, Australia's best but not its most committed player. Hiddink recalled later: 'He came in with, "Oh I'd like to go to a World Cup but it's going to be difficult. We've never made it and I'm not fit."' Hiddink sent the Socceroos' physio-therapist to work with Viduka at his club, Middlesbrough. This didn't merely get the player fit. It made him feel wanted. Hiddink also made Viduka his captain, to make sure he would be inside the tent pissing out rather than outside pissing in.

It was striking how quickly the Socceroos learned EEC football. Once again, 'culture' seemed to be no obstacle. In November 2005, only a couple of months after Hiddink had started part-time work with them (he was also coaching PSV at the other end of the globe), they beat Uruguay in a play-off to qualify for the World Cup. Suddenly the *Melbourne Herald Sun* found itself wondering whether Aussie Rules football could survive as the dominant sport in Australia's southern states. Already more Australian children played soccer than Aussie Rules and both rugby codes combined.

The newspaper's worries appeared justified when a few months later, just before the World Cup of 2006, an Australia v Greece friendly drew 95,000 people to the Melbourne Cricket Ground. In no city in Europe or Latin America could such a game have drawn such a crowd. Australia had also just become approximately the last country on earth to acquire a national professional soccer league.

And then Hiddink led the Socceroos to the second round of the World Cup of 2006. Great crowds of Australians set their alarm clocks to watch at unearthly hours. What had happened on Uist over a century before was now threatening to happen in Oz. A century from now, Aussie Rules might exist only at subsidised folklore festivals.

2006–2009: HIDDINK TO GHIDDINK IN A MOSCOW HOTEL SUITE

After Australia, Hiddink could have had almost any job in football. In an ideal world, he would have liked to manage England. Of all the world's marginal football countries, England had the most potential because it was rich, large and had recently rejoined the network of core countries.

Hiddink also relished the specific challenges of managing England. He had the psychological expertise to inspire tired multi-millionaires. He loved dealing with difficult characters; Wayne Rooney would be a cinch for him. And he would have improved the thinking of a team that had everything but intellect. As a lover of the bohemian life, he would have been happy in London, and his girlfriend would have been an hour from her beloved Amsterdam. But Hiddink couldn't bear the thought of British tabloids crawling over his family, and so he decided to spread his EEC know-how to Russia instead.

Admittedly Russia's population was collapsing rather than growing, as Russian men drank themselves to death. However, when he took the job the country's economy was moving the right way. In the decade from 1998, Russian income per capita nearly doubled. The country's new oil money bought Hiddink's brain.

As in Korea, Hiddink's job was to force his players to be free. Traditionally, Russian footballers had the 'I only work here' demeanour of *homo sovieticus*. They feared their coaches as much as they feared the mafiosi who stole their jeeps. They shoved safe sideways passes into each other's feet, because that way nobody could ever shout at them. There was *zaorganizovan-nost,* over-organisation.

Ghiddink, as the Russians call him, joked with his players, relaxed them. As a 'punishment' in training, a player might have a ball kicked at his backside, while the rest of the squad stood around laughing. The times helped: this generation of Russian players could not remember the USSR. Armed with iPhones and SUVs, they had left the periphery and joined the global main-stream.

As he had in Korea, Hiddink practically ordered his players to think for themselves, to give riskier passes, to move into new positions without him telling them to. Marc Bennetts, author of *Football Dynamo: Modern Russia and the People's Game,* said: 'It's as if he's beaten the Marxism-Leninism out of them.' At Euro 2008, Russia's hammering of Ghiddink's native Holland was the ultimate triumph of a marginal country over a core one. It also provided the almost unprecedented sight of Russian footballers having fun. They swapped positions and dribbled, knowing that if they lost the ball no one would scream at them. After the game, their best player, Andrei Arshavin, muttered something about 'a wise Dutch coach', and cried.

Russia lost in the semis of Euro 2008 to another former marginal country, Spain. By then, after 22 years in the European Union, Spain was so networked that it didn't even need a foreign coach to win the Euro.

Spain, Russia and Turkey, another semi-finalist at Euro 2008, were all beneficiaries of the spread of football know-how to marginal countries. When all countries have about the same foot-ball information, and converging incomes, the countries with the most inhabitants usually win. Three of the four semi-finalists at Euro 2008 (Russia, Germany and Turkey) had the largest popula-tions in Europe. This was bad news for small core countries like Holland, Denmark or the Czech Republic. Their populations and economies are almost static, and they have exported their football knowledge. What made them unique between 1970 and 2000 was their network. Now that that has expanded to include much of the world, they are probably doomed.

2009–: THE PERIPHERY WINS THE WORLD CUP

Until the late 1990s the cliché in football was that an African country would 'soon' win the World Cup. Everyone said it, from Pele to Walter Winterbottom. But it turned out not to be true, mostly because although African populations were growing, their incomes remained too low to import much good football experience. A better tip for future World Cups might be Iraq. If the country remains halfway stable, it's likely to do even better than it did in its years of madness. However, the best bets for the future are probably Japan, the US or China: the three largest economies on earth, which can afford coaches like Hiddink, where potential footballers have enough to eat and don't get terrible diseases. There are already omens of their rise: the US has the most young footballers of any country, and has reached a World Cup quarter-final; Japan says it aims to host the World Cup again by 2050 and win it; China topped the medals table at the last Olympics. These countries will get to the top sooner than the Africans. In the new world, distance no longer separates a country from the best football. Only poverty does.

ACKNOWLEDGEMENTS

Dozens of people helped make this book possible. We would like to thank Dave Berri, Joe Boyle, Dennis Coates, Rod Fort, Bernd Frick, Brian Goff, Jahn Hakes, Pauline Harris, Brad Humphreys, Paul Husbands, Kai Konrad, Dan Kuper, Markus Kurscheidt, Mike Leeds, Wolfgang Maennig, John McMillan, Roger Noll, Andrew Oswald, Holger Preuss, Skip Sauer and Lia Na'ama ten Brink.

We got ideas and information from Kevin Alavy, Rob Baade, Vendeline von Bredow, Carl Bromley, Tunde Buraimo, Pamela Druckerman, Russell Gerrard, Matti Goksoyr, Adam Kuper, Hannah Kuper, Kaz Mochlinski, Ignacio Palacios-Huerta, Ian Preston, Andreas Selliaas and Paul in 't Hout; from Benjamin Cohen, Jonathan Hill, Mark O'Keefe and Alex Phillips at UEFA; and from David O'Connor and Andrew Walsh at Sport+Markt.

The following were fantastic collaborators: Kevin Alavy, Wladimir Andreff, Giles Atkinson, Tunde Buraimo, Luigi Buzzacchi, David Forrest, Filippo dell'Osso, Pedro Garcia-del-Barrio, Steve Hall, David Harbord, Takeo Hirata, Tom Hoehn, Georgios Kavetsos, Stefan Késenne, Tim Kuypers, Umberto Lago, Stephanie Leach, Neil Longley, Susana Mourato, Susanne Parlasca, Ian Preston, Steve Ross, Rob Simmons, Ron Smith, Tommaso Valletti and Andy Zimbalist.

Jonathan Taylor at HarperCollins had faith in the book before we had even written it, and was a thoroughly supportive presence throughout. Steve Dobell was a most literate copy-editor who saved us from many errors. And our agents Gordon Wise and Kate Cooper masterfully overcame their lack of interest in football for the sake of this book. Thanks to Gordon for listening so patiently to our early, confusing accounts of what we wanted to write.

We also want to thank all the interviewees quoted in the text.

SELECT BIBLIOGRAPHY

BOOKS

Andreff, Wladimir, and Stefan Szymanski, eds. *Handbook on the Economics of Sport*. Edward Elgar, Cheltenham, 2006

Andrews, David L. *Manchester United: A Thematic Study*. Routledge, London, 2004

Bellos, Alex. *Futebol: The Brazilian Way of Life*. Bloomsbury, London, 2002

Bennetts, Marc. *Football Dynamo: Modern Russia and the People's Game*. Virgin Books, London, 2008

Burns, Jimmy. *Hand of God: The Life of Diego Maradona*. Bloomsbury, London, 1996

Burns, Jimmy. *When Beckham Went to Spain: Power, Stardom and Real Madrid*. Penguin, London, 2004

Dobson, Stephen, and John Goddard. *The Economics of Football*. Cambridge University Press, Cambridge, 2001

Drogba, Didier. *"C'était pas gagné"*. Editions Prolongations, Issy-les-Moulineaux, 2008

Exley, Frederick. *A Fan's Notes*. Yellow Jersey Press, London, 1999

Ferguson, Alex. *Managing My Life: My Autobiography*. Hodder and Stoughton, London, 2000

Foot, John. *Calcio: A History of Italian Football*. Fourth Estate, London, 2006

Ginsborg, Paul. *A History of Contemporary Italy*. Penguin, London, 1990

Gopnik, Adam. *Paris to the Moon*. Random House, New York, 2000

Hall, Matthew. *The Away Game*. Harper*Sports,* Sydney, 2000

Hamilton, Aidan. *An Entirely Different Game: The British Influence on Brazilian Football*. Mainstream Publishing, Edinburgh, 1998

Hill, Declan. *The Fix: Soccer and Organized Crime*. McClelland & Stewart, Toronto, 2008

Holt, Richard, and Tony Mason. *Sport in Britain, 1945–2000*. Wiley-Blackwell, London, 2000

Hornby, Nick. *Fever Pitch*. Indigo, London, 1996

Kapu ci ski, Ryszard. *The Soccer War*. Vintage International, New York, 1992

Kok, Auke. *1974: Wij waren de besten*. Thomas Rap, Amsterdam, 2004

Kolfschooten, Frank van. *De bal is niet rond*. L.J. Veen, Amsterdam/Antwerp, 1998

Lewis, Michael. *Moneyball*. W.W. Norton & Company Ltd., New York, 2004

Lever, Janet. *Soccer Madness*. University of Chicago Press, Chicago, 1983

Mandela, Nelson. *The Long Walk to Freedom*. Abacus, London, 1995

Montague, James. *When Friday Comes: Football in the War Zone*. Mainstream Publishing, Edinburgh, 2008

Mora y Araujo, Marcela, and Simon Kuper, eds. *Perfect Pitch 3: Men and Women*. Headline Book Publishing Ltd, London, 1998

Nieuwenhof, Frans van de. *Hiddink, Dit is mijn wereld*. De Boekenmakers, Eindhoven, 2006

Norridge, Julian. *Can We Have Our Balls Back, Please? How the British Invented Sport and Then Almost Forgot How to Play It*. Penguin, London, 2008

Oliver & Ohlbaum Associates and Fletcher Research. *Net Profits: How to Make Money out of Football*. Fletcher Research, London, 1997

Orakwue, Stella. *Pitch Invaders: The Modern Black Football Revolution*. Victor Gollancz, London, 1998

Peace, David. *The Damned United*. Faber and Faber, London, 2006

Simons, Rowan. *Bamboo Goalposts: One Man's Quest to Teach the People's Republic of China to Love Football*. Macmillan, London, 2008

Szymanski, Stefan. *Playbooks and Checkbooks: An Introduction to the Economics of Modern Sports*. Princeton University Press, Princeton, 2009

Szymanski, Stefan, and Tim Kuypers. *Winners and Losers: The Business Strategy of Football*. Penguin, London, 1999

Szymanski, Stefan, and Andrew Zimbalist. *National Pastime: How Americans Play Baseball and the Rest of the World Plays Soccer*. The Brookings Institution, Washington, DC, 2005

Taylor, Peter. *With Clough by Taylor*. Sidgwick & Jackson, London, 1980

Turnbull, John, Thom Satterlee & Alon Raab (eds). *The Global Game: Writers on Soccer*. University of Nebraska Press, Lincoln, 2008

Varley, Nick. *Parklife: A Search for the Heart of Football*. Penguin, London, 1999

When Saturday Comes. *Power Corruption and Pies: A Decade of the Best Football Writing from 'When Saturday Comes'*. Two Heads Publishing, London, 1997

Vergouw, Gyuri. *De Strafschop: Zoektocht naar de ultieme penalty*. Uitgeverij Funsultancy, Antwerp, 2000

White, Jim. *Manchester United: The Biography*. Sphere, London, 2008

Zirin, Dave. *A People's History of Sports in the United States*. The New Press, New York, 2008

ARTICLES AND RESEARCH PAPERS

Baade, R. 'Professional Sports as Catalysts for Metropolitan Economic Development'. *Journal of Urban Affairs* 18, no. 1 (1996): 1–17

Gabaix, Xavier. 'Zipf's Law for Cities: An Explanation'. *Quarterly Journal of Economics* (MIT Press) 114, no. 3 (August 1999): 739–767

Hicks, Joe, and Grahame Allen. *A Century of Change: Trends in UK Statistics Since 1900.* House of Commons Library Research Paper 99/111. London: House of Commons Library, December 1999

Hirshleifer, J. 'The Paradox of Power'. *Economics and Politics* 3 (1991): 177–200

Kavetsos, Georgios, and Stefan Szymanski. 'National Wellbeing and International Sports Events'. *Journal of Economic Psychology* (forthcoming)

McGrath, Ben. 'The Sporting Scene: The Professor of Baseball'. *New Yorker,* July 7, 2003

Palacios-Huerta, Ignacio. 2003. 'Professionals Play Minimax'. *Review of Economic Studies* 70, no. 2 (2003): 395–415

Szymanski, Stefan. 'Income Inequality, Competitive Balance, and the Attractiveness of Team Sports: Some Evidence and a Natural Experiment from English Soccer'. *Economic Journal* 111 (2001): F69–F84

Szymanski, Stefan. 'A Market Test for Discrimination in the English Professional Soccer Leagues'. *Journal of Political Economy* 108, no. 3 (2000): 590–603

Tapp, A. 'The Loyalty of Football Fans – We'll Support You Evermore?' *Journal of Database Marketing and Customer Strategy Management* 11, no. 3 (April 1, 2004)

Tapp, A., and J. Clowes. 'From "Carefree Casuals" to "Professional Wanderers": Segmentation Possibilities for Football Supporters'. *European Journal of Marketing* 36, no. 11 (2002)

MAGAZINES

Hard Gras (Netherlands)
Johan (Netherlands, now defunct)
Voetbal International (Netherlands)
So Foot (France)

INDEX